VANCOUVER — FROM MILLTOWN TO METROPOLIS

VANCOUVER

FROM MILLTOWN TO METROPOLIS

ALAN MORLEY

Mitchell Press, Vancouver, Canada

Printed and bound
at Vancouver, Canada
by Mitchell Press Limited

Copyright 1961

First edition 1961
Second edition 1969
Third edition 1974

PRINTED IN CANADA

Table of Contents

For H.B.M.,
one who knew
The Golden Years

Preface

THIS BOOK is not a history of Vancouver. It is obviously less, and I have tried to make it something more.

This is the city in which I was born and in which I have spent the greater part of my life, much of it as a working newspaperman. In my work and as a citizen it has been of importance to me to know what my city is—and why it should be what it is. History does not have the answer; as far as it has rules and design it requires a larger stage to display its pattern. A city is alive and individual; it demands a biographer.

To tell the story of a city one must love and understand it. This is not a science, but a mystery and an art. Like loving and understanding a woman, it requires a sensual and emotional receptivity the historian cannot permit himself, and at best only a partial success can be attained.

It is this personality of the city which prevents either the historian or the social scientist from understanding it. The one looks at the past, the other plans for the future. Accurate records of the past are invaluable, wise plans for the future essential, but the city lives in the present—this instant of the here and the now. In this, too, it is feminine—illogical, unpredictable, contradictory—but with a fine pragmatic realism. Immortal, as Max Weber said of nations, it has neither regret for the past, nor fear of the future. It is as it is —now.

So, without regret for its past or fear for its future, I have tried with as much love and understanding as I have to paint a picture of the living Vancouver, as I know it. I have looked in the past for those parts of it I feel still live in the living city. As in a portrait, much detail is passed over; its professions, its sports, its industries, its religious life, its politics are rich tapestries of intricate design, but here hinted at with a mere touch of occasional color in the background. If the portrait is true and reveals to you something of the character and vitality of the city that is my subject, I have done all I could hope to do in the confines of a single volume.

Nor have I done it alone. One cannot deal with Vancouver's past without being indebted to the late City Archivist, Major James S. Matthews. 1 have used material accumulated by the many students of the city's early years, owing most, perhaps, to Mr. Norman Hacking and the former Miss Darrell Gomery. Those who have read my manuscript in whole or part and assisted me by their comments include Mr. Roy Mah, Mr. Paul St. Pierre, Mr. A. R. D'Altroy, Mr. Francis Dickie and Mrs. M. A. Lyons. The work never would have been undertaken had it not been for the encouragement of my publisher, Mr. Howard Mitchell. Quotations from Dr. Margaret A. Ormsby's *"British Columbia—a History"* are by permission of the author and of its publisher, The Macmillan Co. of Canada, Ltd.

My account of the Great Fire of 1886 was first published in the *Vancouver Sun* in somewhat similar form; that of Seraphim "Joe" Fortes in the *Vancouver Province* and *The Bajan,* of Bridgetown, Barbadoes.

My acknowledgement is due to Mr. Donald Cromie, formerly publisher of the *Sun,* for first turning my attention to and subsequently encouraging my study of Vancouver's past.

Available sources are numerous and often conflicting; it has often been necessary to select that version of an event which seems most likely to be correct, or even merely most plausible. I do not hope to escape criticism and contradiction, and do not presume to have avoided all error. With this confession I abandon all the paraphernalia of footnote and bibliography, so dear to the academician, as calculated only to intensify scholarly disputation, while wearying the average reader. I have, however, made liberal use of quotation marks to identify phrases from contemporary reports or eyewitness recollections. With these explanations, which are not to be construed as apologies, Ladies and Gentlemen, I present to you my City—Vancouver.

A.M.

Prologue

IN THE LAST unknown quarter of the habitable globe, a river roared through a waste of mountains, then slid between sullen forests to an inland sea.

The river was brown with mud and heavy with gold.

The mountains stood in the sea, with their heads in the clouds a mile and two miles above the water. When the clouds blew away, the glittering ice-caps stood like a thousand-mile wall between earth and heaven.

Where the forest fell back from precipices, rains leached metallic color from hidden lodes and painted great aprons of naked rock.

Along the mountain wall, the forest was unending. The trees ran up the slopes, stood ranked along the shore, and clustered on every islet and in every gully. They were immense trees, in bulk and in age little less than the redwoods of California; but the redwoods were measured in groves, this forest in hundreds and thousands of square miles.

The inland sea was whipped by storms. It stirred and muttered with a life of its own. Four times each day it ran into or out of its maze of inlets, passes, channels and sounds. It grumbled around the points, dashed over the reefs, piled up and roared through the narrows. Here and there it plunged over deep-hidden ledges, whirled in fury, dragging down and gnashing to bits everything afloat, even whole trees.

When it tired and ebbed away, whispering through the beds of bobbing kelp, it left these fragments of its rage littered yards deep on miles of stony beaches.

This inland sea was cut off from the open ocean by a great flotilla of thickly wooded islands. The islands were the rugged peaks of a drowned mountain range, as massive and forbidding as the mainland mountain wall. The ocean tides, piling up and jostling through tortuous funnels between the islands, became the lashing rips and furious currents of the inland waters.

The sea swarmed with salmon, cod, herring, halibut, crabs, seals, whales and deep-furred sea-otter; the mountains with bear, goat, deer, marten, beaver, mink and wild sheep; the shores and the shallows with ducks, geese, herons, eagles and gulls.

It was a vast, rich, abundant land, crawling with life. It was a huge, grim, violent land; everywhere over it hung the imminent shadow of death.

When the 18th Century was half gone, the Spaniards were in California, the Russians in Alaska; even then this northwest coast of North America was unmapped, unexplored, and unknown to the rest of the world. No white man had seen it.

There had been a map, of course, drawn by some forgotten illustrator for Dean Swift's *Gulliver's Travels*. With the unconscious truth that lies in jests, he had placed in this far corner of the Pacific, Brobdingnag—the Land of the Giants."

Truly it was a land fitted for giants. But before the century was out, the men it waited for would find it. And having seized the land, in fewer than one hundred years they would build in a setting of surpassing beauty one of the great cities of the world.

Vancouver they would call it.

CAPTAIN GEORGE VANCOUVER, R.N.
*His name lives with
the seaport he surveyed*

3

SIR WILLIAM VAN HORNE

*As general manager of the new Canadian Pacific Railway, Van Horne named
Vancouver to commemorate, through the great city he then foresaw, the
British navigator, Captain George Vancouver.*

1

The Finding

IN 1774, CANADA was 171 years old. The thirteen British colonies scattered along the Atlantic seaboard of America were on the verge of revolution. The Russians had reached east through Siberia and in a weak, isolated post at Sitka were embroiled in a death-struggle with the Alaskan Indians. Thirty-two years before, the La Verendryes had seen the Rocky Mountains from the east.

The Spaniards had consolidated their empire on the coasts of the South Sea; the North American colonists were reaching westward for more lands and more furs; the British traders still battered their ships against Arctic ice in search of the Northwest Passage.

In Mexico, the viceroy decided it was time to set the Spanish seal on the northern coast of Spain's private ocean. First Perez, then Don Bruno Heceta, came bucketing up into the "Graveyard of the Pacific" in tiny schooners, and Heceta, at least, saw the unknown land as he ranged to the north of the Queen Charlottes. But he did not land before he was blown back south.

The British, barred from the eastern door of the mythical passage to China, decided to look for the western one. And in 1778 Captain Cook landed in Nootka Sound—the first white man to reach the western shores of what is now Canada.

He found no passage there but his men traded for sea-otter skins, using them for bedding and for clothing. When the ships reached China on their homeward passage (Cook long dead among the Hawaiian savages) the prices they got for rags and tatters of fur amazed them all.

5

The news spread, and the world reached out for the northwest coast.

They came, first, from India; James Strange, with two ships and the blessing of "John Company." Strange left at Nootka the Irish surgeon, John Mackay, first white man to see the inland sea, for Maquinna's Indians took him to the top of a high mountain from which the Strait of Georgia was visible.

Or so says Mrs. Barclay's journal. Barclay sailed the Austrian ship, *Imperial Eagle*, into the sound named after him the year after Strange reached Nootka, picked up Mackay, and took him back to China.

From England came Dixon and Portlock, ranging down the outer coast from the Queen Charlottes south; Meares, the "monumental liar" and sharp dealer, who built a ship in Nootka; and the Bristol brig *Jenny*, that mysteriously appears once and vanishes from history.

From Mexico, still vainly attempting to assert Spain's wilted sovereignty, Martinez settled in Nootka, arrested Meares and sundry others, and then abandoned the settlement.

Amazing adventurers they were, boldly sailing cockleshells in some of the world's most dangerous waters. Yet it was not until 16 years after Perez' voyage that, in 1790, Sub-Lieutenant Don Manuel Quimper found a way into the inland sea.

Out of San Blas, Mexico, Don Manuel sailed the little sloop *Princesa Real* north to Nootka, back south to Barclay Sound, into Port San Juan, into Sooke, and into the continent-splitting—so the legends said and so he thought—Strait of Juan de Fuca. He sailed into Esquimalt Harbor, into Victoria Harbor, had a brush with fierce Indians in canoes off Saanich Peninsula, and sailed back home to tell His Christian Majesty's viceroy, El Conde de Revilla Gigedo, that God had been good and it had been left to His faithful Spaniards to discover the long-sought Northwest Passage.

Before he turned around off Saanich, he saw and put on his map the snow-clad peaks of "El Gran Montano del Carmelo." He had seen from afar the mountains north and northwest of Howe Sound and Burrard Inlet.

Quimper's exciting news made it worthwhile to send the next year, under Lieutenant Don Francisco Eliza, the impressive flagship *San Carlos*, all of "75 feet long, 24 in the beam and of 14 feet draught," and the less impressive *Santa Saturnina*, 36 feet over all.

Unfortunately Don Francisco became ill and the *San Carlos* never got farther north than San Juan Island. But Don Juan Pantoja y Arriaga did.

He pushed the *Santa Saturnina* north through Haro Strait, between Orcas and (time has changed the name) Saturna Islands, into the inland sea. Don Juan had the Spanish gift for fine, melodious, rolling, impressive names. He called it:

"El Gran Canal de Neuestra Senora del Rosario del Marinera" —the Great Channel of Our Lady of the Rosary of the Seafarers —perhaps a more fitting name for this "grand and extended canal" than the one it got the next year.

Back went Pantoja to report to Eliza and take charge of the *San Carlos* for his ailing superior. Two weeks later it was Second Mate Don Jose Maria Narvaez who brought the *Santa Saturnina* north again and on into El Gran Canal.

For eight days, Narvaez in the *Saturnina* and Brevet Second Mate Don Jose Verdia in the longboat pushed north.

North past the Isla de Zepeda (Point Roberts). North past the place where the great river flowed between the forests to the sea. "There must be some copious river here," recorded Narvaez, "for we sailed two leagues through water more sweet than salt."

He called the channels of the Fraser delta the Bocas (mouths) of the Floridablanca.

And then he anchored off the Isla de Langara.

Narvaez' Isla de Langara was Point Grey, now all, except the university district on the tip of the point, part of the City of Vancouver.

Whether Narvaez was or was not the first white man to set foot inside the city limits will probably never be known. Certainly he talked to the Indians there. The Salish, probably from Musqueam Village, told him there was flat land for many miles up the course of the river and at the head of the valley were passes through which came strangers (the interior Salish) to fish and stay for two moons, bringing with them goods to trade on "large quadrupeds with round hooves and long tails and manes." The coast Indians had no horses, which Narvaez assumed these to be.

Our knowledge of Narvaez' exploration is third-hand, for we have only a report of Pantoja's report of Narvaez' report to him. The only direct evidence in favor of a landing by Narvaez is that he mapped three Indian villages on Point Grey, one of which must have been invisible from the water. Perhaps he went ashore and saw it—or perhaps the Indians told him it was there and he took their word for it.

At least, on the 5th and 6th of July, 1791, the first Europeans visited the site of the city-to-be. Don Jose Maria Narvaez and Don Jose Verdia were the discoverers of Vancouver's site.

From Isla de Langara they sailed on north to the mouth of Jervis Inlet, passing and mapping English Bay, the entrance to Howe Sound, landing at Roberts Creek or Wilson's Creek for water, and mapping the shores of the Strait of Malaspina, including Lasqueti and Texada Islands, before they returned.

The following year was of such historic note that for a century and a half the work of Narvaez and Verdia was forgotten, and 1792 became accepted as the year of discovery of the city's site.

The arrest by Martinez of British traders in Nootka has been noted. When the news reached Europe, it precipitated an international crisis. Britain and Spain came close to war before—with some give and take on other issues as well—a settlement was reached which included the formal cession of Nootka to Britain. In effect, it is under this agreement that Canada holds her Pacific coast today.

Don Juan Francisco de la Bodega y Quadra was back with a Spanish garrison in Nootka. The British Admiralty had commissioned Captain George Vancouver to circumnavigate the world with His Majesty's Ships *Chatham* and *Discovery*, stopping on his way to accept from Bodega y Quadra the surrender of the northwest coast of America, seek the western entrance of the Northwest Passage and, at the end of three years, return home.

About the time Narvaez was anchored off the Isla de Langara, Vancouver's ships were running down the Atlantic coasts of Africa. Since then he had rounded the Cape of Good Hope, crossed the Indian Ocean, passed south of Australia, run eastward through the Pacific, wintered in Hawaii, and in April of 1792, made his North American landfall on the coast of California.

On his second visit to this coast (he had been one of Cook's midshipmen in 1778), it was his duty to examine meticulously the mainland shores, to make sure no possible passage to the Atlantic was overlooked.

Running north he surmised the existence of, but did not examine, the Columbia River (a river could not be the Northwest Passage). He put off its exploration until his return trip in the autumn. This was an omission which eventually played its part in depriving Britain of possession of the present States of Washington and Oregon, and helped to facilitate the extension of the United States to the Pacific Ocean. Amongst its lesser consequences, it helped to make necessary the founding of the City of Vancouver and assured its growth. For if Lieutenant Broughton had rowed up the Columbia in May, instead of September, the American, Gray, following hard on Vancouver's heels in the ship *Columbia*, could never have made his claim to discovery, by which the United States in part justified its annexation of the vast Oregon Territory a half-century later.

If the British had held the territory which they first occupied there would have been no border at the 49th Parallel, no necessity to drive the Canadian Pacific Railway through the grim northern passes of the Rockies, and no possibility of the City of Vancouver becoming the great Canadian gateway city of the West. Today's metropolis of a million souls may well owe its existence to a favorable off-shore breeze a century and a half ago, which made Captain Vancouver shrug his shoulders and bowl on northward instead of delaying to poke into a suspected river estuary on a desolate coast.

So came the *Chatham* and *Discovery* to the great Strait of Juan de Fuca, which Vancouver imagined he was the first to find. With the boats out, crawling day by day along the shore, they explored the depths of Admiralty Inlet and Puget Sound, anchoring June 10 in Birch Bay.

With Vancouver himself in the yawl, and Lieutenant Peter Puget in command of the launch, the two boats set off northward.

9

Forced westward from Point Roberts by shallow Roberts Bank, they veered across the strait and spent the night on an island off the western shore.

Tuesday, June 12, they sailed again at 5 a.m. in beautiful summer weather and in seven hours, "about noon", Captain George Vancouver landed on Point Grey, little dreaming that here, one day, would rise a great city bearing his name.

"As we suspected," he says, "the point formed the south point of an extensive sound."

Point Roberts and Point Grey he correctly identified as parts of the mainland, rather than islands, but dismissed the Fraser River as "only navigable for canoes." The great navigator's experience with rivers was largely unfortunate.

From the point, the boats crossed English Bay and entered Burrard Inlet's First Narrows, now known as the Lions' Gate, from the two sphinx-like peaks standing guard on the mountains to the north of it. Stanley Park he considered an island, and False Creek a southern branch of the inlet. In this he was not mistaken; before the head of False Creek was filled in, at high tide there was a "canoe pass" from the creek to the inlet about the present Columbia Street.

As they passed through the narrows, they were met by about 50 Indians in canoes, "who conducted themselves with the greatest decorum and civility, presenting us with fish cooked and undressed . . . resembling smelt" (oolichan or candlefish) "and . . . finding we were inclined to show some return for their hospitality, showed much understanding in preferring iron to copper."

They stood on up the inlet under easy sail, accompanied part of the way by their new friends, and stopped for the night a mile or two from the head of the inlet, sleeping in the boats because the shore was steep and rocky.

Some of the midshipmen, however, preferring the rocks to the ribs and thwarts of the boats, "found themselves incommoded by a flood tide . . . and one of them slept so sound that I believe he might have been conveyed to some distance had he not been awakened by his companions."

At 4 a.m. of June 13, Vancouver roused his crews and set out to retrace his way, passing Indian Arm without investigating it, the encampment at the Capilano before his Indian friends were awake, and reaching Point Atkinson by 7 a.m.

"The shores of this canal," said Vancouver, "which after Sir Harry Burrard of the navy, I have distinguished by the name of Burrard's Channel, may be considered on the southern side, of a moderate height, and, though rocky, well covered with trees of a large growth, particularly the pine tribe.

"On the northern side, the rugged, snowy barrier, whose base we had now nearly approached, was only protected from the wash of the sea by a very narrow border of low land."

Having rounded the point and started up "the main branch of the sound," which he named Howe Sound, Vancouver paused to contrast "the sublime though gloomy spectacle" of its soaring peaks with "the low, fertile shores we had been accustomed to see" no further south than the far side of Burrard's Channel. He thus identified a geographical feature which was to play a considerable part in the social, political and economic life of the city that now bears his name.

While Vancouver and his boat crews rounded Point Atkinson, unknown to him and knowing nothing of him, two colleagues of Narvaez and Verdia were close on his trail.

They were Don Dionisio Alcala-Galiano in the brig *Sutil*, and Don Cayetano Valdes in the schooner *Mexicana*.

What men—what seamen—these Spaniards were! With 24 men in each of these rickety, patched, worn-out tubs of 45 tons burthen, they had driven their way north through the spring gales and into El Gran Canal—now, by grace of Captain Vancouver's harsher tongue, the Strait of Georgia. The cabins were so small, only four of the crew could eat at one time. At Acapulco both boats—they were scarcely more—had been sawed in two and "made more commodious" by "insertions" which lengthened them.

This Wednesday, as Vancouver reached the head of Howe Sound, they were driven, as he was, across the strait by Roberts Bank, and spent the night on Galiano Island near Active Pass. The rest of the week, while Vancouver threaded the stupendous gorge of Jervis Inlet, they found and explored the Bocas de Winthuysen —modern Nanaimo—and spent five days in the intricate navigation of the Vancouver Island shore.

But at 3:30 a.m., Wednesday, June 20, they had crossed the strait again and anchored on Sturgeon Bank, just off the southwest tip of Point Grey. (Vancouver was rousing his tired and starving crews from rest on the east shore of Texada Island during their return from Jervis Inlet.)

The Indians swarmed out from Musqueam to greet their Spanish friends again.

Some wore basket hats, some brandished spears in friendly greeting. They brought a fine, fat salmon for a present. The Spaniards admired "their liveliness, grace and talent."

"They combined unequalled affability with a warlike disposition, and had good arms, such as iron-pointed spears half a yard long, quivers full of arrows . . . bows and clubs, stone harpoons, boxes and baskets in their canoes and seaweed fishing lines."

The Spaniards traded copper for a good canoe, up-anchored and closed the point, to reanchor fairly in the North Arm of the Fraser, about the present booming grounds, where they spent an uneasy night fending off the huge logs that floated down the river.

Thursday morning, June 21, Vancouver met them, thinking them at first the *Discovery* and *Chatham*, come north to meet him. However, the Spaniards gave him and his hungry crews "a very hearty breakfast," which they badly needed.

They gave him a shock, as well.

"On this occasion I experienced no small degree of mortification in finding the external shores of the gulf had been visited and already examined a few miles beyond where my researches had extended. . . ."

They showed him their charts and gave him all the information in their power. The two parties agreed to continue their exploration in company.

While waiting for Vancouver to return from Birch Bay with his ships, Mates Juan Vernaci of the *Sutil* and Secundino Salamanca of the *Mexicana* took two small boats to explore the "arm to the northward" Vancouver had passed in Burrard Inlet. At the head of Indian Arm they met a few curious Indians, named it Canal de Sasamat, and returned to the ships on the morning of Monday, June 25, sailing northward with Vancouver later in the day.

Vancouver noticed as they left, "a very great number of whales."

He also recorded of the Spaniards that he was "not more pleased with their hospitality and attention, than astonished at the vessels in which they were employed to execute a service of such nature." It was a fitting tribute from a great British seaman to the valiant mariners of Spain.

It was also their swan song, for after Galiano and Valdes, the Spaniards never returned to this coast.

As they sail away into the north, one minor footnote to history remains. The City of Vancouver has dated some monuments and celebrates Vancouver Day one day behind the correct time. Sailing eastward around the world, Vancouver failed to drop one day at what is now the International Date Line and did not alter his calendar until he reached the Island of St. Helena in the Atlantic, his voyage nearly over. So the "June 13" he records as the day he discovered and landed on Point Grey was actually June 12. The dates in this narrative have been corrected.

For 16 long years, no other white man is known to have seen the site of Vancouver.

In 1793, Alexander Mackenzie crossed the continent, missing Captain Vancouver on his northern survey by only a few weeks. The Spaniards eventually surrendered Nootka. Yankee traders swarmed along the outer coast, and the "Boston men" made enemies of the Indians where the British and Spaniards had made friends. The North West Company pushed into northeastern British Columbia on the heels of Mackenzie's exploration. They sought the sources of the Columbia River in order to get their furs out by sea.

Simon Fraser founded Fort George (modern Prince George) in 1807. In 1808, believing the Fraser to be the headwaters of the Columbia, with John Stuart, Jules Maurice Quesnel, 19 other white men and two Indians, he started out to follow it to the mouth.

Their gruelling voyage is one of the classics of Canadian adventure.

Having passed the terrible canyon of the Fraser, they rented canoes from the Chilliwack Indians at Yale, and on July 2, floated quietly and watchfully down past the place where New Westminster was to be.

But the Musqueam Salish were no longer friends of the whites. When Fraser already could taste the brackish tide of the estuary, he landed on the north bank "to take an altitude" and determine his position.

The Musqueams, "howling like wolves and brandishing their clubs," descended on the party. With some difficulty Fraser's men got their canoes off the muddy shore with whole skins. They retreated with what dignity they could muster, and started the long trek home.

Despite enthusiastic modern Vancouver pageantry, Simon Fraser never saw the Strait of Georgia, he never rounded Point Grey, and he never paddled across English Bay to land on Kitsilano Beach amid the plaudits of friendly Indians.

He did see and land on the southern slope of South Vancouver or Marpole somewhere along the river bank.

For the rest, having made sure the Fraser was not the Columbia, he snorted that it was "this useless river," and left in disgust, convinced his work was wasted. But they called the "useless river" after him, and so his name endures, part of the daily nomenclature of today's Vancouver.

2

Closing In

FOR 50 YEARS after Simon Fraser was chased ignominiously from its southern river-bank, the site of Vancouver was left to its forests, its bears, its wolves, its deer and its Indians.

Metropolitan Vancouver—as an economic and social unit, even if not yet a political one—takes in the whole of the Fraser delta and the north shore of Burrard Inlet. Roughly, it runs some 25 miles north from the United States border, and some 30 miles east from the Strait of Georgia. Civic planning experts more and more tend to envision it as including the entire lower Fraser Valley, from the strait 90 miles east to Hope, where the river finally emerges from its mighty Coast Range canyon.

However, for most of its first 100 years, the metropolitan population of Vancouver, its suburbs, and New Westminster has been concentrated on a long, sprawling peninsula, some 20 by 10 or 12 miles, bounded on the north by Burrard Inlet, the south, by the Fraser River and on the west by the Strait of Georgia. The peninsula is composed largely of alluvial deposits, with two parallel east-west rock spines, the northern running from Stanley Park easterly to Pitt River, the southern from Point Grey to Brunette Creek. A cross-barring hump connects the two where Grandview now lies.

The primitive inhabitants consisted of the Musqueam and Sko-ko-mish (Squamish), two tribal divisions of the Salish people, estimated to have been from 3000 to 5000 in all, including those of Howe Sound. More than 100 "village" sites have been identified in Greater Vancouver alone but, aside from the main villages, these

15

were mostly hunting or fishing camps occupied temporarily at certain seasons by families or small groups of families which held hereditary territorial rights to hunt or fish in certain locations. These rights were jealously maintained, but they were solely the rights to exclusive use of the territory for certain purposes. The Indians had no conception of land ownership as such.

The Salish were one of the seven great language divisions of the west coast Indians who occupied the coasts and islands from farthest Alaska to the mouth of the Columbia River. The coast Indians differed culturally and physically from the Amerinds who inhabited the remainder of the continent north of Mexico. They were more akin to the Siberian tribes than to the mountain or plains Indians, and had definite Mongoloid characteristics.

Their political organization was benign, their social system intricate, their arts and crafts profound in concept and expert in execution. Inheritance in some of the language divisions was matriarchal, though not among the Salish; in none did women occupy a position of inferiority.

Theoretically, there were no hereditary chiefs—the rulers of the tribes were "hegas" men—those distinguished by generosity and wisdom. In practice, a propertied man of the ruling oligarchy would assist his designated heir to perform the tribal obligations of generosity and thus assure him, in his turn, of "hegas" status.

Raiding for slaves was common, and retributive killing or blood-payments atoned for murder. Young men in the springtime commonly went raiding, more out of sheer high animal spirits than deliberate malice, and such raiders were often regarded as temporarily insane. The concept of organized war was unknown.

Slaves were not, as a rule, unkindly treated, being regarded as inferior members of the family, but they were liable to sudden and brutal elimination in times of scarcity, and occasionally became ritual sacrifices. The Kwakiutl and the Haida regarded the Salish as their natural source of slaves, and were feared accordingly. Among the Salish tribal divisions there was a similar gradation, and the Sko-ko-mish and Musqueams took their slaves from the Coquitlam and other Fraser Valley groups. Retaliation was virtually unknown.

The Salish, while the lowest in status of the northern language divisions, were the most numerous of all, their territory taking in both sides of the Strait of Georgia from Cape Mudge south, with an enclave on the coast at Bella Coola, and—the only one of the groups to penetrate inland to any extent—the Okanagan and Similkameen Valleys. As we have seen, their inland cousins came yearly to the lower Fraser to fish and trade "for two moons."

This inferiority of status was definite and concrete. Not only did they fear and flee the northern slave raiders, but the Kwakiutl held and exercised social and religious privileges over the Salish, who were obliged to buy from their fierce neighbors not only permission to create and use certain forms of ritual art, but even the designs of their canoes.

Cannibalism, often charged against them by early explorers, was never more than an occasional symbolic religious ritual, such as sharing among the men of a village the heart or liver of a particularly courageous or distinguished enemy slain in battle. It was a matter of character, not calories, and the victim's mourners would cherish the manner of his end with a certain melancholy pride.

Such was the native population of Vancouver before the white men came. The main concentrations were at Musqueam, where there was a numerous population and a "long-house" over 90 feet wide and 1500 feet in length. A similar village was at Squamish. For the rest, we know of populous centres at Kokopai (Locarno Beach), Snaq (Kitsilano), Whoi-Whoi (at Lumberman's Arch in Stanley Park) and Whumulcheson (mouth of Capilano River). Other major sites were known; whether then occupied or not, we do not know.

During the 50 years following Simon Fraser's brief visit, the outside world was slowly closing in on the Vancouver-to-be. The Hudson's Bay Company had early taken over the North West Company, and extended its operations south to the mouth of the Columbia River.

After the War of 1812, it became obvious the United States would take over Oregon and Washington eventually, and "The Company" began to look north of the 49th Parallel for new bases.

In 1827, Fort Langley was founded. Steam navigation came to the North Pacific in the 1830s with the advent of the famous *SS Beaver*. Coal was found near Nanaimo in 1835; and the company's Pacific headquarters moved to Victoria in 1843.

By this time the Ṣko-ko-mish and the Musqueams were no strangers to the white men's appearance, habits, trade goods, or guns, but Vancouver itself lay largely untroubled and unknown. The Indians have a tradition that during these years, when the company was actively seeking new mines, "Two white men with Indians in a canoe came looking for coal." But nothing else is known of them.

The Sko-ko-mish and Musqueams had a reputation for ferocity, whether deserved or not, it is hard to tell now. At least, Vancouver was avoided by white men. As shadowy as the "two men in a canoe" is the tradition of one Supple Jack, who lived near Siwash Rock, and was credited in the reminiscences of oldtimers with "the murder of a dozen prospectors." The legend could be—as Supple Jack's defenders aver—wholly slanderous, of course.

We do know that in 1851 new-made Governor James Douglas (later Sir James) reported coal found in surface beds along the shore of Burrard Inlet. And in 1854, a mining engineer named Grant reported to the London Geographical Society on these and other British Columbia coal deposits. In 1855 one A. K. Isbister mapped and reported on the coal beds in the society's journal.

That year, other prospectors were abroad.

On the Fraser, they raised the magic cry—"Gold!"

It took almost three years for the world to hear and answer, but in 1858, more than 22,000 men passed Fort Langley on their way to the gold fields.

Contrary to a common belief, the gold rush did not spawn Vancouver, unless you count her tiny twin, New Westminster, an integral part of metropolitan Vancouver. And even New Westminster began as a by-product. It was the administrative capital of the colony the gold rush brought into being.

New Westminster also fiercely resents being considered a part of Vancouver, no matter what the facts of life may be, economically, socially or geographically.

So it should be soothing for the Royal City, and salutary for Vancouver, to remember that Vancouver began life as New Westminster's back door.

All Vancouver saw of the 1858 gold rush was a few miners camping on Second Beach in Stanley Park while they waited for the Fraser freshet to subside. Early in the summer, one MacLean, a Scottish farmer from California, sailed his schooner, the *Rob Roy*, into the inlet, looking for land to settle on. The Indians proved hostile, and he sailed back to the Fraser with Mrs. MacLean and his young son standing by the schooner's two little brass guns.

On Christmas Day, Colonel Richard Clement Moody's famous detachment of Royal Engineers arrived in the new Crown Colony of British Columbia, and founded the establishment that was first Queensborough and later New Westminster.

Colonel Moody was not only senior military officer in the colony (proclaimed the previous August 25) but also chief commissioner of works and chief commissioner of lands. With Admiral Baynes, the senior naval officer, he took a load of responsibility off Governor Douglas' shoulders—not, it was whispered, altogether to Douglas' delight.

Since the Fraser was an unruly river, and in those days often froze over to the mouth in winter, Admiral Baynes late in 1858 had *HMS Plumper* survey Burrard Inlet, and chose English Bay's south shore and the extreme head of the inlet as naval anchorages.

Colonel Moody concurred. As senior military officer, he set the Royal Engineers to work early in 1859 on a road to Port Moody (the source of the name is obvious) at the head of the inlet. As chief commissioner of works, he let civilian contracts for a road to Jericho Beach on English Bay. Today these routes are the North Road and, approximately, Grandview Highway.

The admiral wanted coal, as well as anchorages. The *Plumper* returned in June and dug two tons "of very good quality" from exposed seams on the shore, about the present north foot of Bute Street, "in a very few hours." Richards Street recalls the name of the *Plumper's* captain, Brockton Point that of her engineer, and Coal Harbor that of her mission. Ironically, the British-American

Oil Company's distribution depot stands today on top of Vancouver's only coal mine.

Early in July came Walter Moberly, explorer and son of a Hudson's Bay Company factor, and Colonel Moody's secretary, Robert Burnaby, to survey and map the coal beds. Rumors soon reached New Westminister that the Indians had attacked the survey party.

The *Plumper* came racing to the rescue, found all well and Captain Richards brought the crew ashore with a keg of navy rum for Vancouver's first recorded beach party.

Some mystery, a distinct probability of arbitrary dictation from Colonel Moody, and wild allegations of corruption from Vancouver Island politicians surround Moody's first allocation of land in Van-couver.

Moberly was instructed to make extensive surveys, and Moody reserved for naval and military purposes 788 acres on Point Grey, 11 acres at Jericho, 155 acres on Burrard Inlet opposite the head of False Creek, 110 acres at Port Moody, 354 acres in Stanley Park, 950 acres opposite on the North Shore, and 190 acres north and 127 south of the inlet at Port Moody.

The Indian inhabitants, of course, received no consideration in this. They were discontented, as a result, and when shortly after-ward Moody took the necessary and humane step of freeing all their slaves, they became even more discontented.

The North Road was completed in 1859, the Jericho Trail in 1861, and the River Trail, from New Westminster along the Fraser to Point Grey, in 1863. The Royal City had her back door.

In January, 1860, Douglas proclaimed the new colony's land law. Burnaby and Moberly, evidently partly paid in land script, immediately filed on inlet lands. Burnaby filed for 128 acres "near the coal site," and Moberly, on his way upcountry to the gold fields, for the south shore of False Creek.

Moberley's application was filed on behalf of Admiral Baynes before Patrick O'Reilly, J.P., at Fort Hope.

Over these, and a number of other filings outside the Vancouver area, mostly by Moberly on behalf of military officers and main-

From a painting by L. A. Hamilton

THE OLD HASTINGS ("New Brighton") HOTEL — *Pictured here as it looked in 1885. Built in 1864 near what is now Exhibition Park, this was one of the earliest permanent structures on Burrard Inlet. It served the well-to-do of New Westminster as a holiday resort. It housed the first post, customs, revenue, and telegraph offices. The C.P.R. established its construction offices there.*

ONE HUNDRED YEARS AT KITSILANO BEACH — *In the upper reproduction of a painting made in 1861 by Lieut. Willis, R.N. of H.M.S. GANGES, white sailors are depicted helping Indians to net fish at about the foot of today's Maple and Arbutus streets. This was later Greer's Beach and Kitsilano Indian Reserve at the entrance to False Creek. The modern scene is the same strip of beach, with bathers unconscious of this once having been a happy fishing and hunting ground of Chief Khahatsalano's Squamish Indians.*

Vancouver City Archives

LOST LAGOON IN 1868—*Looking north from about the foot of today's Robson Street (produced), with Indian huts of split cedar in the foreground.*

LOST LAGOON TODAY — *A group of weeping willows is seen on the shore in the middle distance standing on the site of the Indian shacks built some 100 years ago.*

Photo by George Shaw

G. W. HAYNES   SEWELL MOODY   JOSIAS C. HUGHES

First industrialist on Burrard Inlet was Sewell Moody who, with Yankee shrewdness and enterprise, founded in 1864 a thriving sawmill community at Moodyville on the North Shore. George Haynes was a brother of Laura Haynes, Burrard Inlet's first school teacher at Moodyville. Josias Hughes was a clerk at the mill and the founding master of Mount Hermon Lodge, first Masonic lodge in the Vancouver area.

JOHN MORTON   WM. HAILSTONE   SAM BRIGHOUSE

Coming as goldseekers in the Cariboo gold rush, these three were the first landowners in what is now Vancouver. Their "Brickmakers' Claim" covered the entire west end area from modern Burrard Street to Stanley Park and from Burrard Inlet to English Bay.

land businessmen, Moody came into conflict with Douglas and the Victoria politicians, who denounced "the military clique building roads and appropriating land to enrich itself."

Nevertheless, the new land laws had set the stage for the first appearance of Vancouver. At last it was possible for a businessman to invest in property, a farmer to own his farm, a citizen to own his home.

3

The Potter

Now WE SHALL SEE the giants of Vancouver's early days come and build the city which in the end dwarfed them.

Giants, as "Jack and the Beanstalk" tells us, can be mad, bad and stupid; or, as Gulliver found them, sensible, kind and noble. They differ from the rest of humanity in being more, perhaps only a trifle more, than life-size, and usually just a bit out of proportion. Some facet of their personality or character does not quite fit the human norm.

These are the pioneers of history, the men and women who hear the relentless call of the strange, the violent, the new, the challenging lands. These are the Jews of the Exodus, the Norse of Greenland and Vinland, the Voortrekkers of South Africa, the Forty-Niners of California, the pioneers of British Columbia. Such were the men and women who built Vancouver.

To appreciate their work, it is necessary to remember what both citizens and strangers often forget—Vancouver is the work of one human lifetime. There were men alive here in the 1960's who were born before any white man felled a tree, built a cabin or hewed a trail anywhere between Point Grey and Coquitlam, Howe Sound and the Fraser River.

In the winter of 1861-62, floating ice closed Fraser River navigation in December. The year-old "stately screw-steamer" *Emily Harris* was chartered to run from Victoria to Port Moody. Mails and passengers were sent over the North Road to New Westminster, justifying Colonel Moody's first project. Traffic was light (only

50 passengers in all of February) and March 18 the river was open again, ending Burrard Inlet's first commercial shipping episode.

Now we go far afield. May 8, 1862, the world's largest steamship, *Great Eastern*, began her maiden voyage from Milford Haven, England, to New York. Aboard was John Morton, younger son of a noted family of Yorkshire potters, "bound for the gold fields." He, his cousin, Samuel Brighouse, and a shipboard acquaintance, William Hailstone, took passage from New York to the Panama land crossing, from Panama to San Francisco, from San Francisco to Victoria, and on June 25, arrived in New Westminster.

In the Royal City, Morton, a man who liked to have two strings to his bow, saw a block of Burrard Inlet coal in a shop window. His potter's mind ran from coal to clay, clay to bricks and bricks— building material was at a premium—to money. He hired an Indian guide and set out for the inlet.

Part way they crossed the peninsula on the incomplete Douglas Trail, the third Fraser-Burrard Inlet access road, designed to reach the inlet about Second Narrows. From its end they struck through the bush to about the present north foot of Main Street. The Indian unearthed a hidden canoe and paddled Morton to the coal seam, of which Morton approved.

From there, possibly intending to cross English Bay and strike the Jericho Trail, they rounded Stanley Park, but at Lumbermen's Arch found some 2000 yelling, dancing Salish preparing to repulse an expected raid by Haida slavers, so they kept close to the shore, landed near the south foot of today's Denman Street, followed a dim Indian trail back to where they had first struck the inlet, and went home by their outward route.

In October the three young Englishmen returned from the Cariboo gold fields, "owing to the inclement weather and the fact all the good claims were taken up," says Brighouse.

At the end of the month they were back at the coal seam and found good clay upon the bank above. November 3, Morton filed in the names of all three on what later became District Lot 185— all of Vancouver's West End, from Burrard Street to Stanley Park, and from the inlet to English Bay.

November 4, legally seized of the homestead, the three were hard at work clearing a cabin site on "the bluff," just west of the site of the new Guinness Tower Building on the north side of Hastings Street, between Thurlow and Burrard. They built a cabin, long known as "Morton's shack," a small barn, and cut a trail which joined the Jericho Trail near the head of False Creek. The preemption consisted of approximately 500 acres at four shillings, two pence an acre, a total of $555.75 for land worth hundreds of millions today. (Sterling was then the "money of account" in B.C. but the local currency, in which payments were made, was dollars.)

Their claim was later disputed by Robert Burnaby on the basis of his 1860 filing, but Judge Brew, not informed of Burnaby's name, pronounced the claim that of "either of knave or a liar," and it was not pressed.

The next year, Brighouse "packed the first cooking stove on the inlet on his back from New Westminster." In a rough kiln, the partners baked the first bricks made on the mainland coast of British Columbia.

Early in the year, Indians stole some of their tools. When they complained, Colonel Moody called old Chief Capilano to New Westminster and gave him a dressing-down which prevented any further trouble.

Nevertheless, the partners, who could not speak the Chinook *lingua franca* of the coast, were uneasy one morning when an aged Indian and two sturdy young women appeared at the cabin. Since neither side could understand the other, the elderly gentleman and one of the girls seized the bench that sat in front of the cabin and raised it successively higher and higher as the remaining girl leaped to and fro over it until exhausted. The girls changed places and the performance was repeated. When this failed to elicit any response from the settlers, the Indians retreated in high dudgeon.

Later the mystified partners learned the old man was displaying the energy and talents of two "servant girls" he hoped to hire to the homesteaders. Being honorable men, it is as well they escaped this particular snare in their relations with the Indians. With primitive innocence, the Indians naturally expected the arrangement to include bed as well as board, but where the contract and its in-evitable results impinged on the social system of the whites there were deplorable consequences which we shall have to examine more than once in the development of Vancouver.

The brick trade lagging, that summer Morton and Hailstone set off for the Cariboo to work as hired hands in the mines. Brig-house remained to satisfy the residence requirements of the pre-emption, and planted a vegetable garden. In the name of the three, he also rented a large plot of farm land on the Fraser River.

Thus the "three greenhorns" (as New Westminster called them) and "the Brickmakers' Claim" (as Vancouver called it) came to be the first settlers and the first settlement in Vancouver.

As the city expanded, others might dispute their claim. Hugh Magee, William Shannon, William Catchpole and Henry Mole were farming in or near Marpole in 1863, Magee possibly in 1862, and one Gariepy possibly first of all. The McCleery brothers, Sam and Fitz, were not long after them. But it was not until more than half a century passed that Vancouver would engulf that dis-trict. Morton, Brighouse and Hailstone are fully entitled to the honor of "first settlers."

In reality, they played little part in the early development of the city. By the time they proved-up on the pre-emption in 1867, the inlet settlements had by-passed them. Hailstone later returned to England in moderate circumstances, convinced his partners had "done" him in the eventual disposition of the claim. Morton spent long years in California in search of the fortune that eluded him, returned to Vancouver to dig ditches on Lulu Island, a widower with a daughter in a convent and a son boarded-out in a private home.

Only Sam Brighouse became a man of mark in the community, and for nearly 20 years to come his main interests lay in New Westminster and on Lulu Island.

It was left to others to bring Vancouver into being, though Brig-house and Morton profited immensely from it in the end.

4

Timber-r-r-r!

IT WAS THE forest, not the land, that gave birth to Vancouver.

"On Burrard Inlet grows the finest stand of easily accessible timber in British Columbia," declared John Robson in his New Westminster *British Columbian*. That meant the finest in the world.

Vancouver was the child of the timber beasts. The long-drawn groan and crash of the trees falling before their saws saluted the city's birth.

Robson's contemporaries in the three-year-old mainland capital were not behind him in recognizing the opportunities the inlet's timber offered. In the autumn of 1862, T. W. Graham and Co. of New Westminster pre-empted 480 acres of rich timberland on the north shore of the inlet, some quarter-mile east of the foot of present-day Lonsdale Avenue.

Through the winter, while the "three greenhorns" cleared their claim on the opposite shore, gangs under David Ramage began to open the skidroads, fell the timbers, and build the mill to which the grunting ox-teams hauled the great logs.

In February, surveyor Corporal George Turner of the Royal Engineers came across by still-incomplete Douglas Road (raised in status from "trail" now the inlet was opening up) to lay out, on the south shore from Second Narrows west, District Lots 181, 182, 183, 184, two Townsite Reserves and Lot 185, the last being the Brickmakers' Claim.

In April, G. Tranfield sent a party of men to the inlet to fish for cod for the Royal City market. And in June, on the north shore, Graham Co.'s Pioneer Mill was complete, with "two centre-discharge waterwheels of 50 horsepower and the 22-inch planing mill." The infant scream of the mill's puny (by later standards) head saws was the birth-cry of the city.

When "The Song of Vancouver" is written, its theme will be the shriek of giant saws biting into timber, the clang and thud of the sawyer's "nigger" tossing huge logs like jackstraws, the clatter and twang of limber planks on the sorting chains.

In August, Captain William Moore's crack river sternwheeler, the *Flying Dutchman*, with an "all-day excursion party, P. Hicks, agent," of New Westminsterites aboard, nosed through the narrows to load Pioneer Mill's—and Burrard Inlet's—first timber cargo. It consisted of 50,000 board feet of 3-inch planking for the Royal City's river levee.

Later in the month, *SS Governor Douglas* brought 150 excursionists to watch *HMS Sutlej* carry out a marine survey of the inlet. The land business was booming, too. Thomas Ranaldson bought District Lot 183 in October. Henry Pering Pellew Crease, later attorney-general, still later Mr Justice Crease, and later still, Sir Henry, bought Lot 182. Robert Burnaby, now a New Westminster merchant, took Lot 181.

Pioneer Mills sawed its steady 40,000 feet of lumber a day, but in December, the company went broke. Royal City grocer John Oscar Smith bought the mill and one million feet of logs at auction.

Pushing the bidding up in $100 jumps, from $6000 to $8000, was a brash young Yankee, Sewell Prescott Moody (no relation of the colonel) who had been rafting logs on the inlet. Moody's day was not yet.

The year 1864 was a quiet one. John Graham, clerk of the treasury to the mainland colony, bought up the last open land on the inlet's south shore—Lot 184. Smith's re-named Burrard Inlet Mills shipped steadily to New Westminster, Nanaimo and Victoria. John T. Scott, on contract, pushed Douglas Road through to the inlet. It was a bad year for forest fires; they burnt out the bridges on the North Road, leaving Douglas Road and the Jericho Trail the only links to the Fraser River. Hugh Burr, first settler on the North Shore, took up Lot 193, at the mouth of Seymour Creek, and began to clear a farm.

One event of note broke the monotony—November 9, the barque *Ellen Lewis*, under Captain Hellon, cleared the inlet with 277,500 feet of lumber and 16,000 pickets for Adelaide, Australia. It was the first "foreign trade" export shipment ever made from Burrard Inlet, and John Oscar Smith's swan song in the lumber business.

Burrard Inlet Mills went broke in December.

Sewell Moody's chance had come. For much less than the $8000 he was willing to pay the year before—some say he bought the mortgagee's $5000 bond for $40—S.P. Moody and Co. took over Burrard Inlet Mills.

Now for Burrard Inlet came the year of years.

So far the little millsite "up the coast" had been a mere appanage of New Westminster—a pleasant little backwater where one could catch codfish, where there might be a little coal, and where Mr. Graham and Mr. Smith had managed to lose a lot of money in the impenetrable, dark, dank forest.

Then three notable men moved in on the scene and—presto! —Burrard Inlet was a lusty, brawling, booming little community singularly ungrateful to the unamused mother-city on the Fraser.

They were shrewd Sewell Moody, bumbling, fuming Captain Edward Stamp, and legendary Jerry Rogers, "greatest woodsman of them all."

"Sew" Moody fired the first shot of Burrard Inlet's War of Independence in February, 1865, when he reopened an altered and improved Burrard Inlet Mills.

Graham's and Smith's white elephant got into the black and never looked back.

At the middle of May, Moody and Captain Hall walked the road to the Royal City customs office to clear Moody's first export shipment, on the barque *Glimpse*, for Sydney, Australia. By the end of the month, the *Envoy* was at his wharf, loading 300,000 feet for Adelaide. July 29, the *Metropole* took out a cargo consigned to Mexico.

The *Metropole* cleared through a newly appointed deputy customs collector for Burrard Inlet, and the inlet was on its own.

For the next 20 years its timber era built up in constantly
quickening tempo until the inlet was ranked among the greatest
timber ports in the world.

Moody showed the way. Restless, energetic, scheming, sharp, he
was regarded as "a typical Yankee," but there was more to him than
that. There was a Yankee strain of Puritanism in him, a Puritanism
he sometimes turned to profitable account in his business, yet his
schemes and stratagems occasionally sailed close to the wind of the
law, and, in pioneer parlance, he was "not exactly married" to his
Indian wife. He was at once a stern master and a kind employer.
He was anathema to the ultra-British official set, and generally
regarded by the rest of the colony as a good fellow.

From the first, Moody ruled his mill and milltown with a strong
hand. At once it became known as "Moody's mill," and soon the
little North Shore settlement became Moodyville, and so remained.
It was the first of the three Burrard Inlet settlements, and, for almost
a generation, the leading one.

It was a temperance town. In an age of hard-drinking, savagely-
brawling "timber beasts," Moody's men went dry and worked sober.
They were not without the consolations of religion; June 19 of
that year, Reverend Ebenezer Robson, far-travelled Methodist fron-
tier parson, held Burrard Inlet's first religious service at Moodyville, preaching to 15 men from the mill and the ship *Metropolis*.

As far as Moody could make it, it was a family town. He employed married men when possible, and encouraged them to build
their homes there. In 1868, Moodyville celebrated the Inlet's first
wedding—Ada Guinne to Peter Plante, by Reverend Edward White,
Mr. Robson's Methodist successor. In 1870, with a $500 grant
from the colony, Moodyville opened the Inlet's first school. Miss
Laura Haynes, sister of a mill employee, was teacher.

The quiet annals of Moodyville are outshouted by the rowdy
history of Gastown, but for the 20 years of the timber era it remained
the leading, most influential and most progressive of the inlet
towns. And when Moody drowned in the disastrous wreck of

the *SS Pacific* off Cape Flattery in 1875, he was universally mourned. The pioneers remembered his irrepressible humor and his secret kindnesses; his "sharp Yankee tricks" became a cherished legend, no doubt embroidered upon.

Most shadowy of our three pioneers is Jerry Rogers, the Paul Bunyan of Point Grey, though his name is the only one still daily on the lips of Vancouverites. "Jerry's Cove" naturally became Jericho, and Jericho Beach it is today.

By all accounts, from present Granville Street to the tip of Point Grey grew one of the most magnificent stands of virgin timber the world has ever seen. "Big sticks", in these days of steel girders and pressed and laminated composition boards, are an embarrassment, rather than an asset, to lumber mills. Not so in Jerry's time, when great sailing vessels called for masts and spars, Chinese emperors built palaces of wood, and the stately homes of England demanded beams of baronial proportions.

In May, when Moody was loading the *Envoy*, his men brought out of the woods and sawed the framing timbers, 70 feet long and 20 inches square "without a knot," as Moody's gift to the construction of Holy Trinity Church bell-tower in New Westminster. At the same time, Rogers' axemen were working into the forest from Jerry's Cove, felling trees incomparably larger.

They worked on "springboards" notched into the butts of the trees eight to twelve feet from the ground. A day's work by two expert fellers would scarce serve to make the undercut that guided the tree's fall. From the opposite side, whirring crosscut saws 10 and 12 feet long then ate into the heart of the 800 or 900-year-old tree, bringing it to a thunderous downfall that bared to full sunlight for the first time in a millenium the pale forest undergrowth.

August 15, the ship *Aquila*, Captain Sayward, took on board Jerry's first shipment—251 gigantic spars—before moving in to complete loading at Moodyville. Jerry's second shipment—early in 1866, on the *Egeria* for Glasgow—gives us some notion of the value of these huge timbers. Two hundred and fifty-seven spars brought $50,000, about $195 each. These were probably smaller than usual, as the average spar was valued at $230.

Their reputation spread. In July, 1866, Rogers loaded the *Astarte* with spars for the French Navy. The *Astarte's* master declared them "the finest cut anywhere in the world" and the commercial magnates of New Westminster entertained him and Jerry at a formal banquet.

From January, 1867, to July, 1868, Rogers shipped no less than 2000 spars. Two years later, in 1870, the American ship *Martha Rideout* took a number of timbers 101 feet long and 24 inches square, "the finest ever shipped anywhere." Jerry's logging was so selective "the point was twice logged off after he went, before it was clear" of merchantable timber.

A progressive operator, in 1873 he built his own tug, the *Maggie*, 20 horsepower, 72 feet long, 16 feet beam, 4 feet 6 inches draught. By 1874 he was using a steam tractor, a number of which had been imported for use on the Cariboo Road, but failed in that onerous duty. The solid rubber-tired wheels cost $500 each, and he bought and dismantled others of the tractors to use the pairs of wheels as log trucks. However, the bulk of his hauling power was still oxen; Jim Grouse, Indian resident of Brockton Point, weekly ferried him out by dugout canoe 40 sacks of feed from Hastings Mill. At this date Rogers was logging the productive Fairview slope south of False Creek.

He died in Gastown in 1877, leaving little personal information behind. Except for his titanic labors in the woods and his reputation for harboring "busted" hand-loggers in his camps free of charge, the pioneers remembered little of him.

Some idea of the conditions under which he worked, however, may be gained from the fact that Angus Carmichael Fraser, who took over the south-shore bay camps after him, in 12 months cut and put in the water 9,470,000 feet of timber off only 80 acres, and in 1884 by special order shipped to Peking beams for the Imperial Palace 112 feet long, 28 inches square, and, in accord with the usual specifications of perfection, "without a knot."

Jerry is also credited with being the originator of the harmless fraud the inlet timber exporters worked on the British Admiralty. The Admiralty, unacquainted with forests where a tree three feet in the butt was considered a "sapling," called for masts and spars hand-hewn, to save every last inch of length and girth of the largest trunks. Jerry's spars were towed to the mills, sawed down to Admiralty dimensions, and then supplied with a laboriously hand-hewn finish. Thus everybody was satisfied.

Well, peace to his ashes—he was "the greatest woodsman of them all," and who would want a better epitaph?

Captain Edward Stamp was of different kidney. Well-connected, hand-in-glove with the Victoria political clique, captain probably by courtesy (since he once bought a ship he was afraid to sail in) he had unfortunate intervals as a merchant in Victoria and a mill-owner on Alberni Canal. "The colonies" weren't panning out.

He selected Burrard Inlet as his next venture.

The exact political implications behind his activities probably never will be known, but they offer scope for speculation. Colonel Moody, recalled to England, had been succeeded as commissioner of lands by Joseph William (later Sir Joseph) Trutch. Governor Douglas had retired in 1864, and Governor Frederick Seymour of the mainland colony was preparing to assume office as governor of the united colonies the following year. Captain Stamp was an Island—not a Mainland—notable, and possibly Seymour wished the goodwill of the Island magnates.

Whatever the background may have been, Commissioner Trutch on November 30, 1865, signed the document around which Vancouver was built.

Hastings Mill Land Lease (the title is an anachronism) conveyed to British Columbia and Vancouver Island Spar, Lumber and Sawmill Co. (in effect, Captain Stamp) for £50-13-6, Lot 196, Group 1, of 243 acres, 37 perches, in fee simple, to be known as the Sawmill Claim, in the heart of future Vancouver; also 5254 acres on the south shore of English Bay, 2897 acres on the North Arm of the Fraser River, 1920 acres on Howe Sound, 1280 acres at Port Neville, as timber leases; the right to select for purchase 1200 additional acres at four shillings, twopence an acre; the right to select 15,000 additional acres of timber leases, and whatever water rights necessary to the company's undertakings.

The total payment was $244.04. In 1929 a very small fraction of the original Sawmill Claim alone was resold to the Federal Government of Canada for $2.4 million. Mathematically, over 64 years, this fraction had each year increased in value 153 times the total cost of the entire Hastings Mill holdings.

Government "giveaways" are not a new invention.

Not that Captain Stamp made much out of it. Not only was he too proud to follow the leadership of "damned colonials," he went out of his way to make enemies of them.

The captain's first effort was an abortive mill and wharf about where Lumbermen's Arch is now. Neither the wharf nor their own anchors could hold ships against the strong First Narrows currents.

This attempt was made in 1865, and obviously before the mill lease was drafted, for it was not until after this preliminary failure that he settled upon the spit at the foot of modern Dunlevy Street which is the site specified in the lease as the Sawmill Claim. Some previous agreement, official or unofficial, must have been made, for by the date of lease, construction of the second mill was well under way. In December, the barque *Kent* brought direct from Glasgow the mill machinery, and was able to unload it at Stamp's wharf.

The *Kent* was piloted by the newly-appointed inlet pilot, Captain A. J. Chambers, and after discharging was towed to Moodyville to load for Mexico—Moody's fifth export cargo of the year.

As the New Year dawned, Stamp found an essential piece of the machinery was lacking. He sued and won damages from the shippers (the inlet's first civil lawsuit) but the mill did not begin operation until 1867.

Nor had the captain waited for a lease before stirring up trouble with his neighbors. In August, 1865, he objected to the B.C. Coal Mining Co., a firm of New Westminster and Burrard Inlet men, sinking a test hole on the south shore of False Creek, even though under the mill grant his claim to that area was a timber lease only. The mining firm sidestepped trouble and moved to the inlet shore on the border of the Brickmakers' Claim. There John Dick and his drillers reached a depth of 500 feet by April, 1866, without encountering any substantial seams. This ended the dream of coal mining in Vancouver. The only other reference we have to it concerns one Ostrander, who for a brief period worked by himself a small surface seam near Second Beach, and peddled the coal in Gastown.

An unpleasant man he was, but Stamp's contributions to the inlet were by no means negligible. In '65 one of the chief drawbacks to the inlet as a lumber port was the cost of loading ships, a process that averaged six weeks and involved inward and outward tows by tugs from Victoria. While Moody improved his wharfage, Stamp ordered built in Victoria the inlet's first tug, the *Isobel*, a sidewheeler 146 feet long, 24 feet beam, 9 feet draught, with Scottish engines. She was launched in May and her first recorded tow was the ship *John Jay* in August, by which time Moody had cut the loading time to four weeks. Captain Chambers commanded the *Isobel*; Pamphlet and Devereaux were later skippers.

Towage was a major problem all through the windjammer era, since the ships had to be picked up anywhere from Victoria to Cape Flattery, as the wind dictated, and returned to that neighborhood when loaded. No sailing ship of large tonnage could safely navigate the intricate passages of the strait.

Stamp's Mill, better known to Vancouver as Hastings Mill, made its first cut June 18, 1867, with the ship *Siam* waiting at the wharf to be loaded.

This was the beginning of the history of Vancouver proper— the city that arose from Gastown, the settlement that grew up around the mill.

For more than 60 years the mill, built and rebuilt, operated profitably in the heart of the city; its waste-burner was a time-hallowed navigation beacon for the harbor.

"By day and by night, the roar of the mill was the pulse of Gastown," truthfully said its first historian, Darrell Gomery.

Captain Stamp continued the uneven tenor of his way.

Unlike Moody, he made no effort to supervise or improve the living conditions of his workers. A higgledy-piggledy settlement of Indians, Kanaka and Scandinavian deserters from the sailing ships and "busted" refugees from the gold mines grew up around the mill and provided his labor force. The captain had more interesting

projects, such as getting himself elected first member of the Legislative Assembly from Lillooet when the two colonies, mainland and
island, were united in November, 1866, as the Crown Colony of
British Columbia.

The *Siam* was loaded and sailed July 25. The mill continued to
cut to capacity, and September 14 the port achieved a record of
four ships loading at once, the *Anna Dorothea* at Moodyville, the
Australind, General Cobb and *Nation's Hope* at Stamp's.

Stamp himself had not neglected his mission of making enemies.
He protested to the colonial government against Jonathan Miller
cutting timber near Brockton Point, on limits to which Stamp laid
claim. Governor Seymour, in a neat minute made December 15
on the back of the protest, suggested Miller be allowed to retain
the logs he had cut. "Captain Stamp has given us a great deal of
trouble," the governor noted.

The following day he added:

"Miller has a perfect right to the logs. Captain Stamp has also
been making trouble with Rogers on English Bay."

By March, 1868, a port record was again set; four ships were
loading at Stamp's, three at Moody's. In May, 10¯ were loading at
once, and the barque *Monita* caught fire at Stamp's wharf. She
was towed away by the *Isobel* and scuttled on a mudflat to extinguish
the flames. Later the same month Stamp's wharf collapsed, cant-
ing gently over on one side as 300,000 feet of sawn lumber floated
away on the tide. The traditional trio of mishaps was completed
July 11, when the ship *Vidette* grounded on the North Shore near
First Narrows and had to be lightened of 50,000 feet of lumber
before she could be refloated.

The great lumber port was now taking shape. Moody was
rebuilding his mill with steam power, to cut 100,000 feet a day,
equal to Stamp's, and providing wharfage for 12 ships. Moody had
also solved his stevedoring problem; in September he completely
loaded the *Princess Royal* with lumber for Valparaiso in two days.

Stamp's record of shipments was the more impressive. In 18
months from January, 1867, to the end of June, 1868, Moody
exported 5,832,000 feet of lumber and 800,000 hand-cut shingles

on 33 vessels. In the little more than a year, from June 18, 1867, to the end of June, 1868, Stamp loaded 4,101,000 feet of lumber and 100,000 shingles on 14 vessels.

Nevertheless, Moody was making money; Stamp was not.

Early in 1869, Stamp returned to England. British Columbia and Vancouver Island Spar, Lumber and Sawmill Co. was broke.

The company and its vast assets were sold to Dickson, DeWolf and Co. of San Francisco for $20,000. "A mere fraction of its value," notes Judge Howay, doyen of B.C. historians.

The captain was not regretted by Burrard Inlet; surviving comments of the pioneers indicate their farewell to him was a polite raspberry. Edward Stamp was typical of a type of Englishman now apparently much rarer than in the palmy days of Victoria's Empire. Upper middle class emigrants with some capital, they "came out from home" to show the "colonials" a thing or two, and usually went back home sadder, wiser and with less capital. Once he had made plain he looked on them as a type of "white nigger," it is not surprising the good people of Burrard Inlet took a great delight in kowtowing to the captain before his face and rooking him on every possible occasion behind his back.

Nevertheless, he was not without his uses. There is no single founding-father of the City of Vancouver, but Captain Stamp must be allowed to stand in the van of the dozen or so men instrumental in its founding. The infant city grew from, by means of, and around Stamp's Mill.

THE BEACH AT GRANVILLE IN 1885 — *Two years before the coming of the railway, this was the scene from the Sunnyside Hotel, looking across to North Vancouver with Stanley Park in the middle distance, left. West of the Sunnyside float was the "Government Float" in front of Constable Miller's cottage.*

THE TOWN FROM SUNNYSIDE FLOAT ABOUT 1884 — *Here is what Granville (alias Gastown) looked like in the area between what is now the foot of Carrall, Abbott and Cambie Streets, later the site of Evans, Coleman & Evans Ltd. wharves and the North Vancouver ferry slip. The little community was astir from the easy-going years between the time Jack Deighton landed on the beach with a keg of whiskey and Granville became the site of the C.P.R.'s transcontinental railway terminus.*

THE BIG MAPLE OF GASTOWN AND GRANVILLE — *Before the name Vancouver was thought of, first residents of Gassy Jack's Gastown—later more dignified as Granville—met to talk politics, make deals or spin yarns under the cover of a wide spreading maple. This picture was taken in May 1886 two months before buildings and tree were destroyed by "The Great Fire". It looks south on Carrall Street at its intersection with Water Street. The steps of Gassy Jack's Deighton House Hotel are to be seen at the right.*

WHEN WATER STREET WAS ON THE WATER—*Gastown looked like a Western movie set in the 1870's when idlers talked away the summer hours on the verandah of Jack Deighton's hotel. From the small settlement, a road ran to the Hastings Mill and a trail to the Brickmakers' Claim and the Kanaka Rancherie on Coal Harbor.*

MOODY'S MILL IN 1872 — *This engraving appeared in the* Canadian Illustrated News *of June 1, 1872 picturing the waterfront scene at Burrard Inlet's first industrial operation. Refugees from "The Great Fire" found shelter here when Vancouver was destroyed. The site was in North Vancouver just east of today's Burrard Drydock location.*

HASTINGS MILL IN 1896 — *Ships of the seven seas filled holds and decks with fir timbers cut from trees logged in the clearing of what are now densely populated areas of Vancouver.*

5

Gastown

Some 45 years after the event, a pioneer described the founding of Gastown:

"Gassy Jack Deighton was a man of broad, ready humor, spicy, crisp and ever-flowing. He was of grotesque, Falstaffian proportions and green-muddy, purplish complexion, with the gift of grouping words and throwing them with the volubility of a fakir. A man who shot at random, but always hit the mark—unlucky the man whom Jack nicknamed, for he carried the word with him to the grave.

"Late in 1867 he left his vocation of Fraser River pilot and headed for Stamp's Mill on Burrard Inlet to make his fortune as an innkeeper. There was nothing at that part of the inlet then but the mill.

"Jack landed at his destination in the afternoon of the last day of September in a light drizzle, with his Indian leman, her mother, her cousin (a big Indian who was the motive power of the canoe and on whom Jack often cast green-eyed looks), a yellow dog, two chickens, two weak-backed chairs and a barrel of whisky. Lookers-on from the mill remarked that it was a doubtful acquisition to the population.

"Gassy, with the craft of a Machiavelli, began to pass the loving-cup with an unstinting hand, telling that he had come to start a little business, that his means were limited and he would be glad to accept any assistance in the way of building the house.

"Saws and hammers fell from heaven, and the populace, led by an errant carpenter named Mike McNarama, joined the work. In 24 hours, Deighton House flung open its doors to the public.

45

"That was the beginning of Vancouver. . . .

"Jack pulled himself to the roof of the building, loosened out the Union Jack and in a homely speech told his hearers that (pointing to the flag) it represented all that was good, the blood and guts of England; it bobbed up on every sea, had been his chum of 40 years, that he had pinned his faith in it and would stay with it, that everybody's help had been most gracious and that the whisky barrel was dry and he would have to postpone the christening for a few days."

So Vancouver was born, and Gassy Jack knocked the head out of the barrel and set it up under the eaves of his shack for a rain-tub.

There is just the touch of malice in the description one might expect from one of the later "respectable" Gastownites toward a business rival and survivor of the unregenerate early years, for Joe Mannion owned Deighton House's competitor, the Granville Hotel, delighted in the strictly unofficial title of "Mayor of Gastown"— and there is no denying the original settlement was a pretty rough, tough and ready sort of place.

Indeed, "brawlings and stabbings were frequent," says a chronicler of the early days of Gassy Jack's saloon—for it was nothing more at the start—and little wonder it was, with the crowd Captain Stamp had collected around his mill. In 1867, apart from the "official clique" in Victoria and New Westminster and a few venturesome merchants, the inhabitants of the B.C. coast were the backwash from the gold rush, disbanded rankers of the Royal Engineer detachment, discharged fur company voyageurs, or deserters from the sailing ships. Angels were few and far between; what diamonds there were, were very rough indeed.

The story of Gastown's first years is the story of the taming of a tough crowd and a tough country.

Jack set up his saloon just near enough to the mill to cater to its crew, and just far enough away to be beyond the company's control. It was about half a mile from the mill, west of the swamp that became Columbia Street, standing on what now is the jug-handled intersection where Water and Carrall meet.

Jack was on his own. Former bucko mate on the tough Fraser River steamships, with his ready tongue and strong arm he controlled Gastown and its hard-case roisterers for four long years before an effective constable was appointed in the inlet. And Gastown grew fast in those years.

Historical "firsts" in the rise of Vancouver are a very elastic class of events. As we have seen, suburban North Vancouver was a mill-town some years before Gastown saw its first inhabitant. There may have been one or more settlers in what is now Marpole before the "three greenhorns" took up the Brickmakers' Claim. But it was on the claim and around Gastown—particularly the latter—that Vancouver grew. It was not until many years later that the city absorbed Marpole and it has not yet legally merged with North Vancouver.

Indeed, another section of what is now central Vancouver was settled two years before Gassy Jack put in his appearance.

Early in 1865 the Douglas Road was completed, reaching the inlet near where the present Second Narrows Bridge rises from the southern shore. May 13, the contractor, Scott, drove Governor Seymour and the colony's Secretary Birch over 13 miles of jolting corduroy from New Westminster to view the completed highway. That summer it became fashionable for the elite of the Royal City to visit "End of the Road" to picnic on the white sands and sea-bathe in the clear inlet waters.

In August, Oliver Hocking and Fred Houston there opened the Brighton Hotel, "with beautiful grounds and picturesque walks" all around. The partners built a floating wharf, entertained steamer excursions, and catered to New Westminster folk of substance who built summer cottages nearby.

In March 1866, Hocking assumed the duties of customs collector of the port. In July, W. R. Lewis put a semi-weekly stage over the road between the Fraser and "New Brighton," as the settlement had become, increasing it to a daily service in October. The stage left New Westminster at 10 a.m., was met at New Brighton's wharf by Captain James Van Bramer's steam ferry, the *Sea Foam*, which made the triangle trip to Moodyville, Stamp's Mill, and back to New Brighton at 3 p.m., connecting with the stage's return trip.

The *Sea Foam* displaced "Navvy Jack" Thomas' sloop, and Navvy Jack took to transporting clean gravel from the Capilano mouth bars to inlet towns. In Vancouver ever since the best quality washed gravel has been known in the building supply trade as "Navvy Jack."

In 1868, as the inlet boomed, Lewis put on two daily stages, and Henry Elliott entered into competition with one daily trip. One of Lewis' stages was a four-horse rig; the others both two-horse.

And November saw New Brighton's most glorious hour—it became the first registered subdivision on the inlet, with 24 water-front sites among its 55 lots. One lot was reserved for government buildings, one for a church, and two for a hospital, none of which ever was built. The townsite was renamed Hastings, after Rear Admiral the Honourable George Fowler Hastings, C.B., who had arrived the year before to take command of the Royal Navy's Esquimalt Station. Hocking and Houston's hotel became Hastings Hotel; the hotel, its stable and one neighboring building outside the subdivision were the only existing structures on the original plan.

As if to celebrate the occasion, the same month the *Sea Foam* blew up at Hastings wharf, severely scalding a Mrs. Bloomfield, her young daughter, and Dr. A. W. S. Black, the inlet's pioneer physician.

Hocking and Houston sold the hotel to Maximilien Michaud in March, 1869; Hocking, disappointed of appointment as a full-time customs officer for the port, vanished from the inlet. Shortly after, Michaud opened the inlet's first post office in the hotel, and Hastings rounded out its role as communications hub April 11, when a telegraph line to New Westminster, financed by Sew Moody, constructed by F. H. Lamb, superintendent for Western Union in B.C., transmitted its first message.

In August, the subdivision's first land sale took place, with Lots 2, 3 and 4 going to Michaud, 9 and 36 to Lewis, and 34 and 35 to Ebenezer Brown, New Westminster merchant. All went at the upset price of $50.

This was the high point of Hastings' history. It lingered on as a stage and ferry terminus and summer resort, with "Maxie" Michaud's hotel enjoying an ever-increasing popularity as its reputation for good food and comfortable lodging grew. One of its attractions was Maxie's consort, golden-skinned Frisadie, whose beauty the pioneers never tired of mentioning. Nor did they omit the monotonous slander, that she and Maxie "were not exactly married."

A slander it was, which British and Canadian immigrants superciliously fastened on almost every native or part-native wife of the early settlers. It was not only self-righteous; it was unjust in itself, and the excuse for much cruelty and often downright robbery.

Previous to the gold rush and the arrival of the "official clique" and their hangers-on in 1858, marriage "according to the custom of the country" was an accepted and respectable—as well as necessary—institution. Such unions were enduring, no stigma attached to the children, and in the primitive conditions of the fur trade life, problems of inheritance were settled on the spot and never — or at least extremely rarely — challenged on legal grounds. The Roman Catholic missionaries encouraged such partners to enter into the religious contract of marriage when possible, but cheerfully tolerated the less formal unions.

That they had the highest official sanction is witnessed by the fact the marriage of Sir James Douglas to the daughter of Chief Factor William Connolly was "according to the custom of the country," remained so for nine years during Douglas' employment under Connolly in northern B.C., through the birth and death of children, and its legality was never called into question until Douglas and his wife returned to Hudson's Bay headquarters on the lower Columbia and two newly-arrived Anglican missionaries, by continued importunity, convinced Douglas a church ceremony was necessary to restore him and his wife to "respectability."

Of course British officialdom, when imported to occupy the high places in the new colony, vigorously supported the church's view. Legally these previously valid marriages were abolished; socially they were degraded; the children became illegitimate and their rights of inheritance abolished in favor of the husband's kin—often distant kin in a distant land.

This is usually what is to be understood when prudish later arrivals referrred to Sew Moody, Maxie Michaud, Gassy Jack and others of their predecessors being "not exactly married." The reproach lies not on these men and their wives, but on the church, the judiciary and the officialdom which condemned them. For the rest, let it suffice that during the early years of Burrard Inlet, this was one of the colony's main social problems, and it did not pass by Moodyville, Gastown or Hastings.

Indeed, Gastown's second resident was also a partner in one of these romantic marriages. Joe Silvey, Joe Silvia, or (most probably correct) Joseph Silvia Simmons, benighted at Musqueam Village in 1867, mistook a hospitable welcome for a hostile reception, and was only reassured after a long and mostly misunderstood exchange in sign language. But a 24-hour stay was enough to let him fall in love with one of the hegas men's daughters, she proved not averse to him, and within the day a marriage which continued happily until they were separated by death, was negotiated and concluded in the same silent gestures. The following year the Delta cattle-drover and his wife opened a combined grocery store and saloon just a city block away from Gassy Jack's, on what is now the south-east corner of Abbott and Water Streets. Simmons' subsequent history is beclouded by Gastown's careless habit of nomenclature, for we can trace, but not separate, the careers of no less than three "Portuguese Joes" in the town. It is probable that he eventually settled on the east coast of Vancouver Island or one of the lesser islands off the coast.

One of his compatriots who managed to escape the universal nick-name seems to have been the legendary Peter the Whaler, who, with a boat's crew of Kanakas and Indians, harpooned whales in the inlet and rendered the blubber at Deadman's Island and later near Deep Cove, to provide oil for the mills and for household lamps. But how a Jose da Costa became a "Peter Smith" is difficult to imagine unless we assume that a seaman who "left" (i.e., deserted) a ship in the harbor, temporarily welcomed any alias. But there are still Da Costas on the Delta who claim Peter the Whaler for an ancestor.

The turning point in Gastown's rather squalid beginning came with the New Year of 1869, when Captain James A. Raymur succeeded Captain Stamp as manager of the mill. Raymur, a veteran master mariner, cold, polite, dignified, pale, ascetic, "a polished gentleman," was the antithesis of Stamp and, naturally, not too welcome in Gastown, for he came armed with the powers of resident magistrate and the determination to reform the settlement. His first words on seeing the disorderly camp around the mill were an earnest of his purpose:

"What," he is reported as saying, "is the meaning of this aggregation of filth? I will not permit a running sore to fasten itself upon an industry entrusted to my care!"

Whereupon the conglomeration of male, female and infant Kanakas, Indians and roustabouts was forthwith banished, with their cows, chickens, pigs, cats and dogs. A company bunkhouse was provided for single men; the happy-go-lucky Kanakas retired to the farthest reaches of Coal Harbor, where their settlement became known as the Kanaka Rancherie or, alternatively, the Cherry Orchard, for in time its cherry trees became one of the springtime sights of the inlet.

Improvement and respectability became the order of the day; Raymur vied with Moody to create a model town. While the Kanakas were being banished from Stamp's Mill, Moodyville was naming its streets—Kanaka Row, Maiden Lane, Brigham Terrace came into being. January 15, Moodyville marked the inauguration of Mount Hermon Masonic Lodge, the inlet's first fraternal organization, with J. C. Hughes, W. O. Allen, P. W. Swett, Captain Van Bramer, Coote M. Chambers, George W. Haynes, Alexander McGowan, S. T. Washburn and Moody as its founding officers. January 23 Raymur countered with the New London Mechanics' Institute, a meeting room and library for mill employees opened by Reverend Arthur Browning. In March it was renamed Hastings Literary Institute, and soon Stamp's Mill also became Hastings Mill, the name which it kept more than 60 years.

But Raymur never had a chance. The essential factor which decreed Hastings Mill settlement would never become as neat and tidy as Moodyville similarly ensured that Gastown would dominate the inlet. Moodyville was a company town. Gastown was not.

Benevolent and progressive Moody might be, but he owned Moodyville; Sew Moody's will was Moodyville's law, and in the last essentials, Moodyville existed to enhance Moody's fortune and serve Moody's mill.

On the other hand, while Raymur undoubtedly had great influence and power, Gastown clung to the unalterable conviction that the purpose of Hastings Mill was to serve Gastown. Let Raymur or "the company" attempt to impose their will one inch beyond the strict legal boundaries of their power, and they had to face the united opposition of a free, independent and (it must be confessed) greedy Gastown.

This basic antagonism was mutually profitable. Both factions were, on the whole, composed of reasonable men. The citizens of Gastown recognized that their livelihood depended on the prosperity of the mill. The management of the mill, warned by the mishaps, shutdowns and all-pervading chaos that had characterized Stamp's operations, realized the prosperity of the mill depended on the good-will and co-operation of the people of Gastown. It was a case of co-existence or no existence, yet there remained sufficient tension and conflict of interests to assure that both Gastown and Hastings Mill maintained the vitality, enterprise and energy which soon pushed these necessarily allied opponents into the domination of their little world.

Sixteen months after the subdivision of Hastings, it was Gastown's turn. The town survey, registered March 1, 1870, included the area between modern Carrall, Hastings and Cambie Streets and extended north to approximately the present waterfront, but of the 29 lots north of Water Street, 21 were entirely and eight partially under water at high tide. Between Carrall and Abbott the shore ran along the south side of Water; between Abbott and Cambie it was slightly to the north of the street. The townsite was officially dubbed Granville (after Earl Granville, British colonial secretary) but the town was Gastown, and Gastown it remained to all and sundry—even, for some years to come, on Admiralty charts.

The land sale took place April 11. Gassy Jack bought Lot 1, Block 2, an out-size piece on the southwest corner of Carrall and

Abbott, for $135. By mischance (or official design?) his saloon was right in the middle of the intersection and later he moved it onto the lot. Ebenezer Brown, also a landholder in Hastings, bought Lot 3, Block 2, for $100; he already had built a saloon on the site, next but one to Gassy Jack's on the south side of the street. Gregorio Fernandez (second of our Portuguese Joes) bought Lot 16, Block 6, on the northwest corner of Water and Abbott for $50; only a small fraction of this was above the high tide mark, but probably he wanted the wharf-site. His building stood just south of the lot and, like Gassy Jack's, in the street allowance.

Successively west of Brown's lot, all on the south side of Water, were George Brew's restaurant (Lot 4), John (Jonathan?) A. Webster's store (Lot 5), Alex McCrimmon's hotel (Lot 6), and Joseph Simmons' ("Silvey", in the records) saloon (Lot 7). These were all at this date in occupation of the land and entitled to buy at the upset price of $100, but failed to do so; Brew and Mc-Crimmon asked but were refused permission to rent. Webster purchased his lot in December; Brew, McCrimmon and Simmons theirs in May, 1871. Here we see the beginning of Vancouver— three saloons, one hotel, two stores.

What Gastown's total population was at this period we do not know. In 1869 ex-Sapper John Scales and his family were living in the shed the coal drillers had put on the borders of the Brick-makers' Claim. In later years his son said his mother and "the women of the settlement" washed clothes at a little creek flowing down the present Cambie Street, heating the water over fires on the beach. He also mentioned a boatbuilder, Charlie House, who lived near the bluff on which was the Morton-Brighouse-Hailstone shack.

The Gastown clearing was about two blocks long, extended in part as far back as Cordova Street, and was connected by rough trails to the Brickmakers' Claim, to False Creek and to Hastings Mill. The trails were little used; the inlet traffic was practically all by water. Deighton House boasted a substantial floating wharf, Brown's Saloon a 40-foot "landing log," and Fernandez' store a float seven by 40 feet, at which Indians traded clams, eggs, vegetables and fish.

One thing was certain, of the seven landowners of Gastown, and their families, lodgers or hired help, not one had the least notion of buying lots away off in the bush—on Cordova Street for $75, or on Hastings for $50. If anyone had wished to do so, 100 years ago he could have bought the present site of Woodward's department store for an even $500.

6

The Quiet Years

GASTOWN'S FIRST ten or twelve
years after it gained legal recognition were a quiet, placid and, on the
whole, idyllic time. As history in the grand tradition, they scarcely
exist; the straggling clump of shacks on the edge of the inlet spent
these years as a humdrum little coast village, unconscious of its
destiny. As a study typical of scores of just such B.C. villages, the
decade is a fascinating and detailed historical miniature.

The artist who painted the miniature for us was the late Major
J. S. Matthews, archivist of the City of Vancouver, a stocky, blunt
and peppery enthusiast. He has been accused of obstinacy, arro-
gance, and even of idiocy, when what possessed him was the blazing white fires of selfless dedication. He has wheedled, importuned
and bullied mayors, councils, commissioners and even the pioneers
he loved, and spent himself and his money, until Vancouver possesses records of its early days unequalled in any other city in the
world. Who the pioneers were, what they did, what they thought,
what they remembered, are in his filing cabinets. Historians may
differ with the Major on the interpretation of his data, but for the
fact it is there at all, they owe him lasting gratitude. His epitaph
is no less than he could desire: A citizen who has given greatly
to his city.

No story of Vancouver would be complete without culling a few
flowers from the quiet meadow of these years.

British Columbia entered Confederation in 1871; some other
things were of greater importance to Gastown. For instance, George
DeBeck was killed in one of the inlet logging camps; his widow

lived on well past the century mark to see her sons and grandsons prosperous citizens of towns yet unborn. When she was in her nineties, schoolboys of Eburne (now Marpole, for Eburne moved across the river), fetching the milk from DeBeck's in the early morning, would wonder to see the old lady exercising at her open window with dumbbells.

Richard Henry Alexander, 26-year-old Scot, arrived with his beautiful wife to be Captain Raymur's assistant. Mrs Alexander, who came to the colony on one of the famous "bride ships," became the social queen of the inlet, as Mrs. Raymur preferred to remain amid civilization in Victoria. Alexander had been one of the few to survive the gruesome overland trek from Canada to the Cariboo goldfields.

For once, Gassy Jack, Raymur and Moody found themselves in surprised accord on the side of respectability. Tompkins Brew had been an ineffective constable; pioneers remembered him chiefly as sitting asleep on the verandah with his long beard fluttering in the breeze. The trio petitioned Governor Musgrave for better protection, and Jonathan Miller, Captain Stamp's old antagonist, was appointed. The government built him a house and tiny jail on the lot between Jack's saloon and Brown's. Brew retained his position as government agent.

Dr. Black, survivor of the *Sea Foam* explosion, was thrown from his horse and killed on the Douglas Road one night when galloping to answer an emergency call.

Moody raised the telegraph tolls to New Westminster from 25 to 50 cents. The barque *Cornelis*, loaded at Hastings Mill for Valparaiso, was lost in Howe Sound, but her cargo salvaged.

Gassy Jack enlarged his saloon and made it a substantial hotel. July 20, Confederation Day, he raised over Deighton House the first Canadian flag seen on the inlet. New Westminster had to wait a month and a half for a similar event, until Jack loaned the flag to Ebenezer Brown and it was hoisted over Brown's Royal City saloon.

The following year Alexander opened a post office in the mill store and the use of Canadian postage stamps became general—

previously mail had been sent out on American ships, bearing American stamps. Deacon Henry Eburne arrived on the Fraser's North Arm and bought an acre of land from Gariepy for $1. The settlement bearing Eburne's name did not become Marpole until 1916. In August, two desperadoes named Brown and Shelley raided a logging camp. Constable Miller staged a running fight with his revolver against their two rifles on English Bay. They fled ashore, leaving Miller with a canoe-load of loot and two frightened Indian women on his hands.

On October 2, the first bridge across False Creek was opened, where Main Street now runs. It led to a trail that ran through Mount Pleasant and down the South Slope to the Fraser. Julius Ceasar, a harmless eccentric with a vegetable patch on the south shore of the creek, had little faith in the bridge; he continued to roll large boulders into the creek in his spare time, so travellers could cross dry-shod at low tide.

Arrival of the year was George Black, Gastown's first butcher. George built a house, shop and abattoir almost opposite Deighton House, projecting out over the water on piles. His Fraser River cattle and local hogs were slaughtered on the back platform, the carcasses hoisted for cleaning and flaying by the same crane that later lowered them into his boat. The boat was equipped with a butcher's block, and with a helper George rowed to the ships in the harbor to sell or deliver meat. His hogs roamed the beach, feeding on offal and mussels and clams. He was a genial "sporting" man who owned and raced horses.

It is also told of George that he once kept a pet bear, but when it grew obstreperous, chained it and shipped it to Victoria on the famous SS Beaver. The bear got loose, the crew took to the rigging, and that ancient sidewheeler experienced a lively hour or two before Bruin was penned up again.

Came 1873 and Captain Raymur scored a major advance in civilizing Gastown. In January, the town's first school was opened at the mill in a building 18 by 40 feet. Georgia Sweney, daughter of the millwright, was teacher. Captain William Soule, head stevedore, Alexander and Constable Miller were the board; the school district included the area within a three-mile radius with the mill as its centre. The school was dedicated by Rev. Mr. Owen, an Anglican, and he and our old Methodist friend, Ebenezer Robson, preached in the schoolroom on their Sunday visitations. There were 16 pupils in the first class, Indian, Kanaka and white.

Miss Sweney married at the end of her first term. The school board, hoping against hope for a more permanent incumbent, appointed Mrs. Richards, a young and pretty widow, as her successor.

As the year progressed, Alex McCrimmon built the Sunnyside Hotel's big float, 200 yards long and a dozen feet wide. At the year's end, Gastown had a population of sixty-five. The mill crew and the married employees living on mill property undoubtedly outnumbered the townspeople.

Among the arrivals at the mill this year were John Peabody Patterson, his wife Susan, and their two daughters. One of the latter has left us a description of the children playing in the mill sawdust pile. On Abbie Patterson's birthday, school was let out early, there were sports and races for all, and Captain Fry of the ship *Niagara* brought a big pan of currant buns from the galley to distribute as prizes. The grown-ups played cards in the schoolhouse that night, and danced to the music of a concertina and a violin.

Mrs. Patterson, a managing woman, was just the sort of hard-boiled angel of mercy Gastown needed. She tended the sick and injured, "never quailed from hardship, danger or disease," and could rout a drunken or brutal husband with a look and a word. In later years she earned herself the title of "the Grace Darling of Burrard Inlet" by going to the aid of Mrs. Erwin, seriously-ill wife of the Point Atkinson light-keeper, on a dark and stormy night when even the boldest tug skippers would not face the wind and waves. But Mrs. Patterson and two Indians did, in a canoe, arriving at the lighthouse just as dawn broke. One of the Indians was named Chinalset; the other's name has been forgotten.

It really was quite an eventful year. The barque *Whittier* carried a piano among its cabin furniture. The master sold it to a Mrs. Schweppe, who resold it to Mrs. Richards, and then the school teacher also gave piano lessons in her rooms in Gastown.

Also among arrivals was the Methodist missionary-pastor, Rev. James Turner, soon known as the Minister of the Interior. A parsonage was built for him on the northeast corner of Water and Abbott, across the street from Simmons' saloon, now called the Hole-in-the-Wall. The Reverend James had a thorny field to labor in, for at this time or soon afterwards, two doors to the west of the parsonage, just past Fernandez' store, Birdie Stewart, Vancouver's first madam, opened an establishment devoted to the oldest profession. However, next the Hole-in-the-Wall, devout Mrs. Sullivan, a mulatto, set up a tiny restaurant. Her son, Arthur, "a fair, handsome Negro," opened a store and soon became the town's leading musician and most popular master of ceremonies. Mrs. Sullivan was "Gastown's first Methodist" and in her kitchen Mr. Turner held his first services.

Dr. William Wymond Walkem was also an arrival. He was the inlet's second (or possibly first) resident physician, employed by the mill and living in a mill cottage.

And still, as the Irishman said, wonders had not done ceasing. The most important arrival of all in 1873 came neither by ship, canoe, stage nor on foot, but by quite another route. Henry O. Alexander, son of Richard and Mrs. Alexander, was born at Hastings Mill, Gastown's (and Vancouver's) first white native. In a long and useful life, he rose to be a judge and an honored and loved citizen of Vancouver.

Whether it can be relied upon or not is uncertain, but one pioneer mentions this as the year in which a famous civic institution began. The Negro cook of the *Red Rover* was detected stealing from Gastown clotheslines, apprehended by Miller, and "put on the chain gang" until returned to the ship when it sailed. If so, a light chain was secured to each ankle, long enough that it could be tucked over his belt while he was working on the roads. This custom was maintained until 1910, long after Vancouver became a city.

Raymur continued his efforts to tame Gastown, advertising in New Westminster's *Mainland Guardian* that as resident magistrate he would oppose the licensing "of any Burrard Inlet houses that keep open after midnight or play cards on Sunday."

Over on the North Shore, farmer Hugh Burr put Henry Alexander in the shade. Mrs. Burr added to their previous four daughters the inlet's first white twins, Emaline and Adeline. Burr and Tom Lynn, godfather of Lynn Creek, both sold milk and farm produce in Gastown, delivering by rowboat.

And then came the *Union*. How a steam threshing machine arrived on Burrard Inlet nobody knows, though a square scow was natural enough there. They were owned by two pioneers (names mercifully lost in the mists of time) who wedded these unlikely consorts and supplied them with a pair of paddlewheels. The culprits then went into the towing business.

The *Union* had one speed—full ahead. Her power was small, so she habitually started off with a long slack line on her tow, gaining speed, and achieved a crack-the-whip effect at the end of the line which set the *Union* back on her heels, but at the same time, imparted a moderate forward velocity to the tow. Then she would gingerly tighten the line and plod solemnly up or down the inlet, steered with a sweep.

Naturally, she was never called the *Union* by anyone but her proud owners. To everyone else she was known as the *Sudden Jerk*.

One final arrival ends the year. As already chronicled, Moody's steam mill burned down December 23. Hired to superintend its reconstruction was a New Brunswick lumberman, already successful in the eastern trade and with a season in the Washington woods behind him. He was John Hendry, aged 20.

Gassy Jack had made his saloon into a hotel in 1871; Gastown had grown large in 1873, and early in April 1874, he completed alterations and refurbishing, advertising in New Westminster papers "the new Deighton House . . . comfortable parlours and commodious single and double bedrooms." Perhaps expansion was a strain on his finances, for shortly afterwards he left the hotel in charge of his cousin, Tom Deighton, and Tom's wife. Jack, his Indian wife and their little son (known to all as "the Earl of Granville") went back to the Fraser, where Jack became master of Captain Irving's splendid new steamer, the *Onward*.

WHERE THE PIONEERS WORSHIPPED — *Vancouver's second church was St. James (Anglican) on Burrard Inlet. Its clangorous bell rang the alarm in the burning of the city. Built in 1881 it was consumed in the fire of 1886 and rebuilt at its present site on East Cordova Street. In this photograph Spratt's Oilery at what is now the foot of Thurlow Street is seen in the distance.*

THE CAUSEWAY TO STANLEY PARK—*First picnickers in the old Admiralty Reserve crossed on boulders and a tree trunk at the entrance to Lost Lagoon. Stanley Park's thousand acres of trees, trails and lawns are famous around the world.*

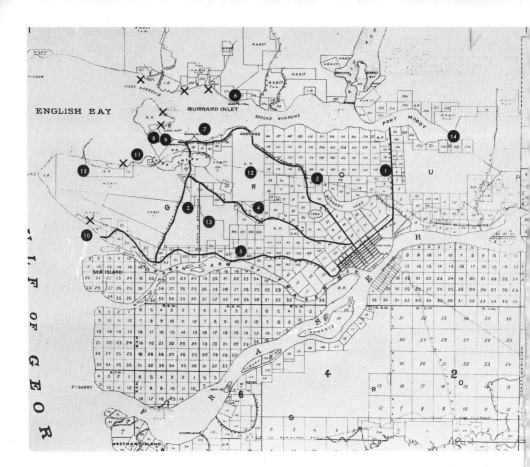

Vancouver City Archives

THE ROADS THAT LED TO GRANVILLE — *This map has historic interest as having belonged to Sir William Van Horne and with his pencilled sketch of a possible rail route (12) for his C.P.R. railway to a terminus at Jericho Beach on English Bay. Some early roads, trails and landmarks are: 1. The North Road, built by Royal Engineers to link New Westminster with Admiralty anchorage; 2. road to New Brighton Hotel and beach; 3. pack trail for farm supplies from Eburne to the Inlet; 4. described as "False Creek Road" this was the route followed by modern Kingsway; 5. River Road to Eburne (Marpole) and a winter loading point for water shipments to Burrard Inlet; 6. Moodyville Mill; 7. Hastings Mill; 8. Kanaka Rancherie, Coal Harbor; 9. area of coal discovery, John Morton's shack, and Spratt's Oilery; 10. Musqueam Indian village where hostile natives in 1808 met and turned back canoes of Simon Fraser's party of exploration; 11. Sam Greer's beach, later Kitsilano and Indian Reserve; 12. hypothetical alternative to C.P.R.'s route down Burrard Inlet; 13. Fraser Road now Fraser Street; 14. Port Moody, first terminus planned for the C.P.R. X marks old Indian village.*

Aerial Map by Hunting Surveys Corpn. Ltd.

VANCOUVER AND ITS SUBURBAN AREAS — *As contrasted with the early days map opposite, when the settlement on Burrard Inlet was still at its beginnings, this is the modern city, seen from a height of nearly six miles. Following are points identified: 1. Vancouver City Area; 2. Burnaby; 3. New Westminster; 4. North Vancouver; 5. North Vancouver District; 6. West Vancouver; 7. Sea Island and Airport; 8. Surrey; 9. Lulu Island; 10. Annacis Island; 11. Fraser River; 12. Burrard Inlet; 13. English Bay; 14. Stanley Park; 15. Kingsway; 16. Point Grey and University of B.C.; 17. Point Atkinson; 18. Lions' Gate Bridge; 19. Steveston; 20. Coal Harbor; 21. Boundary Bay; 22. Exhibition Park; 23. Port Moody; 24. Richmond; 25. Delta.*

VANCOUVER'S FIRST CITY COUNCIL—*Pictured June 16, 1886 three days after the fire that destroyed the city two months after incorporation.* **SEATED**—*Ald. C. A. Coldwell, Ald. E. P. Hamilton, Ald. J. R. Northcott, Mayor M. A. MacLean, Ald. L. A. Hamilton, Ald. P. Cordiner, Thomas F. McGuigan (City Clerk).* **STANDING**—*Ald. Jos. Griffith, Ald. R. Balfour, Ald. Thomas Dunn, J. J. Blake (city solicitor), Ald. Jos. Humphries, George F. Baldwin (city treasurer), Dr. W. J. McGuigan (coroner).*

THE FIRST POLICE FORCE—*Three constables under Chief J. M. Stewart (second from left) were the enforcers of law in 1886. The policemen (left to right) were: J. T. Abray, V. W. Haywood and John McLaren, deputy chief.*

For almost seven years its founder had been the leading citizen of Gastown—for four of the seven its undisputed master.

Before he left, however, he attended Gastown's first wedding. Alas for the school board!—it was the nuptials of Mrs. Richards and Ben Springer, a Moodyville man, later manager of Moody's mill. A Miss Redfern—briefly—succeeded her as teacher. Miss Eunice Seabrook took over as the town's music teacher.

December 2, there was another wedding. Years later, her sister told of the marriage of Abbie Patterson to Captain William Jordan of the ship *Marmion*. It took place in the uncarpeted parlor of the Patterson home, with the Minister of the Interior officiating.

"Abbie made her own wedding dress," she says. "It was beige in color. Mrs. Alexander brought the orange blossoms from Victoria; she was the prettiest woman there—so handsome!

"Ada Miller, the constable's daughter, had a dark blue dress, made from material bought at the mill store, and Mrs. Alexander wore a cornflower-blue silk, her own wedding dress.

"Captain William Soule, the head stevedore, was the best man.

"The ceremony was at half-past seven in the evening, and the wedding was performed in the sitting room. We all went to the kitchen for supper, and afterwards to the mill library to dance.

"It was a wonderful party and everybody was there. George Bone played the concertina and there was a violin, and Mrs. Alexander sang and so did Mrs. Haynes of Moodyville. Captain Pickard read the address to the bride and groom.

"We all, every one of us, drank wine, and there were lots and lots of presents—earrings and a brooch from the crew of Captain Pickard's ship, the *Niagara*, and a case of wine and whisky from Gassy Jack Deighton.

"There wasn't any honeymoon; they just went on board Captain Jordan's ship and sailed away to China. . . ."

Apparently Captain Pickard had succeeded Captain Fry in command of the *Niagara* during the past year.

Some years afterward, Captain Jordan's ship was wrecked off Cape Flattery, and it is pleasant to know that he, Abbie and their children escaped harm and he soon had another command.

That year, 1874, Joseph Mannion, educated, bookish, well-to-do, arrived, built and opened the Granville Hotel, while Joseph Reed also became an innkeeper. Ike Johns succeeded Tompkins Brew as government agent, and one McKendry opened a shoe repair shop.

During the year, a daily steamboat service was established to New Westminster.

The Victoria Directory for 1874, under Moodyville, Hastings and Granville, listed 146 names (males only) "and 14 Chinamen." At a rough guess, this is probably less than a third of the resident men. Indians, part-Indians, Kanakas and men in the logging camps were not included, and many of the familiar inlet names are missing. One change it does indicate, for in Moody's previously bone-dry bailiwick, Henry Hogan was operating the Terminus Saloon. And about the end of the year (after Abbie's wedding) the Pattersons had moved to Moodyville. The Point Atkinson lighthouse was abuilding, to be completed and in operation March 17, 1875.

One notes that at this time there were no "Lions" and no "Lions Gate." The pioneers of the period called the two North Shore peaks Sheba's Paps.

The directory, of course, listed few of such persons living at the mill as "Dumps" Baker who, when not ranging the woods for deer with his pack of gaunt hounds, was a part-time stevedore. Or "Cinch" Smith, the ex-navy mill fireman; "Cousin Jack" Treyenza, the Cornish tallyman; Alex Merryfield, the dignified head sawyer; August Nielson, the Swedish planerman.

Certainly it did not include "Silly Billy" Frost. Silly Billy earned his name when the wharf was being built; he sat on the outside end of a plank and sawed it off. He was the mill's greaser or "dog-fish-oil expert" (all lubricants then came from the local waters) when not patrolling the flume that ran from the Tea Swamp, south and east of the present Kingsway and Main, to the mill. Water from this peat bog was acid enough that the mill never had to be shut down to clean scale from the boilers. Near the mill also lived poor Dick Isaacs, who lost one arm and the other hand one day when the trim-saw broke loose from the guide-rope.

With Gastown we are familiar and need only mention that

George Black no longer slaughtered beasts on his back porch, since he had built an abattoir on False Creek. At the west end of Gastown crews logging around the present Victory Square had opened a skid road down Cambie Street to the inlet.

The Kanaka Rancherie, too, we know. There we get an appeal-ing glimpse of "little Scottsie Two-Tails," always neat and clean with her two pig-tails and natty Glengarry cap of tartan. How life treated the Kanaka-Indian tot as she grew up, we do not know, but once her wise Indian mother told her, "Learn to act like white people—either go up or down, that is your choice. . . ." Too many of the inlet's finest people faced that particular heartbreak-ing choice.

Stanley Park was still the home of many Indians and some whites. Near the rancherie lived Mowitch Jim, who hunted and sold veni-son to George Black. One day, walking through the bush, Scottsie Two-Tails met the legendary Supple Jack; it is rather a come-down to learn the reputed scourge of the prospectors was handsome, neatly dressed, "particular of his clothes and hat" and lived near First Narrows. There he had 24 cows, two horses, many pigs, and his wife, Quy-what, delivered milk to the mill.

On the shore just east of Deadman's Island, Tompkins Brew, the ex-government agent, settled with his Indian wife, and Johnny Baker, a longshoreman, also married to an Indian, had a house about where the Nine-O'Clock Gun is now. When Simmons sold the Hole-in-the-Wall to Pete Donnelly, he, too, settled there and prospered by making dog-fish oil. It sold for 25 cents a gallon.

Donnelly—well, perhaps it wasn't Donnelly, after all. Toward the end of the 70s, Pete went East, came back with a blushing bride, turned ultra-respectable—and insisted his name was James A. Robertson. James A. Robertson he continued to be, and nobody ever knew why.

At Snaq, the present Kitsilano Reserve, there still was a long-house 100 feet in length and 30 feet wide, where Chief Khaht-sahlano ruled a settlement of the Squamish. The chief's grandson, August Jack, who died in 1967, worked at the mill in later years and lived on the North Shore near Lions Gate Bridge.

The plenitude of fish and game on the inlet was unbelievable. Herring shoals in Coal Harbor were so thick "you scoop them up when you row across" and men with herring rakes could quickly fill a boat. Halibut and, of course, salmon were everywhere. Ducks were speared by torchlight at night, and sold by the barrel. Deer and bear were there for the taking. Fresh eggs might sell, as they did that winter, for three dollars a dozen, but nobody in Gastown ever had to starve.

The departure of Gassy Jack Deighton and the coming of Joseph Mannion conveniently mark the end of one era and the beginning of another in Gastown. Gassy Jack was a pioneer; Mannion was not.

Pioneering was not a matter of time, but of function. The pioneering of Gastown was finished by 1875; the pioneers continued to dominate the settlement until the population explosion of 1885 and 1886, after which they adapted themselves to the commercialism of the new city or were submerged by it. There can be no hard and fast date set limiting the latest arrival of pioneers, but a pioneer who rode into a bustling city of 10,000 on the cushions of a CPR passenger coach is a manifest absurdity. Nevertheless, scarcely a week goes by that Vancouver does not bury a "pioneer" who arrived in a Pullman drawing room, took a taxi to the Hotel Vancouver, rarely stepped off a cement sidewalk and never dirtied his fingers with any labor more arduous than accepting a soiled five-dollar bill. For all practical purposes, pioneers were extinct in Vancouver by the turn of the century, in southern B.C. by the end of the 1920s. Since the Second World War they have been dying out even in the far north of the province, their place taken by the organized scientific and technological teams of the great corporations which are "opening up the country."

By 1870 it was a reasonable gamble that British Columbia would join Confederation, and that the terms of Confederation would include a railway. It was possible to start from Canada or Europe, cross North America by the recently completed Union Pacific Railway and proceed by a comfortable steamship service from San Francisco to Victoria. From that time on, by this route there came to the

colony a steadily-increasing number of astute or adventurous men of
the commercial class with sufficient capital to enter immediately
into business, hoping to skim the cream off the colony's coming
prosperity. They were a useful addition to the population, an essential ingredient of its coming expansion; they might be called pioneers
of commerce or pioneers of industry, but pioneers in the strict
sense of the word they were not. If the pioneers had not opened
up the country for them, they could not have existed in it. Of this
type, Mannion is the first we know to have settled in Gastown.

To those of us fortunate enough to have known them, the loss of
the pioneers and the extinction of the pioneer way of life is not so
much a sorrow as a deprivation and a physical and spiritual imprison-
ment. To the pioneer, the roads that opened the countryside for
the city-dweller were walls of a civilization that penned him in. To
him, the townspeople who gathered together for companionship
were invaders bent on taking from him his freedom. Even the facilities of communal life undermined his social and economic independence. When he became subject to the obligations inseparable from
a civic organization, he felt he had lost the rights of a citizen.

In the nature of things, the pioneer was a breed apart. Axiomati-
cally he was self-reliant, because that is what made him a pioneer—
the need to meet Nature on her own terms and to exist by his own
strength, his own skill, his own cunning. The pioneers were
physically strong because they were without machines and without
mechanical transport; what machines they devised and constructed
were merely extensions of their own or their animals' muscular power.
They had an intense feeling of personal ownership entirely apart
from legal possession; the country they lived in was "theirs"
simply because they had proved they were able to exist in it.
Their generosity, hospitality and neighborliness were unbounded
because of their isolation, but they were directed toward human beings
as individuals, not humanity in the mass; to them the community-
chest type of donation would have been revolting.

Their charity was open-handed and unstinting, but it was a personal
service to a known person for a known need. It did not bear the
condescending stigma of modern charity. If your neighbor needed

a dollar, you gave him five; if a down-and-out came to your door for a crust of bread, you asked him in and cooked him a meal. The pioneer knew too well that he himself lived on the ragged edge of disaster and was subject to the inscrutable whim of God.

The pioneers died early and they were little afraid of death. Death was often amongst them; they closed the eyes, bathed the bodies, crossed the hands and buried the corpses of their own dead. To them death was familiar and natural to a degree inconceivable in a generation which banishes its sick to hospitals, abandons its dead to undertakers and is shocked by the sight of a corpse undecorated with cosmetics.

They were intemperate in their drinking, eating and indulgence in sex, but life made upon them such physical demands that occasional intemperance had no lasting effects. The melancholy wrecks of the present-day "skid road" have nothing in common with the loggers, miners, seamen and ranchers who gave that district its name. Their wild debauches—and they were wild—were those of men who worked hard and dangerously from dawn to dusk for six months or a year, and let loose all the repressions of a Spartan and precarious life in one or two weeks of violent self-indulgence. It was an explosion, not a habit.

Finally, the pioneer was not indiscriminatingly accepted by his fellows. He was subject to minute and rigorous scrutiny before his status was determined, but it was a scrutiny of, and a judgment based on, his individual strength of body, character and mind. His society placed him in a niche, but it was his own niche, and there was a niche for everyone; no one was excluded because he did not fall into a predetermined class. Even the feeble-minded, the poor-spirited or the malignant were allowed to contribute what they could to, and draw what they needed from, the community. They were people, not "cases". The pioneer life was hard and demanding; for those very reasons, it was of necessity kind and generous.

It was a life, of course, doomed to extinction. The virtues, the freedoms and the charity of the pioneers could not under any circumstances exist in the society their work was bound to create.

Even as the coming of Joe Mannion marked the dawn of a new

era on Burrard Inlet, the Age of the Pioneers crumbled and blew away in the dust of death.

In 1875, Gassy Jack came off the river for the last time. As he lay dying in New Westminster's summer heat, a dog howled outside the open window, and Jack's mind was on the Indian wife who watched his last hours, and their four-year-old son who was playing outside.

"Look after the boy. . ." was Jack's plea to those who stood near. There was quiet, and the labor of his breathing. And then: "Damn that dog! I wish he'd shut up," said Gassy Jack Deighton, and died.

From far and wide they came to mourn and bury the First Citizen of Vancouver, but the cold, hard wind of the new times and the new settlers was blowing across his Royal City grave. The grave itself was left unmarked and his disinherited wife and child went back to her people; they were "only Indians" and of no importance.

That same fatal year, Sewell Prescott Moody, with his boundless optimism and fertile mind, boarded the SS *Pacific* in Victoria for a visit to San Francisco. How that grossly overloaded ship was rammed in a calm sea, how her plight was ignored by nearby vessels, and how, 24 hours after her gay departure, the corpses of men, women and children began to drift up on the Vancouver Island shore, is a tragedy outside Vancouver's story, except that there died Sew Moody.

There had been giants in the land, but they were going fast. Two years later, the same year that death came in Victoria to that enigmatic man of great strengths and great weaknesses, Sir James Douglas, Jerry Rogers died in Gastown.

Now they were all gone—Deighton, Moody, Stamp, Rogers and the old governor, swept from the stage. Hidden in the wings, of all the great figures of Vancouver's beginning, there remained only Sam Brighouse, busy with his affairs in New Westminster and Lulu Island, and the potter, Morton.

The time of the pioneers was over.

7

Into the World

WITH ALL THE wisdom of hind-
sight, we know now that Vancouver was the only possible place
for the terminus of the CPR. There were known three practicable routes across British Columbia for the road: By the Yellowhead Pass and the Skeena to the present Prince Rupert, by the
Yellowhead and Chilcotin to Bute Inlet, and by the Yellowhead or
some southern pass and the Fraser to the coast. A fourth route by
Bentinck Arm was considered but soon eliminated. It is obvious
that of the three, only that terminating on Burrard Inlet offered
the three essentials, a practicable approach, a large and secure harbor
and room for the growth of a great city.

In 1870 the importance of these factors was not apparent. The
Bute Inlet route had the best grades to the coast and the final
terrible obstacle of Waddington Canyon was certainly no more
difficult to surmount than the Fraser and Thompson abysses. Victoria
and Esquimalt Harbors were ample to accommodate more shipping
than the North Pacific had yet seen; moreover, they were more
accessible than Burrard Inlet, to reach which, windjammers needed
a 100-mile to 140-mile tow. And not for 35 years would some
visionary Vancouver sloganeer prophesy wildly that the city would
have "100,000 men by 1910." A century ago the modern metropolis was not even a pipe-dream. Victoria was the obvious and the
only terminal; best, said Victoria, that the railway come by Bute
Inlet, crossing the inland water barrier by bridges from island to
island with a final span resting on Ripple Rock, or, if necessary,
by ferry from the mainland to Vancouver Island, but if by any

chance it came through the Fraser canyons, the only difference would be the ferry-link located between Port Moody and Nanaimo. For strategic reasons the navy favored the Bute Inlet line; on the same grounds, the army preferred the Fraser.

From 1870 to 1878 the fight to secure the construction of any railway at all, and the dispute over what route it should follow are inextricably mingled. The former is a matter of Dominion-provincial history, the latter of vital concern to Vancouver. Walter Moberly, whom we last saw surveying on Burrard Inlet in 1859, was fanatically determined on the Fraser route. As early as 1865 he discovered the essential Eagle Pass through the Monashee Range and the following year sent Albert Perry to examine the gap in the Selkirks which became famous after its "discovery" by Major Rogers in 1882. To the day of his death, impoverished and bitter, in Vancouver in 1915, Moberly maintained the choice of the Kicking Horse-Rogers Pass route was "a very serious mistake," that Rogers never saw Rogers Pass until he rode through it in a CPR train, and that his own proposed route to the prairies by the Big Bend and Howse Pass was infinitely preferable.

As early as 1871 Moberly was in Ottawa pressing the Fraser route on Sir John A. Macdonald; he had been preceded in 1870 by Dr. R. W. W. Carrall of the official B.C. delegation, who bore Alfred Waddington's plans for the Bute Inlet line. As a fanatic, the Victoria merchant, Waddington, ranked with Moberly. In the early 60's while Moberly was working on the Cariboo Road through the Fraser Canyon, which he helped to locate, Waddington was trying to drive a road through Waddington Canyon, below Mount Waddington, being prevented by the massacre of 19 of his men by Chilcotin Indians in 1864. One of the most unpleasant passages in Moberly's unpublished papers is his fury at the hanging of five of the murderers in Quesnel; he seemed to feel that any measure calculated to hinder Waddington was a public service. Waddington's opposition to the Fraser line continued well on into the mid-70's, when he was associated with a group of Chicago financiers who unsuccessfully attempted to take over construction of the CPR.

73

By 1872, Sanford Fleming had settled on the Yellowhead Pass approach for the railway, but not the line to the coast. Why he later abandoned it and why the Fraser route was chosen will probably never be known. Certainly Fleming's personal memoirs are disingenuous and the official CPR statements issued from time to time were designed to conceal, rather than enlighten. The political pressure was tremendous, the public agitation extreme, the economic considerations were complex and difficult; the railway can hardly be blamed if it extinguished controversy on these and other issues by the brutal announcement from time to time of a *fait accompli*. On the other hand, as we shall see later in the case of Vancouver itself, it was not averse to prolonging suspense and concealing its decisions when it could profit from public uncertainty.

All through the 70's the controversy raged. In public testimony during the inquiry into the Pacific Scandal of 1873, Moberly came perilously close to accusing Fleming of attempted murder of himself and his men by abandoning them for the winter in the Yellowhead Pass without sufficient supplies. By 1874 it was obvious even to Victorians they must reckon with the possibility of choice of the Fraser route, but still the likelihood of a mainland terminal was not considered a serious threat. Not until December, 1877, did Prime Minister Alexander Mackenzie officially announce adoption of the Fraser route. By the summer of 1878, with the return of the Conservatives to power in Ottawa, the matter was up in the air again, but late in the year, Sir John A. Macdonald confirmed his predecessor's choice.

Still the terminus was unsettled. Macdonald had pledged in 1873 it would be at Esquimalt. James D. Edgar, negotiating on behalf of Mackenzie in 1874, went farther—he pledged aid to the construction of the Esquimalt and Nanaimo Railway as the CPR's westernmost section, though some Island politicians feared he might be double-crossing them, for Mackenzie was talking in terms of a transcontinental wagon road and telegraph line instead of a railway. Premier George A. Walkem broke off the talks with Edgar, and Mackenzie's Esquimalt and Nanaimo Railway bill, passed by the Commons in 1875, specifically stated the E. & N. was not to be considered an integral part of the CPR. The bill was rejected in the Senate. In 1876, Lord Dufferin, the governor-general, visited B.C. and attempted to conciliate all factions, but denounced both Macdonald's and Edgar's pledges as "flagrant bribery." Before the election of 1878, Mackenzie rescinded an order-in-council naming Esquimalt the terminus.

But the election of that year changed everything. Macdonald's success seemed to assure, at last, construction of the railway. His personal defeat in Kingston was seen as Victoria's opportunity; he was offered a seat in Victoria and elected. He restored Esquimalt as the terminus. Construction of the B.C. section was started at Yale, May 14, 1880. Victoria's hopes went down again in 1881, when, on an appeal to London, Colonial Secretary Lord Kimberley decided Vancouver Island was entitled only to a light-gauge line, and sank still further in 1882, on the CPR's refusal to take any responsibility for the E.&N. In a fit of pique, the Beaven government of B.C. cut Victoria's throat by rescinding the Island railway grants to the Federal Government and turning the E.&N. over to Robert Dunsmuir to complete. Macdonald took this as relieving both the CPR and the Dominion from any responsibility in the matter. Though the agreement with the Dominion, Dunsmuir's acceptance of the E.&N. offer and substantial federal compensation for Vancouver Island did not become official until 1884, the events of 1882 assured that Burrard Inlet would be the western terminus of the CPR.

Gastown was not excited. To almost everybody, "Burrard Inlet" meant "Port Moody," and it was so stated in all the agreements.

In the furious controversies of the 15 years preceding 1884, the three settlements on lower Burrard Inlet had been notable for saying nothing and sawing wood, the last very literally. As early as September, 1869, Governor Musgrave had been deeply impressed by the commercial activity of a part of the colony scarcely heard from in the political field. When Lord and Lady Dufferin visited Gastown Sept. 14, 1876, the governor-general made a similar observation and remarked on "the floating wooden dangers which carpet the sea" in the inlet.

That, of course, was a tremendous day for Gastown. The vice-regal party arrived in the morning on *HMS Amethyst*, to be greeted by a crowd of 200 on Hastings Mill wharf and a 21-shotgun salute, to which the *Amethyst* dipped her flag. Captain Raymur, supported by the government agent, Ike Johns, presented the address of welcome. A huge log was sawed in the mill as the party watched, and then Lady Dufferin scandalized Captain Raymur by insisting on visiting the small Indian rancherie just east of the mill, where she patted grubby children on the head and talked to an aged Indian woman.

After lunch on the *Amethyst*, the party transferred to the *SS Governor Douglas*, brought around from New Westminster for the occasion, and between Gastown and Hastings landed on the shore by a plank gangway to watch two loggers fell a forest giant six feet in diameter at the butt and 200 feet tall. Officialdom was properly impressed; observing the loggers leaping from their high springboards as the tree began to fall, Lady Dufferin opined they were very brave men; the governor-general shook their hands. The party re-embarked for Hastings and the steamer departed with such celerity Captain Raymur was observed boarding her by an unexpectedly agile leap. The welcome of the crowd at the stage terminal was extended by Maxie Michaud and just before the visitors departed over the corduroy road for the Royal City, His Excellency remarked that it had been a memorable day. "For Burrard Inlet," loyally insisted Captain Raymur.

Continuing to saw wood, during the late 70's and early 80's Burrard Inlet was accustomed to see as many as 40 ships at one time loading or waiting to load timber for Australia, California, China, South America, Mexico, the Hawaiian Islands, South Africa, Great Britain and western Europe. The population of Gastown continued to increase in the measure necessary to conduct the business of the flourishing port, but only to that extent. The inlet settlements had little attraction for the speculators and minor capitalists who, since 1871, had been arriving in considerable numbers in B.C. in anticipation of the coming of the railroad.

Some events of these years deserve to be noted. In 1875, Gastown was re-surveyed by John Jane, who recommended the graveyard be transferred from Deadman's Island (now HMS Discovery) to Brockton Point. Lots 14 and 15 in Block 6, near the northwest corner of Abbott and Water, were granted by the provincial government to William Pollard and transferred by him to a board of trustees to be held on behalf of the Methodist Church. The trustees comprised four Anglicans, two Methodists and one Presbyterian. The 16-by-30-foot church was built by volunteer white and Indian labor and completed early in 1876, being known as the Indian Church. The constitution of the board of trustees indicates the absence of sectarian intolerance; that the majority were Anglicans was probably due to the fact the most "responsible" citizens were of that communion, though Methodism was the dominant persuasion on the inlet. The minister was Reverend Thomas Derrick, successor to Reverend Mr. Turner, and his church the first on the inlet.

That year a road was begun to connect Gastown and Hastings, to be completed in 1877. The timber exports of the inlet for the year were 29 million board feet. And during 1877, Morton, Brighouse and Hailstone divided the Brickmakers' Claim, Brighouse taking the eastern third abutting on Burrard Street, Hailstone the centre section and Morton that adjoining Stanley Park. In 1879, Van Bramer replaced the aging *Sea Foam* with a new inlet ferry, the *Senator*, 51 feet 6 inches long, 12 feet in the beam and 4 feet 6 inches draught.

Funds were raised for the town's second church, Anglican St. James, on the mill property, completed in 1880 and dedicated by Bishop Sillitoe on the fifteenth of May. Its rector was the Reverend George Ditcham.

The following year a two-plank-wide sidewalk, of a type Vancouver was still building in 1915, was laid by the chain-gang from Gastown along the Hastings road, past the church to the mill. The Hastings-New Westminster telegraph was also extended to Gastown. In the fall, Joseph Spratt of Victoria established a herring saltery and fish-oil plant on the south side of Coal Harbor.

The practicability of Burrard Inlet as terminus for a transcontinental railway had changed and improved much in the decade from

1870 to 1880; the steamship had come into its own on the deep seas. Windjammers still dominated the Pacific trade, but the hand-writing was on the wall and undoubtedly the astute tycoons of the CPR had laid their plans long before the events of 1882 made them public. The inlet had now become an accessible, as well as an otherwise ideal, harbor, and in 1881 the now-controlling private railway syndicate sent its engineer, John Ross, to survey the inlet for a port site. There is little doubt that his report of 1882, strongly against Port Moody, settled the question once and for all. Gastown was to be the terminus.

No public announcement, of course, was made. Victoria and New Westminster continued to rely on the prime minister's casual nomination of Port Moody, and the report to the Admiralty by Admiral Richards (whom we·met as captain of *HMS Plumper* in '59) that the head of the inlet offered safe anchorage. Just how secret Ross' report was kept, however, it is hard to say. At least, while the engineer was at work in 1881, Sam Brighouse disposed of some of his Fraser River interests and returned to Gastown. Hailstone and Morton exchanged their thirds of the Brickmakers' Claim (this is the deal in which Hailstone afterwards alleged he had been swindled) and Morton and Brighouse merged the eastern two-thirds of the West End. Brighouse let contracts for clearing part of it, and March 15, 1882, almost twenty years after they had taken up the homestead, the old partners registered the subdivided plan of the "City of Liverpool." Liverpool, B.C., sank almost without trace in the whirlpool of subsequent events, but the plan is not without interest, as it showed a railway line located almost exactly where the CPR eventually laid its tracks.

The obviously incomplete Victoria Directory and the provincial voters' list that year painted the outline of a vastly enlarged Gastown, so much enlarged that it and Hastings were lumped together as if they no longer were separate communities. It listed six general merchants (all in Gastown), seven hotels (two in Hastings), four butchers, eight fishermen, two shoemakers, one harnessmaker, one sail-maker, one wine-merchant (James A. "Pete Donnelly" Robertson), three carpenters, two accountants, one blacksmith, one customs collector, four teamsters, one telegraph operator, three lumbermen, one physician (Dr. George Masters—Dr. Walkem had removed to Vancouver Island), three stevedores, one constable, two longshoremen, one postmaster, one salmon canner, 20 employees of Hastings Mill, 44 loggers, 11 millmen (two Hawaiian), three logging camp proprietors (all on Point Grey), two churches, two ministers, one school teacher, two societies (Hastings Literary Institute and the Ancient Order of United Workmen), three industries (Hastings Mill and the Burrard Inlet Fishing and Oil Companies—the latter two probably comprised Spratt's Oilery), two farmers and two justices of the peace. The stage terminal was no longer in Hastings, but in Gastown.

In July, Captain Raymur, the last of the great men of the early inlet days, died, and Alexander became manager of the mill. The austere and lonely Raymur had won the respect and admiration of the community, but somehow, never quite its affection. Yet for more than a decade, his had been the steadying and reliable hand on its tiller.

One more event, and Gastown moves into the past. The settlement had its second vice-regal visit October 19, when the Marquis of Lorne arrived. A legend grew up that one immense tree at the water's edge was spared at the request of the Marquis' wife, Princess Louise, and for years it stood, known to all as "Princess Louise's Tree." Sad to relate, the princess never saw the inlet. She preferred to remain in Victoria while her husband did the travelling.

With the coming of 1883, Granville was very much upon its dignity, and "Gastown" had become a term of derision, heard only in such bustling places as Port Moody, where town lots were selling up to $2,000 each as the railroad drew near. Gastown had been shut in by its surrounding forest, Granville moved out into the world. And the world moved in on it.

March 15, the ship *Duke of Abercorn* passed on its way to Port Moody with the first shipment of steel for the CPR; June 9, the barques *King Ceolric* and *Kate F. Troop* brought the second consignment; in October, a locomotive purchased from the Panama Railway was landed at the head of the inlet and re-named the Lytton.

During the year, William Irving and his son, Captain John Irving, long active in Fraser River shipping, merged their Pioneer Line with the Hudson's Bay Co. coastwise fleet to form the Canadian Pacific Navigation Co. The CPN replaced the Irving's tiny *Maude* on the Burrard Inlet run with the large *Yosemite* (called locally the *Yo-see-mite*) and from time to time with such famous vessels as the *Enterprise, Reliance,* and *R. P. Rithet.* William Rogers, brother of the late Jerry, built and ran the *Robert Dunsmuir* on the Nanaimo-Port Moody route; she carried much coal for the railway builders and as a consequence became known as the *Dirty Bob.* In all this marine bustle—for the lumber ships kept coming and going as usual—it almost escaped notice that the pioneer *SS Beaver* sank in the inlet, but was raised, refitted and returned to her work as supply vessel for northern logging camps.

Of some historical note was a square-built steam scow, known as *Spratt's Ark,* 145 by 32 feet, drawing 8.2 feet, and carrying a floating salmon cannery. She was built by Spratt in Victoria and anchored in Coal Harbor, to be operated in conjunction with the oilery. Her refuse was discharged overboard and on this pollution of the water was blamed the decline of the fish population of the inlet, which from this time was rapid. Since conservation measures were yet far in the future, doubtless the inlet was much over-fished, as well.

In the final railway settlement of 1884, the Dominion government had withdrawn its reserve from Burrard Inlet lands below Port Moody. William Smithe, the new premier of British Columbia, had conferred with William Van Horne of the CPR while the settlement terms had been arranged early in the year, and replaced the federal reserve with a provincial one. June 14, Van Horne formally opened negotiations with Smithe for extension of the line to Granville, demanding all the reserved lands, with a right-of-way to Kitsilano via False Creek. The terminal docks were to be erected on the present Indian Reserve there. The CPR was asking for a good half of the present peninsula on which metropolitan Vancouver stands.

By September 9, Smithe had whittled the railway's demands down to about 11,000 acres, but they still included the entire foreshore

"THE BUILDERS" — FOUNDING FATHERS OF VANCOUVER
—*On commission of Major J. S. Matthews, later Vancouver's archivist, John Innes, in 1936, painted, from early pictures available, a group composite representing the inaugural meeting of the first city council, May 10, 1886. STANDING—(left to right) three unidentified spectators, symbolic of the pioneers; John Leask, later city auditor; Joseph Mannion, pioneer of 1865, colloquially known as "the Mayor of Granville"; J. B. Henderson, one of the first three school trustees; John H. Carlisle, second chief of the volunteer fire brigade, later fire chief for many years; John Boultbee, first magistrate; His Worship M. A. MacLean, first mayor; W. H. Gallagher, later alderman and longest survivor of the group; Dr. W. J. McGuigan, coroner and mayor 1904; C. Gardner Johnson, poll clerk; John W. Stewart, of Granville and first chief constable; Constable Jonathan Miller, pioneer, 1865, returning officer and later postmaster; Duncan Bell-Irving, M.D., pioneer physician. SEATED—Aldermen J. R. Northcott, Joseph Griffith, Joseph Humphries, Thomas Dunn and Lauchlan A. Hamilton; George F. Baldwin, first city treasurer; Thos. F. McGuigan, first city clerk; Aldermen E. P. Hamilton, Chas. A. Coldwell, Harry Hemlow, Robert Balfour, Peter Cordiner; seated behind City Clerk McGuigan is J. J. Blake, who drafted the first city charter and was first city solicitor. This picture hangs in the council chamber of the City Hall.*

MALCOLM A. MacLEAN
First Mayor of Vancouver
1886 to 1888

DAVID OPPENHEIMER
First president of the
Vancouver Board of Trade
and Mayor 1888 to 1891

BUILDING THE FIRST HOTEL VANCOUVER — When the C.P.R. began preparing the foundations for the first hotel on Georgia at Granville in 1886, dirt was moved with picks and hand shovels — and workmen were not loath to rest and give advice to the photographer. This is now the site of Eaton's department store and the Toronto Dominion Bank Tower.

FIRST TRAIN FROM THE EAST — A band, the volunteer fire brigade and townsfolk turned out for the arrival of the C.P.R.'s much-decorated inaugural transcontinental train on May 23, 1887. Harry Abbott, C.P.R. general superintendent in Vancouver, and Mayor MacLean presided at the welcoming which occurred below the cliff at what is near the end of Howe Street.

from First to Second Narrows. Van Horne declared, "The depth of water necessitates docks along the shore—permanent piers and docks are not practicable." Hastings Mill wharf then, and the CPR's own piers a little later refuted this contention. By October 6, the final terms had taken shape. They included:

Six thousand acres of land, comprising all unalienated lots in Granville Townsite not reserved for government offices or schools; most of Shaughnessy Heights and the remainder scattered through the present city. The right-of-way included the north bank of False Creek in part, and the line to Kitsilano. Title of all these lands passed to the CPR, but the company was obliged to offer to the occupiers at $200 a lot, any land on which individuals had already settled without purchasing. Hastings Mill lease was extended to 1890, on condition the mill give up 4000 acres at once and 1000 more each year. Large private landholders must yield to the CPR one-third of the lots in each block they held. Almost the entire waterfront from Gore Avenue to Stanley Park went to the railway.

No one in Granville or the surrounding area at that time appeared to think these concessions excessive, though today it appears obvious the company had long determined on Granville as the terminus and would have carried through its plans if it had had to buy every foot of land it required.

The agreement included provision for an immediate survey, and Van Horne at once dispatched L. A. Hamilton, who, in 1885, laid out downtown Vancouver on the approximate lines it retains today. Van Horne's final instructions to Hamilton contain words worthy of note:

"Hamilton," the surveyor reports him as saying, "this eventually is destined to be a great city in Canada. We must see that it has a name that will designate its place on the map of Canada.

"Vancouver it shall be, if I have the ultimate decision."

Possibly the decision was his; his wish would carry great weight. However, it is probable the name had been under general consideration for some time previously, since as early as August, 1884, it had been used in a Portland, Oregon, newspaper for the western terminus of the CPR. Whatever the name, the railway's plans for the port were pushed ahead. In October of that year, its president, George Stephen, approached Prime Minister Gladstone in London to ask a subsidy for a line of fast trans-Pacific steamships operating to China and Japan, but the "Little Englanders" turned him down.

By this time, of course, it was public knowledge that the CPR was negotiating for a right-of-way to Granville, but the public reaction was curious. A good deal of the land around Granville was held by prominent citizens of New Westminster; they sat tight and said nothing, and since one of them was Robson, owner of the Royal City's only newspaper, the river city remained generally neutral on the location of the terminus.

Investors and speculators, such as J. W. Horne of Brandon, who had "looked in" at Granville in 1883 and again in 1884, and Frederick Buscombe, Victoria businessman, who emulated Horne in the latter year, generally decided "it was too early yet," and put off their plans for a year or two. The earliest speculator of record was A. W. Ross, M.P. for Lisgar, Manitoba, hard-hit in the Winnipeg "bust," who came west with the idea of retrieving his fortunes in Port Moody, but changed his mind and invested all he had or could borrow in Granville lots in '84. Perhaps his former connection with the CPR syndicate had something to do with his decision. It would seem to have been the natural time for the Port Moody speculators, both local and from Victoria—there was a heavy proportion of the latter—to hedge, but this they resolutely refused to do. On October 11, five days after Smithe and Van Horne had finally come to an agreement and only 45 days before it was approved "in essence," the Port Moody Gazette declared:

"It is well known at Lloyds that Port Moody is safe in every respect, but that in stormy weather, none of the other places is safe for ships. How anyone in his senses could believe the extension would be made, or if made, could be of any use, appears very droll to us."

The Victoria Colonist stationed a reporter at Port Moody to interview newcomers and assure them there was no such place on the inlet as Vancouver—technically correct until April, 1886.

Nevertheless, the CPR pushed the survey of the right-of-way

to Granville all through the fall, with the legendary Major Rogers in charge. At dusk on Christmas Day, Rogers, his nephew, a man named Mitchell and Otway Wilkie of New Westminster reached, and drove a stake on, the eastern boundary of Granville in a heavy snowstorm, before returning to Christmas dinner in George Black's hotel in Hastings. Guests at the dinner included Sam Brighouse, the shoemaker-naturalist Jack Fannin and other inlet notables. The survey party, which included H. J. Cambie, Hugh Walkem, a man named Strong, Tom Smith, Paul Marmette and J. W. Stewart (the last to become a personage of note in Vancouver) finished the Granville end of their work in March, 1885. The CPR offices were in Maxie Michaud's Hastings Hotel, but by this time Maxie had left the inlet, it is said to return to Paris.

The Port Moody speculators might ridicule Granville's pretensions to be the terminus, but did not entirely overlook the threat. A group consisting of Jonathan A. Webster (apparently the "John" A. Webster, New Westminster merchant, who was among Gastown's first landholders), William Johnston, Henry V. Edmonds (after whom a Burnaby district is named), John Johnston, W. A. Duncan, D. Chisholm, H. M. Stramberg and J. C. Armstrong, won an injunction from Chief Justice Sir Matthew Begbie preventing the CPR crossing their property and the case went to the B.C. Supreme Court. While the litigation dragged its slow way along, the main line of the railway was progressing. The Marquis of Lansdowne, in August, was the first governor-general to cross Canada by land. At Revelstoke he rode horseback across a 47-mile gap; on his return, two weeks later, he had to ride only 28 miles. On November 7 the last spike was driven at Craigellachie, and a few days later Robert Mee was at the throttle of the first transcontinental train (a freight) to arrive in Port Moody.

At the same time the Port Moody Gazette was proclaiming, "The true inwardness of the Coal Harbour scheme is being speedily brought to light, proving the same to have been purely a speculation dependent upon suckers." The suckers, however, continued to roll in.

March 10, the SS *Euphrates*, with rails for Port Moody, had been the first deep-sea screw freighter to enter the inlet. During the subsequent months of the year and in 1886, as Brighouse put it, "The mob arrived." Among them, in 1885, were Richards, Akroyd and Gall, real estate agents; T. R. Pearson and Co., branch stationery store, J. Z. Hall, manager; Walter E. Graveley, real estate; E. E. and C. D. Rand; and Henry Allardyce Bell, who "walked over the (Rocky) mountains." Three of the arrivals of the year deserve special notice. The ship *Robert Kerr*, while in tow to Victoria, had been wrecked on East Point the previous winter. She was bought by Captain Soule, the stevedore, towed to Granville and refitted as a barque. With her came Seraphim Fortes, Barbadoes-born son of a farmer of pure African blood and a woman partly Spanish or Portugese, who had signed on in England. "Joe" Fortes became porter and part-time bartender at the Sunny-side Hotel. Taking up his labors in another useful sphere was Reverend H. G. Fiennes Clinton, former domestic chaplain of the Duke of Newcastle, who replaced Mr. Ditcham as rector of St. James. And while the venerable mission church had been built on the North Shore during the previous year, Roman Catholics had as yet no place of worship in Granville. Toward the end of the year, Father Fay arrived, and offered his first Mass in Blair's Hall, at the back of Billy Blair's Terminus Saloon on Water Street. Father Fay became a great favorite in the town and was known as "the Merry Priest."

Seth Tilly opened the first bookshop, in which his son installed and operated for the New Westminster and Port Moody Telephone Co. a "20-point" switchboard, with 35 subscribers on the first list— an indication of the town's rapid growth. The store was on Cordova, near Carrall, a location that earlier in the year when McKendry the cobbler moved his shop there, was described as "quite out of town." Among names first seen this year and later well-known in the city-to-be were Thomas F. McGuigan, T. F. Neelands, George F. Baldwin and M. A. MacLean. J. W. Horne paid his third visit to Granville, this time to remain; he picked up some choice lots along Coal Harbor, where there were "only a few shacks." In that neighborhood, about the north foot of present-day Bidwell Street,

McMahon, Carr and Wright Co. had a 30-man crew busy logging off part of the West End. Their skid road ran south and east to modern Granville and Georgia Streets.

During the year, Granville School presented its first two successful candidates for the school entrance examination, Alice and Ernest Miller. The teacher, W. H. Irwin, who had succeeded the Canadian poetess, Agnes Deans Cameron, resigned June 30 and was succeeded in turn by J. W. Palmer, who was paid $55 a month to educate an enrollment of 58—29 boys and 29 girls—with an average attendance of 37. Total cost of the education system for the year 1884-85 was $710.47, but the trustees were preparing to accommodate 80 pupils in the fall term. In Moodyville, Miss Maude Kirkland was teaching a student body of 39.

Hamilton was proceeding with his survey of the townsite, complaining that the original layout of Granville made it impossible to avoid some irregular corners downtown, and that sale of some "City of Liverpool" lots to Joseph Spratt forced a jog in Hastings at Burrard. Among his achievements was "a mile-long peephole" hewed in the dense forest where Granville Street now runs. Hamilton, as CPR land commissioner, named the streets—those downtown after CPR officials, and those in the West End largely from Admiralty charts and provincial dignitaries. When the survey was complete, selection by the CPR of the lots from landholders involved in the settlement of 1884 took the form of a draw from a hat to decide whether the landholder or the railway would have first choice; Hamilton in later years confessed that he "cooked the draw" in favor of Brighouse, so that the pioneer might retain the lots on which the "three greenhorns" had built their cabin in 1862.

Farther afield, George Stephen was still pressing for the establishment of a trans-Pacific service. For his pledge to build a line of ships to be convertible for Admiralty service in time of war, he asked a £100,000 subsidy. The British postmaster-general went so far as to advertise for tenders for a Burrard Inlet-Hong Kong mail service, but the negotiations fell through. The failure was blamed on the opposition of the powerful Peninsular and Oriental shipping line.

Granville was a hard-boiled, hard-drinking, hard-living town. J. W. Horne remarked that "cards and liquor were everywhere." The night before the land draw, even the great Van Horne was unmercifully skinned in a poker game. The next morning he warned Hamilton, "Keep your eyes open. These damned Vancouver fellows will steal the pants off you." Typical of the tribe were David and Isaac Oppenheimer, who had formed a syndicate, bought part of the Hastings Mill site and were logging off the land between Carrall Street and Gore Avenue, as well as preparing to open a wholesale and retail grocery at the corner of Powell and Columbia Streets. During an all-night poker game, one of the players nodded drowsily, wakened to find four queens in his hand. He looked suspiciously around.

"Who dealt?"

"Ikey."

"Who cut?"

"David."

"I pass," said the drowsy gentleman, and threw his hand in.

The person who recorded this incident also saw Hugh Keefer, owner of a general store at Water and Alexander Streets, bet $100 on which of two flies crawling up a bar mirror would reach the top first. It is not to be wondered at—a man had to be a gambler or he wouldn't be in Granville at all. He was gambling, as a rule, his time, his own future and all his worldly possessions on the future of this hamlet in the wilderness; a trifle more bet on the location of a card or the behavior of a housefly was neither here nor there.

Granville was growing fast, though. Hamilton recorded there were barely 100 habitable buildings in the town at the end of February, 1886, and at least 600 by the middle of May. Besides the speculators, the merchants, the womenfolk and the children, there was a very considerable labor force to erect 500 buildings in a mere 75 days. The boom was on.

In fact, during January, 432 residents of Granville had signed a petition to the provincial Legislature asking that the City of Vancouver be incorporated. They were backed by 18 citizens of Victoria, headed by Isaac Oppenheimer, who had business interests in the town. There was opposition from representatives of New Westminster, but the act received third reading April 2, at 7:30 p.m., and Lieutenant-Governor C. F. Cornwall gave it royal assent April sixth.

Ninety-five years after Narvaez and Verdia talked to the Indians of Musqueam, the City of Vancouver came into existence. It extended from Heatley Avenue on the east to Trafalgar Street on the west; from Burrard Inlet on the north to Sixteenth Avenue on the south.

Its first business was to form a city government. Of the more than 400 persons who signed the incorporation petition, few could claim a year's residence. All of Burrard Inlet had only 175 names on the provincial voters' list. Qualification of the city voters was set at land ownership, or the possession of a cabin, room or lease of the value of $5 a month. Four hundred and sixty-seven votes were cast in the election of May 3. Hastings Mill manager R. H. Alexander ran against real estate dealer M. A. MacLean. It was the old-timers against the newcomers, and Alexander had the additional handicap of being an employer of Chinese labor at a time when Chinese released from railway construction were in active competition with white workers for available jobs. In addition, Alexander or his supporters made the blunder of attempting to vote the Chinese workers at the mill, marching them in a body to the poll. Stage driver Charlie Green charged the procession with his vehicle, and the whites drove the bewildered Orientals back to the mill with clubs and fists. At the close of polling, Poll Clerk C. Gardner Johnson declared Malcolm A. MacLean elected by 242 to 225 votes. The newcomers had taken over. More, the Canadians had taken over.

From the very beginning, as colony and as province, British Columbia had been bedevilled by the bitter feud between the official clique and its supporters—more British than the British—and the Canadian element that grew larger and larger. New Westminster and Victoria had been their battlegrounds for two decades; Burrard Inlet had been too insignificant, fortunately for itself, to be greatly involved. And in its first election, Vancouver made its choice—

Canadian it would be. When Alexander taunted the newcomers with being "North American Chinamen" and opposed them at the polls with real Chinese, it was the last flare-up of the old vendetta, and the embers were stamped out with ballots.

Its ingrained Canadianism and its opposition to the "Little B.C." faction bred in Victoria was to cost the city dear in the future, but it gained as much in internal unity and cohesion by taking a determined stand at the start. Moreover, it was the only logical and sensible position for the terminal city of the great transcontinental railroad. Vancouver was the child of Canada and the CPR its navel cord. The city has never quite forgotten this essential fact, nor has the rest of the province; it is not by accident that Vancouver has often had to bear the reproach of being a "foreign city" in the land.

The old-timers did not accept defeat gracefully; they petitioned to have the election voided and MacLean unseated, and there were threats of violence, but it came to nothing. The new city council held its first meeting May 10. Besides the mayor, it consisted of 10 aldermen; Joseph Griffiths, Robert Balfour, Thomas Dunn, Charles A. Coldwell, E. P. Hamilton, Joseph Northcott, L. A. Hamilton, Peter Cordiner, Harry Hemlow and Joseph Humphries. They met at 2:30 p.m. in Jonathan Miller's house; with the creation of the city, the constable's post was about to lapse, but he was already invested with the office of postmaster. The city archivist has recreated the scene:

"Mrs. Miller cleared the dining-room table. Some laid their hats upon it, others got more chairs out of the three or four jail cells (the jail was behind the house), an oil lamp swung above, the tiny room was crowded, the audience, such as could, peered through the open door.

"The poll clerk, the late Gardner Johnson, swore in the mayor-elect, then the mayor swore in the ten aldermen. A bystander . . . went around the corner and came back with a pad of paper, a pen and a bottle of ink and wrote 'City of Vancouver' across the top of the first sheet."

The main business of the meeting was appointment of officials.

J. Huntley was appointed city clerk pro-tem at $75 a month; John Boultbee police magistrate, unsalaried; J. P. Lawson assessment clerk and city engineer, at $75 a month.

"As for city treasurer," observed the mayor, "I do not see any particular hurry for this appointment, having no cash to deposit in his hands."

The first communication dealt with was an offer from Silsby Manufacturing Co. of a second-hand fire engine on reasonable terms.

Later in the month Dr. A. Harrison Thomas was appointed medical officer, George F. Baldwin city treasurer, J. J. Blake city solicitor and T. F. McGuigan city clerk. The police commission consisted of the mayor, the magistrate and the city clerk; Boultbee proposed his brother-in-law, Gardner Johnson, for chief of police, MacLean his old Winnipeg acquaintance, James M. Stewart, and— alas for Gardner Johnson!—the city clerk was sparking Mr. Stewart's pretty daughter. Chief Stewart commanded a force of four, himself, an assistant chief and two constables.

Another essential force was organized May 28 at a public meeting, when Sam Pedgrift, a shoemaker, was elected chief of a volunteer fire brigade. Among the other 13 members was J. H. Carlisle. Members paid dues of 25 cents a month and a fund of $200 was collected in voluntary contributions; the city council undertook to provide a fire engine.

Granville had long been the passive target of Port Moody, Victoria and New Westminster newspapers, but Vancouver was not be without its own press. In January, William Brown established the *Vancouver Herald*, a four-page weekly of Liberal leanings, with an office at Water and Cordova Streets. At the end of May, N. Harkness and J. H. Ross started publication of the *Vancouver News*, and R. W. Gordon the *Vancouver Advertiser*, with a Conservative policy. Francis Carter-Cotton was the *Advertiser's* editor.

When Van Horne had declared he would "run the railway down the middle of the inlet on a trestle" if the Port Moody speculators won their lawsuit, it was no idle threat. Even before the survey was finished, men were working on the grade west of the disputed right-of-way; during the spring 2000 were employed, with a large construction camp in the small bay where Hamilton Street met False Creek. Wives and families of the superior employees lived in the old Hastings Townsite, where the CPR construction offices remained. March 6, the company held its first land sale, setting June 10 as the deadline for persons in occupation of land previous to the 1884 agreement to buy their lots at the reserved price of $200. Walter Graveley was the first buyer of unreserved land, paying $700 for Lots 1, 2 and 3 on the southeast corner of Carrall and Oppenheimer (now East Cordova) Streets, and the company was flooded with claims "almost in excess of the entire population of Gastown in 1884," from persons claiming to have been in occupation at that date. No wonder Van Horne had warned Hamilton to keep his eyes open when doing business with the people of Vancouver.

The railway was also clearing the land along Water, Cordova, Hastings and Pender Streets as far west as Burrard, much of it by the "bowling-pin" method, which consisted of sawing rank after rank of the close-packed trees half-way through and then felling another of the forest giants against the first few, with the result that scores would fall at once in an awful welter of smashed trunks and branches, undergrowth and jagged stumps which would be left to dry out through the summer and burned the following wet season. This district was known as "the CPR Townsite." Among all this activity, H. B. Abbott was appointed general superintendent of the Pacific Division, and Cambie chief engineer; both took up residence in Vancouver. Stephen, undeterred by his previous failures in England, pressed on with his trans-Pacific plans, chartering a number of sailing ships to make passages connecting with transcontinental passenger trains later in the year.

The furious activity of Vancouver in those first days of June, 1886, is almost beyond our imagination to picture. The bare 100 habitable buildings at the end of February, which had become 600 at mid-May, only two weeks later numbered 800, with hundreds more under construction. Lots that brought less than $300 in the March land sale were changing hands for $1000. Coastwise boat schedules included the SS *Teaser* on the Victoria run, the *Dirty Bob*, Nanaimo; the *Gladys*, New Westminster, the *Evangel*, Seattle, and the *Senator* for all inlet points. A telegraph cable had been laid to Victoria. Vancouver's first County Court sessions had been scheduled for June 15, a colossal Dominion Day celebration for July 1. A new and larger Methodist church had been opened on Water Street May 2, a Presbyterian church on Oppenheimer Street June 6, the same day that Frank Fooks completed Columbia Hall on Powell Street, the first beer garden and cabaret licensed in Vancouver. Over 300 Vancouverites attended the opening of the hall at which the New Westminster Brass Band played, Pearl Anderson and C. E. Dunbar sang, Miss Grayson recited and the "acrobatic song and dance experts" Webster and Steel charmed the crowd. "Big George" of the North Shore reserve had recently thrown a potlatch which attracted 4000 Indians and whites and aroused much pious comment among the latter on the extravagance of Indian ways. Joe Mannion, having enlarged his Granville Hotel, sold out at a handsome profit and retired to private life. Sam Brierly died and was buried on Deadman's Island, already crowded with 25 graves, and Vancouver opined it was high time the provincial government came through with the 25 acres promised as a cemetery.

The Bank of Montreal May 27 tried to make up for missing the boat a few months previously by buying a lot at Granville and Dunsmuir Streets. General manager Buchanan, who got stuck in the Granville mud earlier in the year and went back east with a bad cold, had declared Vancouver "would never amount to anything." Export lumber prices, which during the past decade had varied from $12.50 to $40 a thousand, had settled at a moderate $20, but lumber was at a premium, due to local consumption.

Retail trade, naturally, boomed with the town. Flour was $6 barrel, rice $2 a sack, corn meal four cents a pound, bacon 15 cents, coffee 20 to 30 cents, tea 50 to 75 cents, porterhouse steak 15 cents, rib roasts 12½ cents, leg of mutton 15 cents, cod five cents, salmon 65 cents each, smelts 50 cents a bucket. Nails were $4.50 a keg, cross-cut saws $1 a foot, sad-irons 10 cents each and grindstones four cents a pound. Seth

Tilly had in stock the San Francisco, Portland, Seattle and Toronto newspapers, the London News and Graphic, Frank Leslie's Illustrated Paper, Harper's Magazine, Weekly and Bazaar and Gody's Lady Book. Captain J. K. Ritchie of the Tivoli Saloon had introduced the 5-cent schooner of beer. John Hendry's Royal City Planing Mills Co. (he was the youth who in '73 and '74 rebuilt Moody's steam mill after it burnt down) was building Vancouver's second lumber mill.

On Water Street there were 36 considerable buildings, residences, halls, saloons, hotels and stores, between Carrall and Cambie, with the new Regina Hotel west of Cambie. Cambie itself boasted the town's largest structure, the three-storey Carter Hotel, also the Edinboro Hotel, the Scots Greys and Stag and Pheasant saloons and a few stores. Only a few buildings were on Abbott Street, but Carrall rivalled Water, with 29 business establishments, the new post office, and the Ferguson Block, housing the CPR and B.C. Express offices. Cordova Street was the select residential district; Hastings ran to hotels and boarding houses; Powell was the "gay" street, with the Tivoli and Cisne saloons, Fook's Columbia Hall, McLennan and McFeely's tinware and plumbing shop and Oppenheimer's store. At Water and Alexander were Hugh Keefer's store and Andy Linton's boat-building works. Oppenheimer Street (East Cordova) was residential, Westminster Road (Main Street) was "Blue Blood Alley," where high society resided. Buildings were rising in the Dupont Street area (under the present Georgia Viaduct) and on Pender. These were the main concentrations—completed and half-completed buildings were scattered all over the town where streets-to-be were rutted trails winding between stumps. The Eagle and Bridge Hotels rose on the north shore of False Creek.

The town's water supply came entirely from wells, many of which in June were in danger of running dry; there had been no rain since May 26, when a brisk shower helped to put out a bush fire at Fred Little's camp in the Brighouse-Morton subdivision. On that occasion, people at Spratt's Oilery and John McDougall's camp nearby had packed up, ready to leave if the flames spread.

8

Holocaust

ON THE FINE, peaceful Sunday afternoon of June 13, 1886, Art Sullivan and a companion were lazing in a half-decked pleasure sloop just off the Burrard Inlet shore near the Indian Mission Church west of Moodyville. The Vancouver boom had done well by the "fair, handsome Negro" of Gastown days; he and his mother were proprietors of prosperous Gold's Hotel on Water Street.

Without warning, a fierce, freakish western squall swooped down on English Bay and the inlet.

On the south shore, clearing fires to the west of the town bloomed into ominous life and Sullivan swung the sloop across the wind to make for the new city wharf at the foot of Carrall Street. With two reefs in the mainsail, the jib blown away and his shipmate bailing furiously, he could not make the long slant to the wharf; scudding past and half-foundering, he brought up at Hastings Mill wharf half a mile further on. They had made the passage in less than twenty minutes.

In that time, Vancouver was wiped from the face of the earth.

First warning was the dense cloud of smoke from the western clearing. Second was the shouts of running men from the clearing camps beyond Cambie. Third was the clang and jangle, jangle and clang of the bell of St. James' Church at Powell Street and Westminster Road; Father Clinton had correctly interpreted the pillar of smoke in the west.

There was no question of fighting the fire. In seconds rather than minutes, it had routed the men in the clearing gangs, was sweeping across the terrible tangle of "bowling-pin" clearing and the brush along the inlet shore, crown-firing through the dense timber still standing south of Hastings Street. It sped ahead of and cut off the men from the clearing gangs and they rallied on the Regina Hotel in its cleared area west of Cambie Street.

For those in the town there were four avenues of escape; to the city wharf at Carrall, along the CPR embankment or the road to Hastings Mill, to False Creek at Pender and Carrall (now filled in) or out the Westminster Road and across the bridge to the south shore of the creek. On that shore, Sam Brighouse and George Black had been racing their horses Sunday morning. Among the spectators was Lewis Carter, owner of Carter House, who tried to make his way back into the city by the last route, but had no more than crossed the bridge when he was forced into False Creek by the flames.

For the rest, the burning was but a record of wild and hurried flight. Houses did not "catch fire." Paint or the pitch on new, bare boards blistered and ran, walls and roofs shimmered with heat waves for a second or two, then the whole exterior of the building was a single mass of white flame. "Vancouver did not burn—it exploded," said an eyewitness.

People saved what they carried, and no more. J. Z. Hall and Sam Greer's daughter were on their way to teach Sunday school. Hall had forgotten his Bible and stepped back inside to get it when Miss Greer saw the smoke and called. After the fire his worldly possessions were the Bible and the clothes on his back. Miss Greer helped Mrs. Ben Wilson, next door, to carry her sewing-machine into the water of the inlet, and there she, Hall, Mrs. Wilson and the sewing-machine waited until the fire had passed. Miller, the postmaster, ran for the mill with the post office cash-box, his spectacles carefully balanced on top of it. Ike Johns saved only the customs register.

Along Cordova, a young man lashed a horse harnessed to an old buckboard, with a canvas tied over its load. The canvas blew away to reveal the corpse of his mother, a huge, 300-pound woman who had died the day before. Laughing crazily, one man ran, swinging a dead goose by the neck. Another struggled along burdened with a mattress and half a brass bed, only to drop them in the street and rush back for the wife and child he had forgotten. Two men running by a house forced a mother and her little girl to flee, the woman weeping distractedly over the little shoes they would not let her wait to fit on the ringleted child. These, and the bulk of the fugitives, made for Hastings Mill.

There were explosives stored in the town—a major peril in case of fire, and the responsibility of drivers employed by the merchants involved. On Water Street, near Cambie, Hugh Campbell refused to join the flight until he loaded amid falling sparks seven cases of dynamite, which he drove to the mill. Farther down the same street teamster Harry Berry, with the help of two men, put 20 barrels of blasting powder on his dray, wrapped them in wetted blankets and forced his team through the flames down Carrall to False Creek, where he drove out into the water.

Among those who made for False Creek were Magistrate Boultbee, C. Gardner Johnson, Bailey, the bartender of Balfour's Hotel, and a stranger who was carrying a valise. They had been surrounded by flames while taking part in an attempt to save the hotel. On their way, they passed a man throwing water from the side of the road onto a woodpile; he refused to join them and was burned to death. At Pender and Carrall they could go no farther and lay down in a small patch of gravel. "To the westward side," said Gardner Johnson, "a large frame house was burning and it was so near that the burning timber came falling about us, causing us agonies I cannot describe. Bailey said he could not stand this and said he was going to get through at any cost, but he could not penetrate a foot in the flames, and after running around for a few seconds, he dropped and burned up before our eyes."

Gardner Johnson, on the windward side of the three, borrowed the stranger's valise to shield his head. Inside it, the heat exploded the cartridges in a loaded revolver. As the fire roared past and burned out, they made for the creek and scrambled along the shore, half in and half out of the water. The deep bay in the creek, which then penetrated north to Pender Street, shielded that part of the town built out on the Westminster Road where Gardner Johnson lived; when he arrived at his cottage, his wife was standing outside anxiously waiting news of him. He in later years recalled: "I could not go and speak to her, but I remember sitting down on the steps and beginning to cry."

Known dead were more than a score, but in the crowded state of the city, many more could have shared the fate of Bailey; human bones are still turned up in the area of the fire and counted as its victims, but with what justice, no one knows. The morning after the fire a mother and child were found in a well where they had taken refuge, smothered when the flames ate the oxygen out of the air above. A few calcined horse and human bones were found amid the iron tires and ashes of a wagon on Hastings Street. One account tells of "a man named Fawcett with a magnificent team of bays and a face like stone" driving directly into the heart of the fire, where no one could have lived.

The heat was so fierce, in many places iron melted, and the bell of St. James Church was a pool of bronze slag where the steeple had stood. The deck timbers at the shore end of the city wharf began to burn and were torn up and thrown into the water by the survivors who crowded the structure. Old Captain Dyer, watchman on the refitted *Robert Kerr*, lying off *Spratt's Ark*, lowered two boats and took many off the wharf and out to the *Kerr*. Boats from the *Southern Cross* and the *Von Moltke* at Hastings Mill wharf removed others; both the ships were crowded with refugees and ready to put out into the inlet if the fire approached the wharf. Andy Linton launched 20 boats from his shed and filled them with survivors. Most of the people arrived safely at the mill and many, among whom was Father Clinton with a boy of nine in his arms, stood in the water as the flames approached. But the wind died down, and there, at the mill clearing, the fantastic, terrible holocaust stopped and smouldered out.

There remained the men from the clearing gangs who were cut off at the Regina Hotel. Penned in on all sides by fire, they ranged from room to room, soaked in water every blanket they could find, and literally swathed the hotel in them. A bucket brigade sluiced

CAPT. EDWARD STAMP
Sawmilling Pioneer

RICHARD H. ALEXANDER
*Vancouver grew on lumber from
his Hastings Mill*

L. A. HAMILTON
*C.P.R. land agent
who named many
Vancouver streets*

HARRY ABBOTT
General Superintendent for the C.P.R.

WATER STREET AND CORDOVA — *In* 1901 *Vancouver was spreading west from old Granville's main corner at Water and Carrall streets. Sailing ships still loaded at the Hastings Mill and the Union Steamship Company and Evans, Coleman & Evans had wharves at their present locations. The C.P.R. still reached its station by trestle. Building in centre is that of the Hudson's Bay Company. The "flatiron" building remains, near Eaton's store.*

ON CORDOVA STREET IN 1898 — *The Klondyke gold rush temporarily made a mining outfitting town of Vancouver and helped it recover from the depression of the 'Nineties.*

FROM TANGLED LOGS TO TRAFFIC TANGLE—*This was the scene in 1886 at what is now Georgia and Granville streets. The huge Douglas Fir lay across the land where the Hudson's Bay Company's store now stands in busy downtown Vancouver. Its stump was said to measure 14 feet 4 inches across.*

HASTINGS AND SEYMOUR ABOUT 1888—*Looking east on Hastings street, which was junior to Cordova street as a business thoroughfare. The vacant land to the left became the site of Spencer's store, then Eaton's. To overcome the mud, planks were laid in the centre of the road. Sidewalks are wood plank on raised stringers. Cast iron pipe for the first water from Capilano River will be seen awaiting laying between the plank road and the sidewalk. Building in right foreground housed the pioneer Bank of British Columbia.*

TODAY'S GRANVILLE STREET AS IT LOOKED IN 1895—*Then known as North Arm Road, it connected the farming area on the North Arm of the Fraser River with the settlement on Burrard Inlet, having replaced a packhorse trail. The spot here pictured is in the vicinity of what is now 37th Avenue and Granville.*

down the roof and others beat out with wet blankets every spark and blaze. Aided by the wide, unoccupied clearing around the hotel, they succeeded in their fight. When the summer hurricane died down, they occupied the only standing building in all but the fringes of Vancouver. And of it, they occupied the bar and drank beer in silence and thankfulness; an Irishman among them crossed himself and prayed as he opened the first bottle.

The burned and injured were attended at the mill and at Spratt's refinery, where their burns were dressed with oil and flour and wrapped in leaves. An improvised morgue was established at the north end of the False Creek bridge, and a refugee camp at the south end. For the rest, "He was a rich man who had his life and a blanket that night." The people of Vancouver slept amid its ashes.

The smoke of the burning was seen in Port Moody and New Westminster. By 3 o'clock, unable to raise Vancouver on the single telephone line, the Royal City knew what had happened. The smoke was overhead and bits of burned paper and ashes sifted down out of it. The cloud drifted past Mission, 40 miles away, and north of Sumas an hour later, and shortly afterward the same dread tokens were falling from the sky on Chilliwack. Then was seen how the people ignored in time of need the petty squabbles that bulked so large in press and politics.

In New Westminster the council was summoned, $9,000 voted out of the public funds. Doctors and women collected medical supplies and bandages, food, clothing and household goods were donated, and by 6 o'clock in the evening an unending relief caravan was crawling over the Westminster Road and in sight of Vancouver. It passed crowds of refugees making their way to the hospitality of the neighboring communities, where every door was open to them. By 3 o'clock in the morning, lumber wagons were jolting in from the Fraser communities; nails and tools were unloaded by the light of lanterns and the flickering of still-burning stumps. By daylight, tents and building frames stood in the dawn, with the smoke curling around them and the ashes puffing wherever a man trod.

In twenty minutes, Vancouver had been wiped off the earth. In twelve hours, it was rising again.

9

From the Ashes

FIFTY YEARS AFTER the great fire of 1886, one of its survivors was asked what rebuilt Vancouver. "Faith," declared the old gentleman. "That was all we had left."

In the comfortable sunset of his declining years, he had boiled down the heroic myth of Vancouver's destruction and rebirth to one apparently unassailable phrase. The only trouble with it is, it doesn't happen to be true.

Dramatic, spectacular, disconcerting and even expensive, the fire was, but not catastrophic. The money loss has been estimated at about $800,000, but it was a mere drop in the bucket compared to the resources ready and waiting to pour in for reconstruction. Where one man was wiped out financially, ten sprang up in his place with money in their pockets to undertake the same gamble. Few, if any, already established were unable to find sufficient credit to re-establish themselves; this was a boom town setting a mark to shoot at in the history of booms and a man who rolled up in his blanket Sunday night to sleep beside the ashes of his store or office might wake up Monday morning and find the land alone worth more than all he had possessed when the fire swept down on him.

The tiny city was a scene of devastation, but it was far from being set in a desert. Money and goods were poised to pour into it before the fire; the conflagration speeded rather than retarded the flow. Strong and willing hands abounded for the work, there were 2000 men working on CPR projects alone on the inlet and False Creek; every boat, every stage and every footpath swarmed with more to compete for every available job. Machines on the modern scale were undreamed of, the city was to be rebuilt with hammers, saws, picks, shovels and muscle—of these there was no lack.

It was a city of men—young men. Women and children were few, and the town that had 3000 homeless after the fire, according to the mayor's telegram to Sir John A. Macdonald, had only 58 children on its school rolls. The patriarchs of its business community, David Oppenheimer and Jonathan Miller, were 52 years of age when the fire struck; Mayor MacLean, 44; his opponent and standard-bearer of the "old timers," R. H. Alexander, was 42; the speculator and M.P., Ross, 40; its chief financier, J. W. Horne, who had already made two fortunes and lost one, 33. John Hendry had made himself a lumber magnate at 32, E. J. McFeely was just 23 when he lost his tinshop, and C. D. Rand, 28, when his real estate office went up in smoke. Fire, flood or economic catastrophe were all in the game for these men; McFeely and Rand were back in business inside a week. So was Robert Clark, who had lost his drygoods business in Nanaimo during the depression following the strike of 1877, moved to Yale and was wiped out by the fire of 1881, and had opened shop in Vancouver on April 5, 1886, to be burnt out two months later.

At the very outside, 1000 completed buildings were lost in the fire. Only one was of three storeys, all were frame buildings, and the vast majority of them were little more than shacks. Stocks of goods were not large, they could be replaced easily, usually on 90 days' credit (time for a complete turnover in a boom town) and many of the businesses were branch stores of prosperous firms in New Westminster or Victoria which re-established them immediately. Under these conditions and with this type of citizen, Vancouver was bound to be back in business in short order. Nevertheless, the speed with which it occurred was amazing.

The resilience of the people was tremendous. Before dark, Gardner Johnson, whom we last saw in tears on the steps of his home, was west of the town organizing a refugee centre at Spratt's Oilery. Father Clinton and Mrs. Alexander converted the Hastings

Mill cottages into temporary hospitals. By daylight, the city council and a relief staff were functioning in tents and lean-tos; for want of a jail, city police chained prisoners to stumps. Between 200 and 300 families required immediate relief, but funds and supplies poured in from neighboring communities, eastern Canada and the United States.

In three days on Water Street a clothing store, a three-storey hotel, a public hall and a hardware shop were open for business; on Carrall, a saloon, a real estate office, six stores and a hotel; on Oppenheimer, an auction house, a butcher shop and several other stores. These were obviously of flimsy construction, but in its haste Vancouver did not miss the opportunity the fire gave it of improving itself. The Saturday after the fire, the city council passed its first building by-law, requiring more solid construction and certain precautions against fire. On August 15, all insurance firms operating in the city refused to write additional fire risks until streets were cleared and dumps of inflammable material removed. With Provincial Government assistance, a program of street clearing was set in operation. After the first emergency construction, many of the buildings erected were of brick or stone, so that in 1890 a travelling correspondent of a London newspaper was moved to remark on the fine structures incongruously set among old shacks and remnants of the burned forest.

By July 30, the city was "a going concern" once again. By the end of the year the *News* declared: "The city has changed so much for the better in the short space of six months we look upon the disaster as an event of the past." Completed construction totalled $521,000, incomplete, $524,000; in values of today, somewhere between $7 million and $10 million—this in a city which on New Year's Day counted its population at 5000. On three streets alone, Cordova, Water and Carrall, there were 14 office blocks, 23 hotels, 51 stores, nine saloons, one church, two livery stables, one roller-skating rink, one mill and one wharf completed. Construction was under way on Hastings, Granville, Dupont, Homer, Beatty, Cambie, Pender, south of False Creek and as far west as Thurlow.

Citizens who in July had petitioned against construction of a new post office on Hastings between Homer and Richards as "away out of town", now thought of it as being in the city centre. The CPR had spent $200,000 clearing lots and grading streets as far west as Burrard, and had sold $290,000 worth of lots; its executives were building big, rambling wooden houses, palatial for Vancouver, "on the bluff" west of Burrard.

The amazing thing is, that amidst all this incredible turmoil, the people of Vancouver were laying the solid foundations of an organized city. July 27, the council had moved out of its tent into the relief office. Quite naturally, its first occupation was with fire protection. Following the building by-law of July 19, on the 30th of the month the 5000-pound steam pumper "*M. A. MacLean*" arrived over the road from New Westminster, "looking awful" after three weeks on a flatcar, and two days later four hand reels with 2,500 feet of hose were delivered. That evening the fire department turned out on Cambie Street Wharf, the fire was lit in the pumper at 7:19 p.m., in three minutes she had steam enough to blow the whistle, and in seven pressure enough to throw a stream over the rebuilt Stag and Pheasant saloon and to douse the mayor and Alderman Dunn. Ten days later the engine stood guard on the same wharf in case a fire that burned down Spratt's Oilery should again burn east and spread to the town, but only the oilery was lost; nevertheless, the council hastened construction of a number of 50,000-gallon water tanks through the city, to be filled from nearby wells and kept ready for use by the pumper. The fire brigade was increased to two hose companies, "Invincible" and "Reliance," and August 24, sponsored Vancouver's first formal ball in Gold's Hall, "a brilliant sight" declared one reporter, commenting on the bunting and evergreen decorations, but for which —shades of Gassy Jack and his Confederation Day flag!—a Canadian ensign was "kindly lent by Mr. Powers of Moodyville." There was an elegant supper in the neighboring St. Julien Restaurant, and, continued the chronicler; "The costumes were in many cases both elegant and chaste and considering the very short notice the ladies of Vancouver showed themselves equal to any emergency."

With $200 from the ball and $200 from a provincial grant, the volunteers were outfitted with helmets, badges, shirts (Invincibles, blue; Reliances, red) and seven speaking trumpets. By the end of the year, Chief Pedgrift had left town and J. H. Carlisle headed the department—to remain chief for many years and create an organization that has brought Vancouver Fire Department international recognition. Its first real test came the following July, when clearing fires again broke away and a forest conflagration extended from Hastings and Howe Streets to English Bay. Pumping from the new tanks and assisted by a citizen shovel-brigade, firemen conquered the fire in two days' hard fighting and the city was spared a repetition of the 1886 disaster.

The council's main difficulty, of course, was with the city finances. The Provincial Government agreed to assist with grants for road-building, school construction and a cemetery, but resolutely refused to rebate any local tax money. For street clearing, Alderman Hamilton proposed local improvement assessments, to which Water Street businessmen unanimously agreed in August, less than two months after the fire. The Bank of British Columbia came to the rescue with a $10,000 loan at the same time, which was devoted to a fire hall and reconstruction of the Carrall Street wharf. The council exacted a $200 licence fee from all liquor retailers, $50 from wholesalers. In August it licensed cabs, omnibuses, dairies, livery stables, hotels, restaurants and employment agencies at $5; sales and feed stables, bowling alleys, billiard rooms and shooting galleries at $10; theatres and halls at $25, and peddlers and auctioneers, $100. Rates were set for cab and omnibus fares, horse hire and stabling, and employment agency fees. Contracts were called for improvement of Carrall, Cordova and other streets by the construction of 18-foot planked driveways and three-plank sidewalks; in wet weather the roadways developed an unusual agility in citizens, who had to leap fast and far to avoid the jets of water that spurted up between the planks as heavy vehicles rolled past.

In September, the city acquired from the Provincial Government Mountain View Cemetery site, a grant of 20 acres of the present area. A month later it was considering "the burial of Joe Butterfield, colored, on account of his sudden expiration, in the Cemetery on Deadman's Island," and a consequent wave of public protest against further use of that crowded resting-place. Clearing of the Mountain View Cemetery was expedited but the council just couldn't win— another tempest sprang up when it was ready for use; from a pious faction which objected to a suicide being the first occupant, and from a practical body of opinion which pointed out that it took a four-horse team to haul the hearse through the mud of the North Arm Road.

By October, the city borrowed another $20,900 for the fire department, to install oil-burning street lamps, for construction of a city hall and jail and more street work. Citizens were pressing for additional funds for the hospital—a four or five-bed building taken over from the CPR construction organization, and already over-crowded with patients who could not be made comfortable, and for whom the city "does not even supply the necessaries." Charitable women were appealing for 50 yards of unbleached cotton to make nightshirts for the patients.

In October the coroner, Dr. W. J. McGuigan, met a man in the last stages of typhoid fever staggering along the street—there was no room for him in the hospital and the hotel in which he had been living had thrown him out; typhoid was epidemic, with 25 cases since the fire, which were blamed on the digging of shallow wells into which surface drainage penetrated. This brought down on the harassed city council new demands for a civic water system and a sewerage system, and the council pressed Victoria for additional loans and hastened preparation of the civic assessment rolls. In the meantime, construction of the new school was under way, but classes could not be opened until November 15 because of nearby land clearing and the danger from blasting stumps; assorted fragments of defunct fir trees dropped through more than one citizen's roof that summer at inopportune moments.

The town was dark and dismal that fall; public illumination was restricted to the lamps each saloon was obliged by law to display outside its doors and crowds gathered to gape at the handsome octagonal beacon of the reconstructed Stag and Pheasant, first in town, when it was lit in the dusk of August 6. H. B. Abbott, G. A. Keefer and W. F. Bullen had incorporated the Vancouver Electric Illuminating Co., Ltd., in April, before the fire, but all that winter controversy raged over whether the city should be lighted with the new-fangled electric lights or by proved and reliable gas; the Vancouver Gas Co. offered three months' free light and free mains against the illuminating company's demand for a subsidy. Council decided in favor of electricity in January, 1887, and many serious citizens questioned the decision on the grounds that it would be three months before the lights were operating—and what use were expensive street lights in the summer?

In the gloomy nights, law enforcement was perilously near a breakdown. Life itself was unsafe. During July, a knee-high boot with a leg and foot in it was found near Lamey's sawmill on the south shore of False Creek, that "very terrible neighborhood" where two badly battered bodies had already been discovered; the boot with its gruesome contents was hung from a pole on the police-headquarters tent for two weeks, but nobody identified it and it was disposed of with the garbage. Eleven months later, confronted with a decomposed body in a hollow stump, Coroner McGuigan declared, "So many bodies have been found during the past year, foul play is the only explanation."

As long as the bodies were those of unknown and friendless newcomers, they excited little comment, but the demise of a well-known citizen required more formal recognition. In one such case, after loud altercation, cursing and stamping in his third-floor room, the victim was found dead on the sidewalk below next morning. The only pertinent witness had remained quietly in his room next door; "It was none of his business." The jury found the deceased had unfortunately fallen out of his window when drunk. A young woman died in violent convulsions after drinking in a cafe with a mysterious stranger. Her father declared she had been poisoned; there was no autopsy and the jury found "natural causes."

Burglaries were numerous and Vancouver had its first "hood-lums," for such was the way the chief of police described gangs of boys who roamed the streets all night. He excoriated the parents concerned. The city also had its first narcotics problem; the chief estimated there were, in the population of 5000, "fifty white opium-users past redemption." Opium could be legally bought and consumed—usually in the form of laudanum—but the police were severe with unlicenced Chinese dealers who interfered with the white trade. They were hunted down "without mercy" and fined $250 or three months in jail.

It did not come out until the inquiry by Mr. Justice Drake in 1889, that the police were having themselves a wonderful time. (Ex-Mayor MacLean was, by the time of the inquiry, police magistrate.) The chief had been instructed to "go easy" on responsible citizens—"There has been one law for the rich and another for the poor," observed Mr. Justice Drake—but otherwise the sky was the limit. Informers were entitled to half the fines levied, but not if they were members of the force; Chief Stewart hired a civilian assistant jailer, in whose name practically all informations were laid; the jailer got a flat two dollars of every "moiety," the police split the rest.

Saloon keepers and other influential citizens were allowed time to pay fines, and the fines were never collected. Prisoners stayed in jail overnight and were quietly freed next morning on payment of half or less of their fines—payments which were never, of course, turned in to the city. One of Constable Fife's activities was collecting $8 a month from the Chinese prostitutes on Dupont Street; white madams and their busy staffs were rounded up regularly in court and on the jailer's information the madam was commonly fined $50 and each girl $15. Mattie Davis, keeper of one of the more plush lupanars, "regarded it as an exceedingly good jest" when she shelled out and was told to go and sin no more. She had, she explained, just paid for her sinning licence.

Mr. Justice Drake grew exceedingly critical when he found no record of evidence given in police court and even more so when it became impossible to untangle records of time served by prisoners, or find out when they were released; the chief explained he often cut a few days off the sentences of men on the chain gang when they had done extra work. It was a fine state of confusion. On one occasion the magistrate on the bench had ordered a batch of seized liquor destroyed, but when court was adjourned he, the prosecutor and the chief decided it would be a pity to waste good gin. It was sold to a tug boat captain for $47, of which $20 went to the constables who made the arrest.

In the end, the chief and Constable Fife were fired, the city auditor resigned, and Mayor Oppenheimer, after long consideration, asked for the prosecutor's resignation. The magistrate remained on the bench, and when it all blew over, the chief and the prosecutor were readmitted to office.

The madams continued to pay their sinning licences, but the new auditor saw that the fines were collected and a new system of jail records assured that prisoners who did not pay served their time. The three constables on night shift were hustled out on their beats and forbidden to meet in their favorite saloon for long midnight suppers.

With its suddenly crowded jail, council decided 50 cents a day was too much to pay for a prisoner's keep—it called for tenders at a lower scale.

Oh, it was a gaudy show! Corpses were turning up here and there, the bawdyhouses were running full blast, typhoid cases staggered in the streets, drunks were beaten up in saloons ($5 was the standard court charge for "putting the boots" to a helpless man) and tinhorn gamblers operated in the back rooms. But all this was just good for a laugh, it was the smoke and sparks thrown off by the furiously whirling grindstone of the town's real business; the city was really going ahead. Streets were being opened (the chain gang did a lot of good work there), the CPR was ripping the trees off the West End and throwing up a $100,000 hotel at Georgia and Granville Streets while the non-CPR tycoons were developing land east of the city, with both factions snarling at each other. Churches were going up, including a $10,000 Roman Catholic school and church development at Richards and Dunsmuir; Father Fay asked council for a sidewalk from Hastings and when plank and nails were provided, the congregation laid the walk. More than 100 pupils were attending the new school.

The bachelors of Hastings formed a quadrille club at whose meetings the elite of the town danced, the bachelors of Coal Harbor and of the city followed suit and vied in providing elegant entertainment; a dancing club of young married people was formed. A city band, a glee society and a madrigal society were organized. Foundations were laid in December for a YMCA building, and our old acquaintance Arthur Sullivan opened a hall with a pipe organ where, among other organizations, the Young Templars met. The Knights of Pythias lodge was instituted, also the Oddfellows, and Mount Hermon Masonic lodge moved across the inlet from Moodyville.

There was big money floating around. Besides the CPR investment in the West End, the Powell-Oppenheimer-Dupont-Robson syndicate, already in possession of 1460 acres in the East End, bought an additional 85 acres of the Hastings Mill lease for $275,000, just east of Main; the CPR disputed the sale on the grounds of its grant of 1884, and when the syndicate was upheld by the courts, the deal passed into legend as "the 85-acre steal." The city assessment roll was approved in April, 1887, at $2,738,806, and a tax rate of 25 mills struck; a loan by-law for $150,000 was passed by the citizens. Amid all the big deals, a very small, but significant, one took place; January 24, SS *Princess Louise* picked up 50 cases of coal oil from Hastings Mill store for trans-shipment at Port Moody via CPR to the interior; it was the beginning of Vancouver's trade as a vast distribution point for interior British Columbia.

As the winter of 1886-7 boiled with all this activity, another problem that continued to plague the city for half a century came to a head. In the summer of '86, West End clearing contracts had been let at $500 an acre. In the fall, John (henceforth known as "Chinese") McDougall, bid in part of the work at $325 an acre, subletting it to a Victoria syndicate for $150. The Victorians brought in Chinese, idled by the gradual completion of CPR main line construction, to do the work at 50 cents to 75 cents a day, when white laborers were demanding two dollars.

The Knights of Labor, an extremist U.S. primitive type of trade union which suddenly became active in the city, began trouble by trying to run out of town a Chinaman who in November leased a building at Carrall and Water Streets, but the agitation was by no means confined to working men. It was wholeheartedly backed by the press, which excoriated "these yellow-skinned vermin," and by businessmen such as Hugh Keefer, Mayor MacLean, Aldermen Dunn and Humphries and others. After a mass meeting in City Hall January 11, a mob of 1,000 met the Victoria boat and "persuaded" 100 Chinese not to disembark. Similar "persuasion" was exercised for a month to reduce the resident Chinese population. This not proving sufficiently effective, the night of February 23, a Chinese camp on False Creek was wrecked and some 85 inhabitants were run out of town in the direction of New Westminster. Then the mob descended on the clearing camp at "the bluff," on the old Brickmakers' Claim west of town. Here the camp was burned with all the occupants' belongings and bedding; the Chinese were forced out on the CPR right-of-way in the snow. After it was all over, a logger, a milkman and a clerk were arrested by the police force, which made no attempt to interfere with the violence while it was occurring—perhaps wisely.

Except for the Chinese, the aftermath was amusing. New Westminster and Victoria papers were indignantly astounded. The province suspended the city charter and sent in 40 special constables; the mayor swore in 20 specials and told the "foreigners" to go home. Citizens blamed it all on U.S. burglars, who had stirred up the trouble to mask the looting of the Oppenheimer, Abbott, Lefevre and Alexander homes that night. The press congratulated the citizens on having only five Chinese left in town—all laundrymen, who were indispensable.

It also congratulated the Knights of Labor—until the ungrateful Knights promptly turned around and went on strike for a 10-hour day in the mills, which the mill-owners declared would ruin the city's largest industry. The mills, however, managed to survive.

Strike and riots had no effect on the boom. Lots "in the bush" were selling at $200 to $1000, land on business streets up to $55 a front foot, plus, if cleared, the cost of clearing. Mayor MacLean was returned to office in the civic elections, with David and Isaac

Oppenheimer, R. H. Alexander and Joseph Mannion among the aldermen. The city embarked on its first program of poor relief, paying board and lodging for two old men in the Central Hotel. And the whole town turned out to watch the first locomotive steam into town on February 23.

For, of course, over and above and beyond all else, there was the railroad. This was just a construction train, but it was an earnest of what was to come.

Van Horne had been continuously in and out of Vancouver since the fire, pressing on the work on the main line and the yards along the north shore of False Creek, the trestle (now used by the B.C. Electric) across the creek and on the West End clearing and construction, during the last of which the famous Kanaka Rancherie was abolished. In August, Abbott announced and Van Horne confirmed that talk of a trestle down Burrard Inlet to bypass the Port Moody land was no idle threat—the plans for a two and three-quarter mile trestle were drawn and ready for the constructors. As the year progressed, the case was fought up to the Supreme Court of Canada and, oddly enough, a second injuction against the line was procured by G. G. Major, a member of the Oppenheimer syndicate heavily interested in East End property. It can only be presumed Major wanted the terminus to be in the East End, rather than English Bay. Lawsuits abounded. Sam Greer, noted controversialist, claimed to have bought the Kitsilano terminal site from two Indians, Charlie and Joe, before the CPR ever got into the country, and sold lots at $80 each to get money to fight his claim. This became a *cause celebre*, winding up in 1890 with Sam taking a pot-shot at a deputy sheriff trying to evict him, Chief Justice Sir Matthew Begbie refusing to accept a verdict equivalent to acquittal, branding Sam perjurer, liar and forger, insisting on a conviction, sentencing Sam to jail and thus inspiring a vast public protest meeting in which the clergy of the the City of Vancouver led the way in condemning the venerable jurist as a perverter of British justice.

James Orr, M.P., also had a brush with the company. He had built on the right-of-way, the company moved his house off it, he moved it back on, dusted off his hands, adjourned to the nearest saloon for a drink. It must have been a long drink or a small house, for when he stepped outside again, the house had been taken board from board, brick from brick and stacked neatly off the right-of-way.

The transcontinental line was open to Port Moody in November, 1885, and at least token quantities of freight passed over it. On July 4, 1886, the first scheduled transcontinental passenger train rolled into Port Moody, Billy Evans at the throttle, one minute late after a passage of 2907 miles from Montreal. The first eastbound train left the next day and arrived in Montreal July 12. July 27, the barque *W. B. Flint* passed up the inlet in tow of the tug *Alexander* at 3 p.m., with 1,240,753 pounds of tea aboard, the first of seven ships chartered to bring tea and Oriental goods to be shipped east by the new line. The tea arrived in Montreal in 47 days, and in New York in 49 days, out of Yokohama—record time, throwing American lines into a panic. The *Flora P. Stafford* arrived August 27 with a similar cargo, and before the end of the year, the seven sailing vessels had landed 4,000 tons deadweight (9000 bulk) of tea, rice and general cargo at Port Moody— watched by the hungry eyes of Vancouver as they went by up the inlet.

Then came the great news—January 5, 1887, following the Supreme Court of Canada decision in favor of the company, Chief Justice Begbie dissolved the Port Moody injunctions. A last plea from the speculators, that they be paid for their land at the inflated boom price, was rudely rebuffed by Abbott — it was no business of the company, he insisted, if they bought lots at $1500 that were worth only $15, just because they, not the company, assumed Port Moody was to be the terminal.

Only a few last arrangements remained to be made before Van-couver came into its own. The railway secured a 20-year exemption from taxes by offering to place the yards and roundhouse on the north, instead of the south, shore of False Creek. It was a blessing in disguise, for thus the English Bay shore was kept free of industrial blemish, but the reason advanced at the time was curiously short-sighted—"It would be an advantage to have them within the city." In either case, they would have been within the city limits, but apparently in 1887 the city fathers had a very restricted notion of the city's future. The CPR, however, continued with the Kitsilano trestle, and threatened to block off all marine traffic into the creek. After much alarm and many protests to Ottawa, the company was ordered to put a swing span in the structure, and False Creek's future as an industrial centre was assured. The railway's telegraph line had reached the city in September, the docks were being rushed to completion, and all was ready for the long expected day.

That came May 23. Below the site of the Brickmakers' Claim the trackside was lined with the welcoming crowd. Covered with wreaths and greenery, with a transparency of Queen Victoria over the headlight, Engine No. 374 steamed up to the station (near the present Immigration Building) with the first passenger train into Vancouver. Peter Righter was at the throttle, George Taylor firing, Conductor Barnhart in charge, and Mayor MacLean with CPR Superintendent Abbott on the platform to give the speeches of welcome. The whole population of the lower inlet, of course, was on the platform, too. The city band played, the crowd cheered and grown men who had never seen a steam locomotive before climbed on board the passenger cars and shook the seats to see if they were fastened to the floors. It almost put the Queen's Birthday celebrations the following day in the shade, but even so, the miracle was yet only half-accomplished. Through the din, the final blows were still resounding from the wharf nearby as construction crews finished their work. And in far-off Yokohama, the SS Abyssinia was loading 2830 tons of freight, three bags of mail and 11 packages of newspapers for Canada.

The Abyssinia, 3651 tons, the Parthia, 3431 tons, and the Batavia, 2553 tons, were old Cunarders, chartered by the CPR to open its Trans-Pacific steamship service. Contrary to accepted legend, the first two were not sister ships, though similar in appearance, with straight stems and ship-rigged masts, capable of bearing sail. The smaller Batavia had a clipper bow. The Abyssinia had accommodation for 200 first-class passengers and 868 steerage, the others in proportion.

The *Abyssinia* put to sea May 31, and after a speedy passage of 13 days, arrived in the Strait of Georgia June 13, anchoring in English Bay at 9:25 p.m. The city's mayor, band, welcoming party and citizens waited on the wharf. And waited—and waited—and waited. They waited until 11:30 p.m., long after the *Abyssinia's* Captain Alex Marshall was sound asleep in his bunk. The matter-of-fact captain proved to be a sensible man who preferred to make the unfamiliar passage of First Narrows in the light of early dawn, after which the ship's 22 first-class and 80 Chinese steerage passengers quietly walked ashore and the cargo was being discharged before Vancouver woke up.

But if the celebration flopped, the event was none the less significant. Part of that cargo was to be of prime importance to the CPR for the next half-century. A special train stood on the dock to take 65 bales of raw silk, consigned to Montreal, New York and London. With some tea added to its load, and all other traffic yielding way, the train reached New York June 21. The London consignment was transferred to a fast passenger ship and arrived there June 29.

Twenty-nine days out of Yokohama! — and New York only 21! Here was the birth of an era, with a vengeance. The last nail was driven into the coffin of the old clipper ships. The P. and O. tycoons, so long lords of the South Seas, and so determined to club down George Stephen and his grandiose schemes, shook in their boots. Suddenly, on that twenty-ninth of June, 1887, the globe had shrunk to half its size and the CPR made good a boast its trains and ships maintained for 50 years—"Spans the World!" For those 50 years the great *Empresses* would plough the North Pacific, glide up beside the Vancouver docks, and tumble their cargo— costly! perishable! immediate! — into the waiting silk trains that rocketed across the continent, outpacing the finest passenger trains by one and two hours in a division. Here were realized the dreams of those incredible men who hammered the iron highway across the Dominion; here at one essay was established the sole, sure, fast,

FRESH AIR STREETCAR OF 1896—*The city was 10 years old when this picture was taken at the corner of Granville and Dunsmuir streets.*

THE HOLLOW TREE OF STANLEY PARK—*For many years photographers used the hollowed trunk of a standing cedar as a background for pictures. Though the stump still stands on the west side of Stanley Park, the vogue has passed.*

AS THE BIRDS SAW THE CITY IN 1898 — Long before the age of flight a popular method of picturing a city was for an artist to visualize it in what was called "bird's eye" perspective. The city had crossed False Creek to Mount Pleasant and Fairview but the West End was still largely unoccupied. The three bridges were at Main, Cambie and Granville streets. The tide flats east of Main later were reclaimed and an island was built on shallows under Granville Bridge. This drawing was in the Vancouver World in 1898.

Capilano Canyon suspension bridge, part of the Greater Vancouver scene for many years. Generations of swaying bridge enthusiasts have gasped with pleasure as they crossed above the forested slopes of the Capilano River.

George Allen Aerial Photos

BURNABY AND CENTRAL PARK — When Central Park (dark area, middle left) was named for the famous Central Park in New York, it was far from the populated areas. Today, lying between Burnaby, in the foreground, and Vancouver, it is surrounded by Greater Vancouver. One of the early roads from New Westminster has become Kingsway. It is being roughly paralleled on the north by a freeway to speed east-west traffic.

safe Croesus-pipeline to funnel the costly treasures of the Orient into the markets of the West. And as the veteran *Abyssinia* edged through the Narrows in that far-off June dawn, she carried in her holds Vancouver's charter to be one of the great ports of the Seven Seas.

It was a year and one day since the city lay in smoking ruin.

10

Boom and Bust

IT IS HIGHLY unlikely the inner economic history of Vancouver will ever be unravelled. Its most remote beginnings—the Moodyville and Hastings Mill grants—are inextricably tangled with the political intrigues of the colonial period. The city itself was born of the alliance of the Government of Canada with the financial powers of three nations (and possibly more) which became the CPR. The dealings of the CPR and its officials—as officials or as individuals—with the Provincial Government have never been adequately elucidated. And these are only a few of the major whirlpools among a wilderness of eddies, rip-tides, overfalls and undertows in the ever-changing sea of money, power and politics.

To attempt to untangle, even at this time, the threads of such events is still a task for the political controversialist but it can lead to no objective conclusions. Vancouver is only 98 years old; in another century these events may be historical. They are not now.

We can, however, assess roughly some of the forces that were at work in the city when *SS Abyssinia* sailed in through the Lions' Gate and put Vancouver in the world map.

The newcomers had assembled the apparatus necessary to exploit the Pacific shore.

The last and richest untouched land in the hemisphere was waiting to disgorge its treasures, so far untouched. The next half-century, to the beginning of the Second World War, was to be a time of ruthless exploitation. The victors were here; it remained to see which of the victors would enjoy the spoils. There was, as yet, no public conception that naked exploitation was either immoral or uneconomic. For the first time British Columbia felt the full force of the unpredictable winds of world finance. Power and opportunity were divided among a number of groups: There were the colonial nabobs who had managed to secure ownership of a very small part of the Province's natural resources; there was the CPR with its already-vast holdings; there were the large and small capitalists—among them a fair proportion of CPR officials—who flooded in with money to make money; there were the provincial politicians with almost unrestricted control of B.C.'s natural resources; there was the working class, which was only gradually to become conscious of its power and how to exert it during the next half-century.

All these were in conflict, and often violent conflict, for the riches with which the land teemed. That conflict is beyond the scope of the mere story of Vancouver, since it was waged largely on the level of provincial, and often national and international affairs. It can be only a background for the city's story, decisive though it was in the city's future.

Moreover, it was the normal background for the age and the place. Questionable and immoral as many of the events of Vancouver's growth would appear if they took place today, they were the normal and accepted methods of their time. Controversial many of them were, but it was through that very controversy our present standards were shaped and tempered; the early standards were very different. What it is important to remember is, that by those standards, conforming to them, struggling against them, men and women lived and loved, prospered or lost, married, bred children and died, were happy or unhappy, very much as we are today.

Incidentally, they built a great city, but only incidentally; history is not "bunk," but it is 99 percent a lie simply because it tells only one percent of the story. The story of Vancouver is the story of all the lives that have been lived in it, but very little of each life left any mark on the city. That these hundreds of thousands of small and usually unintentional contributions have in a very few years built a large, beautiful and pleasant metropolis is a fair indication it has been a good city to live in during those years. By and large, those lives have not been unhappy ones.

Vancouver, as 1887 opened, still stood in need of almost every-thing that makes a city—streets, water, sewers and lights were the most pressing requirements. The second council was elected by voters with a $300 property qualification and wasted no time pushing ahead with the streets and laying out a sewerage system. By some legislative sleight of hand, the Vancouver Electric Illumi-nating Co. Ltd., had been re-incorporated January 13 with $35,000 capital and with John Boultbee, Hugh Keefer (George's brother), R. Balfour, Jonathan Miller and Ben Springer as officers. Abbott, a member of the original company, was now seeking a franchise for the Vancouver Gas Co., including street lighting; perhaps it was not convenient for his name to appear on both sides of the fight and certainly a similar re-incorporation had occurred in Victoria for just such a purpose shortly before. At any rate, Abbott, the two Keefers and others of the clique were closely allied in the promotion of electric, gas, transit and water franchises, all of which they were successful in procuring. Almost immediately, the council granted the franchise, building started on a generating station at Pender and Abbott Streets in the spring, and on August 6 the first 32-candle-power street lights were turned on. In December, the *News-Advertiser* declared Vancouver to be the best-lighted city of its size in the world, and in February of the next year, 1888, the *News-Advertiser* made history itself as the first newspaper in Canada to be printed by electric power. The hyphenated paper was the fruit of a recent merger of the two pioneer dailies, and continued under the management of Carter-Cotton.

The city had electricity for more than a year before its water system was operating. The Vancouver Water Works Co. was formed in August, 1886, by George Keefer and H. O. Smith, capitalized at $250,000, to bring water from the Capilano River by a submerged main across First Narrows. It, however, met lively competition from the Coquitlam Water Co., which offered to supply the city with a 16-inch main to Heatley Ave. from Coquitlam Lake. City council by a narrow majority April 25, 1887, favored an agreement with the Coquitlam group, but on June 5 a civic by-law for the purpose was defeated 91-53, and council had no choice but to come to terms with the Keefer firm. Work was delayed when an American contractor failed to place the mains across the narrows, but during the summer of 1888 the two Keefer brothers and one McGillivray devised a new hauling apparatus, repaired the damaged mains, and with the aid of an intrepid diver who three times traversed the bed of the channel, successfully placed a 12-inch main, with flexible joints. It was tested at 300 pounds pressure on August 28. Further delays occurred in obtaining pipes from a Victoria manufacturer, but a second submerged link was laid across Coal Harbor and March 26, 1889, a test flow was turned on at Georgia and Granville Streets. April 14, the city tested 60 hydrants, the fire department abandoned its water tanks forever, Thorpe and Co. opened its new soda water factory and innumerable housewives threw out their kitchen pumps.

Vancouver Gas Co. lost out in its effort to get the city street-lighting contract, but obtained an operating franchise and set up a plant at Keefer and Columbia Streets. Construction was pressed on both plant and mains, and by January 1, 1889, services were already well-established, with 24,000 feet of mains in operation.

In February, 1863, Corporal George Turner of the Royal Engineers had first visited Burrard Inlet to survey the original district lots on the south shore of the inlet. In April, 1889, he, Richard Plunket Cooke and Frederick C. Innes incorporated the Vancouver Street Railway Co., under an act of the Legislature of April 6, with a capital of $250,000. It was proposed to operate horse-cars, and contracts were let for laying tracks and for building barns for 50 horses on Main Street, at False Creek. By Aug. 15, rails were laid from the barn via Main to Powell, along Powell to Carrall, Carrall to Cordova, Cordova to Cambie, Cambie to Hastings, Hastings to Granville and south on Granville to False Creek. Horses were bought in Oregon.

In the newspapers of the day, Abbott, George Keefer and Bullen of the original Vancouver Electrical Illuminating Co. were referred to in connection with the new transit firm, as well as its three directors. Whether this had anything to do with it or not, on April 26, 1890, the reconstituted Vancouver Electric Illuminating

Co. and the Vancouver Street Railway Co. merged as the Van-couver Electric Railway and Light Co., simultaneously announcing plans to construct an improved generating plant. What horses had been purchased were disposed of to Gurney's Cab Co., with the original stables. A barn was built for electric cars.

The new plant was built in May and six 1500-pound, 35-passenger open-side cars ordered from George Stevenson of New York, each equipped with two 10-horsepower motors. A test run of the cars on June 26 gave a time of 27 minutes for the 2.12 miles from Granville Street Bridge to the new powerhouse at the foot of Barnard (now Union) Street at Main. Regular service began June 28. The old Pender Street powerhouse was dismantled and used as a warehouse.

By the end of 1888, sewers with outfalls in the inlet and in False Creek were well established on an efficient plan, but until the waterworks were completed the following year, caused a good deal of trouble, as the fire department was unable to flush them properly with the flow available from the city emergency tanks. Garbage was dumped from the city wharf at the foot of Carrall Street.

One more notable public service was instituted by the council of 1886 when during the fall, with extraordinary foresight, it peti-tioned the Dominion government for the lease of the First Narrows Military Reserve as a park. This was approved by Ottawa and a perpetual lease granted at a $1 a year, subject to use of the land for military purposes if required. When the new governor-general, Lord Stanley, visited the city in October, 1889, he viewed the park that is named for him. A shell-surfaced road around the park and a bridge across Coal Harbor on the site of the present causeway had been built in 1888. That summer, as a sequel to a smallpox epidemic, during which there had been a "pesthouse" established on Dead-man's Island, inhabitants of the island and of Brockton Point nearby were ejected and their homes summarily burned. Among those dispossessed was our old Gastown friend, Gregorio Fern-andez, to whom the council granted $150 "without prejudice" as compensation.

It is well worth dwelling on the fact that amid all the furor of rebuilding the city and establishing its essential services, within four months of the Great Fire the civic authorities of Vancouver were already taking steps to establish one of the world's most famous and beautiful civic parks. Whatever faults we can see in them according to our standards of today, they were men with greatness of vision and not without ideals of public service.

And one last note on the reconstruction of public utilities: the telephone service took the fire almost in its stride, but without the dramatic mushrooming of other operations. Toward the end of 1888 its periodical newspaper publication of phone numbers (the directory came later) listed 113 subscribers, mostly business numbers.

For the first three or four years after the Great Fire, the physical act of construction overshadowed the emergence of the real city which was steadily taking place, but no time was lost in making it the great commercial depot of the western coast. Immediately the transcontinental railway service commenced, Vancouver became the supply depot for all the coast and all the Interior served by the main line. The city's wholesale firms, in the latter trade, were assisted by a freight rate structure which made it cheaper to ship goods from Eastern Canada to Vancouver and back to interior points, than to ship direct. Victoria and New Westminster were reduced almost overnight to commercial backwaters. The Royal City maintained a foothold in the lumber trade, but little else. Victoria, threatened with reduction to a mere farming centre, was saved in 1893 when the Theodore Davie provincial ministry "anchored" the capital there by constructing the $1 million Legislative Buildings in spite of loud outcries from the mainland.

Of primary industry, Vancouver possessed only lumber mills and a single salmon cannery on the north shore of English Bay, but in the city were the head offices, the financial control and the physical supply sources for all of British Columbia except the south-eastern interior. With that exception, Vancouver held the purse-strings, and from all, Vancouver took toll. The toll was not collected without protest; political opponents of the city were entrenched in power in Victoria, backed by Vancouver Island and interior voters.

For its first 30 years, Vancouver was much under-represented in the cabinet. It long had fewer representatives in the Legislature in proportion to its population than any other part of the Province, yet it contributes much more to provincial revenue in taxes than it ever receives in return. To justify this, the remainder of the Province has had one solid argument: through financial and commercial control, Vancouver has exacted its toll in return.

The entire growth of Vancouver has been conditioned by this unceasing struggle between the money power of the city and the political power of the remainder of the province. In this 75-year war, no Solomon has yet arisen to define exact justice.

Through the same three-quarters of a century, a parallel conflict has been waged between eastern financial interests and those native to the city. Vancouver has always labored under the reputation of being a "branch-office" city, subservient to financial and commercial firms with headquarters in Toronto, Montreal or even as far afield as London. This charge, too, has not been without justice. Major undertakings were often operated solely for the benefit of "foreign" investors who had no other stake in the prosperity of the city or the Province, and it was not until after the Second World War that the balance inclined noticeably in favor of local control, which even yet is far from a final victory.

Because of a fourth major factor in modern economy, such a final victory may never occur; that factor is the continued trend to consolidation of industry. This is no new movement, for even in the 1880's and 1890's it was under way, and bitter complaints arose in regard to absorption of smaller firms by the salmon-canning "octopus", and similar operations in other fields. So far as the city is concerned, the scale and the impact of this consolidation process has changed in one sense; instead of fearing Vancouver's mills would be entirely dominated by the Hendry interests, it now faces a situation where the coastal forest industry is dominated by five or six Vancouver firms, and in the fisheries field, one Vancouver firm is reckoned one of the largest and most powerful in the world, disposing annually from its B.C. and foreign plants, fish products in excess of the value of the entire yearly yield of B.C. waters.

The fifth theme of Vancouver's growth, the struggle of the labor unions against the employers, was not to become a prominent factor in the city's growth until the B.C. Electric strike of 1917 and the waterfront hostilities following the return of veterans of the First World War. The city was fortunate to escape the bitterness of the early coal strikes against conditions in Dunsmuir's Nanaimo and Ladysmith mines, or the 1900 Steveston strike against the salmon packers. One reason for this escape, of course, was that Vancouver, with its small primary industry, had few single large employers of labor of the types first organized; it is significant the first strike recorded in the city was that of 1887, in the lumber mills, and the first violent outbreak of basically labor trouble was the anti-Oriental riots of 1907. The great strikes of B.C. labor history have been largely outside Vancouver or industry-wide strikes of provincial, rather than civic, scope. By and large, Vancouver workingmen and employers have settled on terms decided by conflicts outside the city itself.

These major factors, however, have conditioned all of Vancouver's growth, and the story of that growth must be read in light of these governing conditions.

From 1886 to 1892, that growth was simply a continuation of the recovery from the Great Fire. Trans-Pacific commerce jumped into full flow after the arrival of the *Abyssinia* on June 14, 1887. Nine trips were made during the balance of the year, with the steamships *Port Augusta* and *Port Victoria* also chartered for the run. The passenger service proved popular; on her second arrival, August 20, the *Parthia* brought Sir Francis Plunkett, British minister to Japan, and Lady Plunkett, and on her return voyage, carried west the brother of the King of Siam and his four sons. So great was the crush on the dock, the CPR excluded the public, a custom still in force when ocean liners arrive or depart in Vancouver. The Dominion made Vancouver a customs port of entry July 1, 1887; previously it had been Burrard Inlet Outport, under supervision of the New Westminster office. Ike Johns was appointed collector of the port.

In 1888, the company added four more chartered ships for

a total of 19 sailings, plus 12 voyages to San Francisco, the latter chiefly to land Chinese immigrants. This traffic was soon cut off by the U.S. exclusion acts, and the steerage passenger lists on eastbound voyages dropped from 6390 in 1888 to 1483 in 1889. Vancouver feared freight traffic might also be diverted to the south-ern port, but the CPR kept a firm grip on it; a Congressional inquiry into the plight of U.S. railroads, hard hit by the new line, showed that in the first 17 months of Vancouver's life as an ocean port, 1,351,382 pounds of silk, 3,677,713 pounds of rice and 23,288,127 pounds of tea destined for U.S. markets were landed here and hauled east by the CPR. Most of the export traffic was Canadian flour and English cottons. The cotton goods cargoes in the first year of operation were 4,660,168 pounds; in the second year, 11,756,504. Both the U.S. imports and the British exports were Vancouver's gain from the Suez Canal trade, and in the 18 months ending at the end of 1889, Vancouver was handling 27 per cent of all Oriental traffic for the west coast of the American hemis-phere. Inward tonnages handled were: 1888, 41,000; 1889, 34,250; 1890, 36,000. Outward: 1888, 24,500; 1889, 25,000; 1890, 37,600. In these days of ocean giants, such a year's freight would scarcely serve to load one vessel; 70 years ago these figures put the tiny port of 8000 inhabitants on the world's commercial map.

In July, 1889, Stephen reached his long-sought goal; the British government granted the CPR a £45,000 subsidy and the Canadian government granted a £15,000 subsidy for a fast trans - Pacific steamship service consisting of monthly voyages to Hong Kong, Yokohama and Shanghai by vessels of a minimum average speed of 16 knots. By October, the company had contracted with the Naval Construction and Armament Co. of Barrow for three such vessels. As a result, April 28, 1891, the SS *Empress of India* arrived in Vancouver after a record-breaking voyage from England via the Orient.

With their long, clipper bows, overhanging sterns, gleaming white paint and lovely, yacht-like lines, the *India, China* and *Japan,* first of the *White Empresses,* are still held in reverence by seamen as the most beautiful steamships ever to sail the Seven Seas. For 22 years they were the bread and butter of many a Vancouver family, the pride and joy of all; it was no uncommon thing for teachers on the scheduled day of their arrival to take their classes down to Prospect Point to watch the lovely vessels, with their long bowsprits, sloping masts and glittering figureheads, glide in through the Lions' Gate. Their solitary memorial, the dragon figurehead of the *Empress of Japan*, enshrined in Stanley Park, is to citizens of Vancouver a precious relic and a reminder that their city's power may also be a servant of beauty.

While the lifeline of trade was flourishing, the city was spreading out from Stanley Park on the west to east of Hastings Mill, and from the waterfront to almost Broadway south of False Creek. A ward system was set up, the West End being Ward One, the city centre Ward Two, the East End Ward Three, and south of False Creek, Ward Four. David Oppenheimer became mayor in 1888, Fred Cope in 1892. During Oppenheimer's administration the city's main business was still the opening of new streets, the building of the first Granville Street Bridge (1888), and the first Cambie Street Bridge (opened 1892) and the provision of schools, of which five, with 1200 pupils, were operating in 1890. There were the new high school, and the East End, West End, Central and Mount Pleasant Public Schools. Over 75 miles of roads had been opened and graded, and people were living as far west as Denman Street, though "separated from the town." The population was counted at 8500 in July, 1888.

A year later, a budding Anglo-Indian author named Rudyard Kipling visited the city and became a landholder—". . . 400 well-developed pines, a few thousand tons of granite scattered in blocks, and a sprinkling of earth. That's a town lot in Vancouver. You order your agent to hold it until property rises, then sell out and buy more land further out of town . . . I do not quite see how this helps the growth of the town . . . but it is the essence of speculation."

"Today," said Kipling, "Vancouver has a population of 14,000 and builds its houses out of brick with dressed granite fronts.

"But a great sleepiness lies upon Vancouver as compared to an American town; men don't fly up and down the streets telling lies and the spittoons in the delightfully comfortable hotels are unused; the baths are free and the doors unlocked. . .

". . . Vancouver possesses an almost perfect harbor. The town is built all around and about the harbor, and young as it is, its streets are better than those of western America . . . The place is full of Englishmen who speak the English tongue correctly . . . avoiding more blasphemy than is necessary and taking a respectable time to get outside their drinks . . . All of them agreed we do not yet know the resources of B.C. and joyfully bade me note the climate, which was distinctly warm."

Kipling was too early to ride the street cars around the Fairview Belt Line. This famous loop consisted of the original tracks, extended out South Granville across the new bridge, along Broadway and down Main to Union. It was completed in 1892. Nor was Kipling able to travel to New Westminster by the Westminster and Vancouver Tramway Co. interurban line, a pioneer enterprise of its kind in Canada.

This company, headed by H. V. Edmonds, Benjamin Douglas and David Oppenheimer, formed in April, 1890, opened 12 miles of track, mostly along the line of the now abandoned Central Park interurban line. It ran into numerous difficulties, chiefly connected with the 10 percent and greater grades out of New Westminster, but by October of 1891 was making two daily round trips at a fare of 50 cents one way, 75 cents return. Stops were made at Central Park (so named because Mrs. Oppenheimer's birthplace was New York City) and Largen's corner (the modern Venables Street and Glen Drive intersection). The company had meanwhile merged with the Westminster Street Railway Co. and both systems were powered by a steam plant at Edmonds. With an improved power plant and six new 35-foot Brill cars with upholstered seats, aided by an improved right-of-way, the company was giving a 45-minute service between the cities by 1893.

At the opening of Cope's mayoralty in 1892 the city had experienced six straight years of boom and was still riding the crest of the wave it had come to regard as unbreakable. The population had reached 15,000; three bridges spanned False Creek; civic property taxes yielded $180,000; liquor licences alone returned $27,000 annually; a police force of 12 men patrolled the city, including the West End and south of False Creek; the Board of Trade was active, having been organized in 1887; an abortive effort to establish a smelter had failed when the completed plant blew up, but a sugar refinery had been added to the city's industries in 1890, and four breweries were working full blast.

The Imperial Opera House had been opened in May, 1889, on Pender Street with a performance by the famous singer, Emma Juch, and such international celebrities as Sarah Bernhardt had appeared on its boards. Five banks, an assay office, a steam laundry and two engineering works were in business. A fine courthouse was opened on the present Victory Square; the Hudson's Bay Co. had opened a second store, this one on Granville Street at Georgia; Gordon Drysdale's new and fashionable ladies' emporium was established across the street, and Charles Woodward was building a three-storey store on Main.

But 1892 was different. When it was over and Mayor Cope was standing for a second term, he was happy to announce that though times were hard and money tight, "there had been few business failures in Vancouver compared to other cities." It was the beginning of the great depression of the early 90's, which culminated in the U.S. financial crisis of 1893.

Vancouver was to feel the chill winds of disturbed international finance for the first time in its experience; Gastown had been largely immune to such phenomena because the sailing-ship lumber trade was, if anything, stimulated by them—when trade declined, idle ships would load timber cargos for long voyages to distant ports, hoping to dispose of them at a profit after months had passed at sea. Now the mills and the canneries were at the end of a telegraph line over which contracts could be cancelled in minutes after a crash in New York, a panic in Paris, or a slump in London. The cancellations came. The supply and wholesale business slumped and staffs were cut. Wages dropped. Men walked to work, when they had work to walk to, and the street-car company discontinued service on the Fairview and Powell Street lines. Vancouver Electric Railway and Light Co. deficits ran up to $1300 a month in late '92, and in February the city council rejected an offer of the system at a price of $477,000. The bond-holders took over in May and on May 30 citizens in a plebiscite rejected a second opportunity to buy the system, this time at $380,000. (What price the B.C. Hydro today?) The West-minster and Vancouver Tramway Co. found its new Brill cars carrying very little traffic, and when lightning struck and burned out the Edmonds powerhouse, it also gave up the ghost. That same May its assets were seized and the Bank of British Columbia filed judgments totalling $280,437 against it. The city cannot be judged too hardly for not taking over these faltering concerns at such a crisis; in 1892 it had already bought out the waterworks system for $400,000, and in all probability considered it had taken on a depression-time utility at a boom-time price.

Main Street's former title of "Blue-Blood Alley" had been trans-ferred by this time to the mansions of Richards and Georgia Streets and "The Bluff". With all the rest, the land boom folded, the speculators fled, and the mortgagees took over. There was more blueness than blood along the alley in the winter of '93 - '94. Houses all over town were boarded up as the population dropped; a large proportion of the working people were from the United States, and to it they returned. The exodus was particularly hard on the smaller merchants along Cordova and Powell, for they went bankrupt where the larger retailers and wholesalers retrenched and survived. Nobody now laughed at nickels, as they had when the Tivoli saloon began accepting them for beers. The saloons themselves were full of idle men, but idle men have no nickels for beer, not even the beer that brings a free lunch with it.

For the first time, Vancouver saw misery on its doorstep and starvation in its streets. By the spring of '94 the churches all through town were feeding hundreds at soup kitchens, and hundreds sought warmth in the public library in the YMCA building, where charitable citizens contributed to the first of a long series of free

Christmas dinners there for the needy and homeless, who were warned to bring their own knives and forks. Significantly a large proportion of these needy and homeless men were former independent "small operators" in the timber business—handloggers and towboat owners and haulage contractors who had lost their all, and were reduced to seeking jobs with the big firms. The process of consolidation into giant industrial combines had begun, and the "little men" who had looked to the new country for freedom and opportunity were disillusioned and broke. The same process was occurring in the fisheries, and by 1901 six firms handled 42 percent of the catch. The floating labor force had largely vanished at the beginning of the depression; those who were left were the men who had had a stake in the country, and lost it.

The depression, reinforced by a disastrous flood in the Fraser Valley in May, 1894, lasted five long years. By 1896 Vancouver was beginning to stir and find itself alive. By 1897 it could announce, "times are mending", but it was still faced by a long, hard, uphill pull.

The bust had followed the boom.

11

The Golden Years

VANCOUVER pulled itself together as the end of the century approached, but that was not all. The hard, grim years had schooled the city as its first cruise schools a ship. An ordered, intelligent, functioning community had taken the place of a chaotic boom-town. The city had developed character, and was self-aware. It had become a city; it had been only a collection of individuals.

It was odd how death seemed to mark the changes in the city's life. Mayor Anderson had succeeded Cope; Collins succeeded Anderson, and Templeton, Collins. As the elections of early 1898 approached, the end came for David Oppenheimer, the very personification of the infant city's rough, rowdy and hard-boiled beginnings, even as it had come for Gassy Jack Deighton and Sewell Moody when the time of the pioneers ended. And two weeks later, Oppenheimer's long-time colleague, Templeton, collapsed and died on the night of election day, even before he knew he had been defeated by J. F. Garden in his second bid for the chief magistrate's chair. Garden was the "new man" for the "new city."

The hard years had not, of course, been dead years. Some things had been accomplished. The $20,000 Market Hall, with a cold storage plant in the basement, had been built at Pender and Main in 1889; it later became the City Hall. The first automobile had been seen in town in 1890, but autos remained a curiosity for another 15 years. That was the year the Duke and Duchess of Connaught first visited the city, and the year council gave B. T. Rogers a $30,000 bonus, 15 years without taxes, free

THE CITY HALL — *Built in the mayoralty term of the colorful G. G. McGeer, the City Hall was a depression project. Commanding a panoramic view of the downtown peninsula, Burrard Inlet and the mountains, it is being extended by construction of an annex tower adjoining the original building.*

COASTERS, OLD AND MODERN — *First steamship on the Pacific, the Hudson's Bay Company's Beaver was a frequent visitor to Burrard Inlet. It ended its career when wrecked at Prospect Point in Stanley Park in July, 1888. Souvenir hunters for years hacked at its wreckage.*

Below is the QUEEN OF SAANICH, *one of the car and passenger ferries in the large government-owned fleet that connects Vancouver Island and the mainland as well as many other coastal points impossible to reach by land.*

Photo courtesy Peter Favelle

water for 10 years and a perpetual guarantee of water at 10 cents per thousand gallons, to establish his sugar refinery here. On his side, Rogers had to agree to employ none but white labor. It was also the year the city parks were put under a park board, instead of a council committee. Carter - Cotton and J. W. Horne in 1891 became the city's representatives in the Legislature; both were Conservatives, though the House had not yet succumbed to the party system. All the "respectable" business people of the city were Conservative, and no young man who hoped to make his way up in the world would think of being anything else.

The province was going railway-mad. In 1892 Vancouver expected soon to be linked to Seattle by one of the few projected lines that ever came into being, but it was years before the Great Northern ran trains into town. The city council, having refused a grant to John Hendry's projected Vancouver, Westminster and Yukon Line, with its proposed grain elevator on the North Shore, finally approved a $300,000 subsidy for the Fraser Valley and Burrard Inlet Railway Co., which was to bring the Northern Pacific in, and $60,000 was spent on constructing a grade. As the depression deepened, the NPR abandoned the scheme. Hendry's VW&Y project came to life again years later as the Pacific Great Eastern. The next 25 years were to be cluttered with grandiose railway schemes; one proposed to tunnel completely under Point Grey, from the CPR's Kitsilano trestle, and build a vast deep-sea port on the western side of Sea and Lulu Islands; another included a causeway across Second Narrows with locks for shipping which would create a fresh-water lake in the upper inlet, thus freeing ships of marine weed while they loaded at docks served by the railway which would run over the causeway and to Port Moody along the North Shore. Still another projected a line up the south side of the Fraser River and through the Coquihalla Pass along the route of the present Kettle Valley line into the Kootenays. Anybody with a friend in the Legislature and the gift of a few shares of stock could obtain fabulous grants of land, timber and mineral rights, and governments rose and fell on railway promises and railway scandals. For Vancouver, it was a pity that the Kootenay line did not materialize until 1917; the Kootenay and Boundary mines became tributaries of Spokane just at the time the hard-hit city was trying to pull itself out of the slump and desperately needed the trade. Mining excitement was intense from 1890 to 1914, and the city papers printed masses of mining news on their front pages, but Vancouver missed the boat.

It was in '92 the first court of civil and criminal assize was held in Vancouver; previously such cases had been tried in New Westminster, and the city did not have a resident Supreme Court justice nor County Court judge until 1901. It did obtain a third representative in the Legislature in '94, but the delegation's political complexion remained unchanged and Carter - Cotton, the *News-Advertiser* publisher, still headed it. The city remained conservative in mind, too, and it was not until 1895 that it adopted a policy of relief works to be performed by day labor. Of course the council was struggling with diminished revenues, for assessments had slipped from a high of $18.6 million to $16.1 million in a single year. That year, local construction included extension of the street railway to Stanley Park, a great deal of work on the water system and construction of a reservoir in the park.

The street railway and lighting systems of Vancouver, North Vancouver and New Westminster had been taken over in 1894 by the Consolidated Railway and Light Co., backed by English capital and managed by Frank (later Sir Frank) Stillman Barnard. Barnard induced Robert Horne-Payne to join the project, more capital was procured, and Victoria brought into the system. In 1896, under the name of the Consolidated Railway Co., the company controlled the entire electrical utility systems of Vancouver Island and the Lower Mainland and was capitalized at $1.5 million. Under the stress of litigation following the Point Ellice Bridge disaster of May 24, 1896, in Victoria, in which 54 street-car passengers were drowned, the Consolidated collapsed, but Barnard and Horne-Payne persisted.

Horne-Payne obtained additional backing in England, and five months later re-purchased the entire system from the bondholders for $2,250,000. The new company was named the British Columbia Electric Railway Co., Ltd., with head offices in London, and local offices in a one-story building on Cordova Street, near Cambie. Thus was accomplished the most rapid and effective consolidation of a single industry in the city's history. The city's most immediate gain was a reduction from 44 cents to 27 cents per light per night in the street lighting rate. In the long run, however, it was Horne-Payne's determination to replace the steam plants with hydro-electric power which was to pay the greatest dividends.

The galvanic shock that brought Vancouver back to roaring life was the discovery of gold in the Klondyke.

Back in 1889, the Irvings' Canadian Pacific Navigation Co. dominated the city's coastwise shipping trade, but that year there arrived here a young New Zealander, Henry Darling, son of John Darling of the Union Steamship Co. of the southern dominion. Darling took over and merged the Burrard Inlet Towing Co., a small inlet business run by Captain Donald McPhaiden, and the Moodyville Ferry Co., an even smaller concern which consisted of Captain Hugh Stalker and the ancient *SS Senator*, old Captain Van Bramer's second inlet ferry. The resulting Union Steamships Co. of B.C. prospered during the decade, owning in 1897 four passenger ships and a tug fleet, among the latter the ill-fated *Chehalis*. The *Chehalis* was run down in First Narrows by the *Princess Victoria* in 1906 with the loss of eight lives, an event commemorated by a small monument in Stanley Park near Brockton Point.

July 21, 1897, the company's *Capilano* became the first British ship to enter the Klondyke trade, leaving for the north with passengers, 68 head of cattle and 20 horses. She was followed in August by another of the fleet, the *Coquitlam*, with cargo and 20 passengers at $30 a head. During this and the following year Vancouver swarmed with Klondyke-bound adventurers, and a detachment of Royal Canadian Mounted Police, still in the old-style pill-box hats, arrived in town on their way north.

". . . a mining madness seized Vancouver," reports B.C.'s official historian, Dr. Margaret Ormsby, "supplies of staples were rounded up; dogs broken into harness; and keels for stern-wheelers and other boats laid in the False Creek shipyards. In 1898, every hotel and lodging-house was crowded to capacity; tents were pitched in every water-front lot; the merchants were prepared to offer free advice on northern wearing-apparel; and stranger sights than ever before were to be seen on the skid road. Everyone from tea merchant to huckster prospered; smart new equipages made their appearance on the city streets; contracts were let for new mansions in the West End and for new business blocks in the heart of the city, and newspapers increased their circulation beyond belief . . . Vancouver had started its climb back to prosperity."

It was the "shot in the arm" Vancouver urgently required, but in cold reality it was a stimulant with no body-building nourishment in it. Seattle and Victoria secured the cream of the trade; Vancouver got the overflow. Once the excitement was ended, the city had to turn to other sources for its daily bread and what Klondyke and Alaskan business remained went to the Puget Sound city. A fair indication of the rise and fall of "the rush" is given by the port's shipping activity, and Vancouver's secondary place is emphasized by the fact that Irvings' CPN boats deserted the port altogether during the most frenzied months to cut in on the Seattle trade, depriving Vancouver of its main coastwise service.

It was, perhaps, a blessing in disguise, for other interests stepped in and filled the gap, becoming effective competitors in the 1900's. The CPR built on False Creek the sternwheelers *Tyrrell*, *Duchesnay* and *Dawson*, placing them on the Yukon River and buying the *Tartar* and *Athenia*, former liners on the UK-South Africa run, for the coastwise route to Alaska. Evans, Coleman & Evans bought the 2078-ton *Ningchow* for the same service. All three ships were taken off the northern route in the fall of 1898, the CPR vessels being transferred to the Pacific service. In the upshot, the Union line was strengthened, Evans, Coleman & Evans was established in the shipping business, and in 1901, the CPR took over the CPN, to begin in 1902, with the building of the *Princess Victoria*, the famous line of *Princesses* which for many years dominated the south coast passenger business. Union added the *Cassiar* to its fleet in 1898, and for 50 years equally dominated the "hole-and-corner" trade of the northern coast with one of the most skilful, romantic and dangerous navigation operations in the world, successfully carried out as a day-by-day routine. "Union" is a proud name in the history of the port.

As far as Vancouver was concerned, the fall of '98 marked the end of the Klondyke rush. No more check-shirted adventurers "mushed" their dogs in the mud of Cordova Street from saloon to saloon, and the flood of supplies that had poured across the docks was reduced to a trickle. Nevertheless, the city was back on its feet and, what was even more important, once more filled with confidence in its own destiny. The boom was on again, and with one hesitation (rather than a break) in 1907, was to last more than a decade. The golden years had come.

And what years they were! Elegance was their keynote— Vancouver had discovered elegance, and elegant she would be, if she had to bust a gusset to do it. Towers, turrets, battlements, gingerbread-work, monkey-puzzle trees, clipped hollies and Chinese houseboys sprouted all over the West End. Bowler hats and beards (the beards soon went out of fashion) crowded the sidewalks of the business district. A varnished gig and a high-stepping trotter were almost equal to an AAA-1 rating in Bradstreet as a guarantee of financial responsibility. Ladies in correct driving habits skilfully drove tandem rigs around Stanley Park on fine afternoons. Every matron had her "afternoon" on which she expected a drawing-room full of acquaintances to tea, and wept with mortification if her "Thursday" or "Tuesday" failed to appear with the 1000-odd others between the chaste blue covers of the Elite Directory. The Elite listed all the members of the Terminal City Club, of the Vancouver Yacht Club, of the Lawn Tennis Club, but—an even superior level of exclusiveness—not those of the Vancouver Club.

Businessmen, once content with the cherry-colored walls and stuffed pheasants of the Leyland Hotel dining room, now lunched at their clubs, or amid the sombre magnificence of Allen's Restaurant or the Strand Hotel; the latter had a cuisine and a wine cellar of truly Parisian standards, even importing French artichokes from California. Service in the cafes and restaurants was impeccable and in homes ladies trained their maids to the peak of perfection; the vagaries and blunders of Chinese "boys" were a never-ending source of conversation and the "boys" were not slow to catch on—many an "old family retainer" just six months off the boat from Hong Kong shamefully bullied his Missee and Mastah, and "no savvee" excused any crime of commission or omission. New standards of excellence arose; to compare Vancouver with San Francisco was no longer popular, Drysdale's delivery service had the finest stable, and C. E. Tisdall's store the largest stock of sporting goods, "west of Chicago." Tisdall, indeed, exemplified a new element in the city's make-up, the sound, conservative, successful businessman of the Victorian tradition. While speculators concocted deals in the bars or over their two-hour-long luncheons, he had worked long hours and slept at night under the counter of his tiny shop, or pored over his ledgers standing at his high, sloping desk. As his business grew, his clerks worked under his eagle-eye; woe betide any wretch who put a gun and the ammunition to fit it on the counter at the same time. In his early days Tisdall had an unfortunate experience with a customer who slipped a cartridge into a revolver and blew his brains out on the spot. No other incident had ever disturbed him so much unless it was the zeal of the green office-boy who swept up two pounds of spilled gunpowder and threw it into the vast stove that dominated the centre of the store. . . .

Honesty and excellence were his hallmarks. Nothing gave him so much pride as the fact that Tisdall's trout flies sold all over the continent, and even in England. Honesty and a sound common-sense were what he brought to his long service in the Park Board. By 1913 the city had poured over $1.5 million into Stanley Park and English Bay beaches and was rightfully proud of the result—all the town swam and picnicked, walked and played there and the beaches were even more crowded than today. Tisdall climaxed his service to the city with two years as mayor and membership in the Legislature. His type is obsolete today, but amid the furor and fireworks of the boom years, it provided a sound core that served the city well, though it added little to the gaudy legends of the gaudy years.

And gaudy they were. Everybody in Vancouver was bound to get rich. (Plenty didn't—but that must have been their own fault.) Land —land—land! Buy a lot today—be a millionaire tomorrow! Sometimes it did happen. A Hastings Street lot bought for $8 a front-foot in 1886, sold for $4000 a front-foot in 1911—$18 a day increase in value, including Sundays and holidays—75 cents each and every hour! Another sold for $5500 in 1889, and $100,000 in 1911. Just before the city burned down, a man named Campbell woke one morning to find himself possessed of a hangover and a $1 raffle ticket. Returning to the saloon for an eye-opener, he found he'd won the lot on the northwest corner of Pender and Abbott Streets. In 1908 he sold out for $50,000; his dollar had earned him $2273 a year over that time. In 1887, the site of the Domininon Trust building sold for $750, in 1889 for $7600, in 1906 for $15,000, in 1911 for $100,000. In 1891 a syndicate bought 64 acres south of False Creek at $250 an acre; in 1910 it sold eight 50-foot lots for $200,000. In 1905 a city block near Stanley Park was sold for $1500; in 1910 a small section of it brought $125,000.

The population was by a liberal estimate, 15,000 in 1892, 20,000 in 1898. In 1904 it was 38,000. In 1905 it was 45,000 and the tourist greeters sang:

> *In nineteen-ten,*
> *Vancouver then*
> *Will have one hundred thousand men.*
> *Move her! Move her!*
> *Who?—Vancouver!*

And they weren't so far off the mark. In 1910, by virtue of annexing Hastings Townsite and District Lot 301, the population was 93,700 and voting took place in eight wards.

In 1906, municipal election candidates advocated completion of streets to all city boundaries, Schumann-Heink sang in the Opera House, the Orpheum Theatre was opened, movies were shown at the Grand Theatre, a by-law was passed to increase the English Bay bathhouse from 116 to 246 rooms, school enrollment had reached 6,103, the city bought a motor-vehicle patrol and ambulance wagon and the Board of Trade was pressing for construction of a grain elevator. In 1907, bank clearings were up 45 percent to $191 million, customs receipts up $1 million to $3 million, building permits up 33 percent to $5.6 million, want ads filled a full page of the *News-Advertiser* and the paper was running a "20 Years Ago" column to show the progress made in two decades. But there was a short, sharp shock in store—in November and December, bank clearings, customs receipts and building were all far below the same months of 1906.

The depression was a flea-bite compared to that of the 1890's. a mere "readjustment" in modern financial terms, but it was severe enough to those who were thrown out of work. Their reaction took a familiar pattern—Oriental immigration had been high, Sikhs were appearing along with Chinese and Japanese, and the wrath of the workingmen was turned against these wage-cutters. The Asiatic Exclusion League, by no means confined to the working class, called a mass meeting for September 7, 1907. Two thousand men assembled on Cambie Street Grounds (the present bus station) and marched out with banners flying, marshalled by Major E. Browne. The procession was estimated to contain 5000 persons by the time it reached Hastings Street, and 8000 at the City Hall, where they burned Lieutenant-Governor Dunsmuir in effigy. Inside the hall, fiery speeches were made by A. W. von Rhein, Reverend H. W. Fraser, Harry Cowan, Reverend G. H. Wilson, C. M. Woodworth, J. E. Wilton, W. A. Young, Gordon Grant, F. J. Russell and W. E. Flumerfelt — by no means persons of the "irresponsible" class. The crowd outside increased to 30,000 and about 15,000 took part in the subsequent action, which started at 9 p.m. with a sortie down Pender Street, in which stores were wrecked and plundered and Chinese beaten.

The Chinese fled. It was a different matter in Japtown on Powell Street. There every able-bodied man and boy turned out with clubs, knives and broken bottles to do battle. After a sharp fight, the mob fled, and when the police arrived at 10 p.m. they found the Japanese organized and alert, with their own patrols out. A cordon was thrown around the area—not so much to protect the Japanese as to prevent any unwary whites stumbling into the hornets' nest. The mob returned to Pender, but the police and fire department set up barricades and by midnight had repulsed several attacks by the mob, the last along the CPR tracks at Carrall Street. During the height of the riot, a Japanese government commissioner, Kikujiro Ishii, arrived in town on a tour of the Pacific coast, and with Consul Morikawa, persuaded the aroused Japanese to remain in their own area, on the defensive.

The next morning, a Sunday, Mayor Bethune, Chief of Police Chamberlain, Ishii and Morikawa held a confused conference in which the consul demanded the Japanese be protected from the whites, the mayor demanded the whites be protected from the Japanese, and Ishii, in the name of the Japanese government, demanded full compensation for all Japanese nationals.

If the situation verged on the comic in City Hall, it was serious enough in the eyes of Ottawa. More than 11,000 Orientals, 8000 of them Japanese, had entered Canada during the year and both Japan and its nationals were cock-a-whoop over their recent victory in the Russo-Japanese war. The governor-general, Earl Grey, wired a demand to Mayor Bethune that order be restored at once. Prime Minister Laurier sent a commissioner to Japan to negotiate a reduction in the flow of immigrants, and dispatched Deputy Minister of Labor W. L. Mackenzie King to Vancouver to examine the local situation. In the upshot, King, Laurier and Grey were converted to a belief in the perils of "the yellow invasion" and Japan agreed to limit immigrants to 400 yearly. But on the fateful Sunday, Ottawa had been merely profoundly shocked at the outbreak of violence. Official reprimands did nothing to soothe the fears of the townspeople and the city was filled with rumors that 5000 armed and organized Japanese were about to capture and sack Vancouver. That night some 5000 whites milled around the streets, but eventually went quietly home. During the day, the mayor swore in a few special police.

Monday, however, the terrible consequences of their rash outbreak dawned upon the citizens amid a quiet and awful hush. Not a single Chinese in Vancouver turned out to work.

Not a laundry in town laundered; not a shingle-mill turned a wheel; almost every sawmill was closed; portly dowagers in the West End cooked breakfast for the first time in years; hardly an hotel, and only one restaurant, opened; meals failed to appear in railway dining cars and ships' dining saloons; tugboats had no cooks, and all up and down the coast logging camps closed. The strike was on, and many Chinese from outside camps quietly filtered into town. No Chinese approached any person in authority, but it gradually leaked out that no Chinese would do a hand's turn in Vancouver until peace and protection were assured him.

The Chinese "forted up" in the shattered remains of Pender Street, barricaded themselves in their homes and collected piles of bricks and stones on the roofs for defensive ammunition. The police seized a shipment of 124 rifles and 5000 rounds of ammunition his New Westminster compatriots tried to smuggle in to Sam Kee of Vancouver. Aggressive patrols of three or four Japanese pushed out from Powell Street, but the whites avoided trouble. The United Services Club marched in a body to the police station to offer help in maintaining law and order, but Chief Chamberlain had already 62 police, 20 special constables and six mounted men on duty. For the rest, the day passed quietly, with Magistrate Adolphus Williams fining two Japanese $10 each in police court for being in possession of deadly weapons, and remanding 18 white rioters, with the reminder that they might get up to seven years in prison. In the evening, the streets were again filled with whites and two or three fires broke out in the city, in which arson was suspected.

Tuesday the Japanese returned to work. The Chinese did not. News filtered into town that a Chinese had been murdered on the River Road, and Consul Morikawa demanded the militia be called out to protect the Orientals. The Asiatic Exclusion League wired Ottawa to demand that approaching immigrant ships be turned back, and threatened to hold a meeting on Thursday despite the mayor's ban. The league's leaders denied any intention of provoking the recent violence. That night it rained heavily, and the police breathed a collective sigh of relief when everybody went home out of the wet. Prime Minister Laurier again assured the Japanese government the rioters would be punished.

Wednesday, the Chinese went back to work; the white cooks who had been brought in to replace them promptly went on strike in turn, but the relieved city scarcely noticed that. It was getting three square meals per day again. The immigrant ship *Monteagle* arrived; 798 East Indians were admitted to the beleaguered city, 103 rejected; 54 Japanese were admitted, two rejected, and 160 Chinese were passed through in bond for Eastern Canada. No one in Vancouver would harbor the unfortunate East Indians and Mayor Bethune wired Laurier for permission to billet them in the Drill Hall on Beatty Street, but the request was ignored. Thursday was quiet except for the stabbing of a drunken white in Canton Alley by 30 enraged Chinese after he had assaulted one of their number; a small crowd of dispirited whites looked on and left it to a Negro woman to rescue him. The banned meeting of the Exclusion League took place, but it was a tame affair, with some 300 curious citizens present and von Rhein in the chair. It contented itself with resolving that publisher Carter-Cotton was a "cur" and that the Vancouver Board of Trade had deliberately encouraged the Chinese to menace the safety of the community. Friday the Board of Trade denied the accusation and declared the AEL a lot of low characters bent on making trouble. The 18 rioters were remanded a second time and a Japanese was fined the regulation $10 for appearing downtown with two revolvers in his belt and a dirk in each sock.

By this time, both the domestic and foreign press were agreeing to blame the recent unfortunate occurrences on American agitators; A. E. Fowler, who had represented the anti-Oriental organizations of the State of Washington at the first Exclusion League meeting, denied ever counselling violence, but declared he would continue to fight the good fight "even if it is necessary to become a martyr to the fury of the yellow heathen." The anti-Oriental riots of 1907 were over.

The aftermath was trivial. During the following week, Laurier and Ishii came to "a satisfactory agreement" on compensation for the Japanese, but the terms were kept secret. Chinese Vice-Consul Owyang King arrived from San Francisco to assess damage to the Chinese community. The New York Evening Post entitled an editorial "Vancouver, B.C.—Yes, 10,000 B.C." Fowler returned to

Washington, was run out of Bellingham and later in the month committed to Stellacoom Insane Asylum, where he was reported by Seattle papers to be a raving maniac. The immigrant ship *Woolwich* landed 238 Japanese.

Compensation for the Chinese community was later settled at $100,000. The Canadian government rejected claims made for two opium factories destroyed during the disorders.

There remained only the real sufferers—648 innocent East Indians, those from the ship *Monteagle* who did not have jobs to go to on arrival. A few found shelter; the rest were existing as best they might, 150 in a 10-room house on Second Avenue, 250 in another house, and 150 in tents on the railway reserve near Beach Avenue. All were suffering from the cold and the wet. A second appeal to the Prime Minister brought only the cold statement that if they could not shelter themselves, they must be paupers, and should be deported at once. The mayor replied that they had money, but no one would rent homes to them.

Leaders of the East Indian Community collected $6000 for their relief, but still no quarters could be found. They appealed to the Governor-General for assistance, and asked him to put an end to what they called misleading recruiting of immigrants in the Punjab by transportation companies. Ottawa continued to ignore the whole affair. The East Indians subsisted through the winter on the charity of the citizens and of their compatriots, many succumbing to the hardships of the unfamiliar climate.

By the end of 1908, the depression was over and the city in full boom pace again. Bank clearings were down to $183 million for the year, but up to a monthly record of $18 million in December. The fire department was gradually being motorized, and 2.16 miles of wood-block pavement, long a unique feature of Vancouver's downtown streets, had been laid. Five candidates sought the mayoralty; C. S. Douglas won the chair, but Louis D. Taylor, publisher of the *Vancouver World*, was runner-up in his first try at the polls. By-laws for $1.5 million were passed, and the voters in a plebiscite approved an eight-hour day for civic workers. There had been 27 failures of business houses, but in view of world conditions, this was considered to have demonstrated the basic soundness of Vancouver business. The city had spent $114,000, plus a $56,000 provincial grant, on its schools during the year, and "with many pupils now earning money," the schools had established a school savings bank system to encourage thrift and responsibility.

All through 1909 the city pushed ahead, until cautious business leaders might be heard quietly deploring "this unreasoning boom," but none spoke out publicly. Assessments shot up from $72 to $106 million and the ratepayers approved by-laws for $413,000 for improving English Bay and securing Kitsilano Beach as a public park; $230,000 for schools; $42,000 for school board offices (they had defeated a $20,000 bylaw for the same purpose two years before); and $50,000 for fire halls. The same voters in a plebiscite intelligently approved expansion of the existing telephone system, decisively defeating a drive to introduce a competitive company into the city. On his second try, Taylor defeated Douglas for the mayoralty by 273 votes and the conservative part of the community shuddered; Taylor was not only Liberal in his leanings but the enigmatic little publisher was reputed to know where many a body in town was buried.

He was the last man, however, to throw any monkey-wrenches into the boom machine; he was already considering plans to erect the tallest building in the British Empire for his newspaper, and by 1913 he completed what is now still a city landmark, the Sun Tower, for it reverted to newspaper occupancy in the 1930's after a long hiatus in less stirring circles. He could afford it, for city newspapers were almost their present volume, with the three department stores running up to three pages each of advertising daily. The city was "built up solid to English Bay;" building permits reached $13.5 million and the imposing Dominion Trust Building was completed by the Von Alvensleben brothers, who were reputed to be backed financially by Kaiser Wilhelm of Germany, himself.

The boom reached its crest in 1910 and 1911. Business was shifting from Hastings to Granville Street. The new swing-span high-level Granville Street Bridge was open, automobiles were common, and "the nobs" were building immense houses on Shaughnessy

Heights, recently opened by the CPR under restrictions embodied in an act of the Legislature, which were expected to render it ultra-exclusive for all time to come. The new "Millionaires' Row" was the creation of the automobile and the plentiful, cheap domestic labor which in 25 years' time had vanished. Nevertheless, the five-year or six-year "old timers" of the West End, already being elbowed by encroaching apartment houses, turned up their noses at the "new-rich" on the "CPR Heaven." (Later they called it "Poverty Heights" —and picked up mansions at a bargain.)

The new-rich revelled in their new riches, sat back and quoted statistics. Bank clearings had rolled up from $147 million in 1906 to $191 million, $183 million, $327 million and $444 million in successive years. Customs receipts were $3.9 million in 1910, $6.2 million in 1911. Stock exchange seats, $250 when the exchange was established in 1907, were sold for $500 in 1908, $1750 in 1910, $3500 in 1911. Building permits in May, 1910, were $941,000; in May, 1911, $2,488,000. The Von Alvenslebens had invested $7 million of German money in two years. The new post office was completed at Granville and Hastings, and doing the fourth largest business in Canada. The city had 12 grocery whole-salers each doing more than $2 million business a year; the turnover of one in 1911 was $4 million. A hardware wholesaler was put-ting up a building one block square and six storeys high; a fine new courthouse was under construction on Georgia Street.

The B.C. Electric street cars and trams were carrying 100,000 passengers a day; they had reached 122,000 during the exhibition week. Point Grey and South Vancouver were filling up with fine houses—annexation to the city was just a matter of time—and Point Grey had at last been chosen as the site of the new University of British Columbia, a matter in doubt ever since 1890. Money by-laws for $2,525,000 were passed at the civic election (but the ratepayers turned down a proposed viaduct linking Dunsmuir and Keefer Streets, and a bridge from the end of Burrard Street to Kitsilano).

Strange new ideas were stirring—all through 1911 the politicians and newspapers smiled at female protests against the way school business was being handled, but in the civic elections of January,

1912, the *News-Advertiser* reluctantly admitted "The ladies turned out in force," and Mary Henrietta (Mrs. P.) McNaughton became the first of her sex to hold public office in the city; she headed the poll for the board with 5169 votes, against 3964 for her nearest male opponent. Mayor Taylor, too, was defeated by James Findlay, after two years in office.

The new Opera House was completed on Granville Street, and 25-foot Granville Street lots were selling for $40,000. There were 12,000 telephones, 52 churches and 13 consular offices in town. The Great Northern Railway had reached the city, and the BCE had pushed a tram line out to Chilliwack. There were three real-estate offices in the city for every grocery store. The Canadian Northern Railway was building down the North Thompson, to a terminal at Vancouver, and the Kettle Valley Line out to Midway.

The social whirl became a whirlpool. Dances, teas, receptions kept the big houses filled to the doors and sparkling with lights. Yachts glided over Coal Harbor and English Bay. The Edwardian Age had come to town, and the young folk broke loose, evoking the tut-tuts of their elders. Visiting aristocrats were submerged in champagne and debutantes; there were reigning belles, and here and there emerged a new species, the playboy, like "Afternoon Tea Charlie" Henshaw, who convulsed a yachting party and scandalized the town by providing his guests with bathing dresses straight from Paris—which disintegrated after 10 minutes in the water. Ladies sat on stools in the shops to be waited on by polite clerks and never carried a parcel too big to slip into their purses. Charming girls swung in hammocks on summer lawns, or sang "The Trail of the Lonesome Pine" in the dusk at beach picnics; mandolins tinkled on front porches in the evenings, and rag-time tunes drifted down the streets.

Oh!—It was a wonderful, wonderful time. . . .

12

King and Country

"THE BLOOD AND guts of Old England . . ." These words, in Gassy Jack Deighton's whisky-bass, growled through the primeval forest of Burrard Inlet as he stood on the roof of Gastown's first tiny building and unfurled the Union Jack to the winds of the wild in 1867.

Vancouver might be the most Canadian, and even the most American, of the cities of British Columbia, but there never was any doubt where her allegiance lay. Through all her turbulent years the blood of Old England ran strong, and when the times of trouble came, she had the guts of Old England, too. Her patriotism might be less suave and ceremonious than that displayed by the rest of "the most British province in Canada," but it stood the test as well as any. When blood was needed, and when guts were needed, Vancouver delivered them.

It is one of the fantastic trivia of the city's history that it fell to that oddly assorted pair, Gassy Jack and Captain Edward Stamp, literally to keep the old flag flying at opposite ends of the British Empire. Gassy Jack's flag fluttered over the saloon in the midst of the forest until the day of Confederation in 1871, when he loyally exchanged it for its newest version—the first Canadian ensign to be flown on the mainland of British Columbia.

From the shores of the Pacific to the heart of London is half the span of the world, but there Captain Stamp was fulfilling the same duty. In 1859, while still logging on Alberni Canal, Stamp cut a gigantic spar and, in the name of lumbermen of Vancouver Island, shipped it to London as a gift to Kew Gardens. The pole fell and

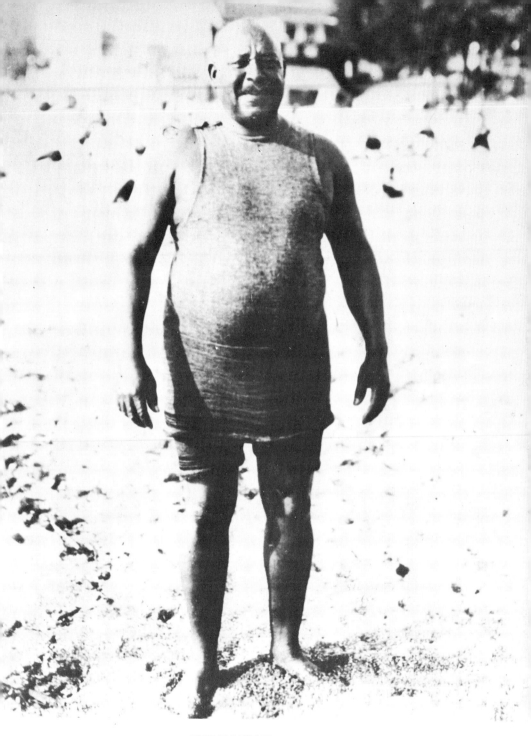

JOE FORTES

He came from the Barbados to Granville in 1884 and adopted English Bay,
its swimmers and its children as his own field of care.

159

MRS. JONATHAN ROGERS

Typical of many women who gave leadership in the city was Mrs. Elizabeth Rogers. She was a founder and early president of the Women's Canadian Club, with her husband a donor to many civic improvement causes. Around her fireplace met the citizens who each gave $5,000 to establish the Vancouver Art Gallery, housed with a donation of $50,000 by H. A. Stone, retired wholesale merchant. She attended the Hague Peace Conference in 1913. Three governments decorated her for Red Cross work in the First World War.

broke as it was being erected, but, nothing daunted, the gallant captain cut and shipped an even larger stick in 1861, before he moved to the inlet. It was successfully placed and for many years remained one of the minor wonders of Europe—the largest single piece of timber ever seen by millions of Londoners and awed visitors. By 1912 the famous pole had become so rotten as to be unsafe, and the curator of the gardens sent an appeal "to the gentlemen of the timber trade of Vancouver and British Columbia" to find a replacement for it.

What Stamp could do in '61, Vancouver's lumbermen could do in 1912, and they resolved forthwith to outdo it. For two years, their timber cruisers combed the woods of B.C. for a tree taller than the tallest, slimmer than the slimmest, true, straight and sound. Eleven such were felled and discarded for trifling imperfections. The twelfth, six feet at the butt, 220 feet long and 18 inches inside the bark at the top, filled every specification. It was brought to Vancouver and shaped by expert broadaxe men—a 33-inch cylinder for the first 15 feet, from there a tapered octagon, 31¾ inches at 25 feet, 30½ inches at 41 feet, 29⅜ inches at 52 feet, 24 inches at 102 feet and 19 inches at 152 feet. At the 157th foot it became round again, at 190 feet, 15 inches in diameter, at 215 feet, 12 inches.

Carriage was a difficulty. The lumbermen refused to ship their gem in October, 1914, on the Royal Mail Steam Packet *Radnorshire*, since it would have been necessary to put a five-foot bend in it to fit the camber of the deck. Finally, in September, 1915, it was hauled through the streets of the city in triumphal procession (there was difficulty getting it around the corner of Hastings and Granville Streets) and loaded on the RMSP *Marionethshire*, perfectly straight on secure blocking. The *Marionethshire* reached Gibraltar, via the Suez Canal, Christmas Day and Spaniards flocked in crowds to view the giant stick, which arrived in London New Year's Day. Thames watermen vetoed a plan to convey the pole to Kew on two large barges; they might have swung in the tide and broken it. It was dropped in the river to float for itself, and in four painstaking days, towed to Kew by tugs, passing under the 12 great bridges of London en route, where more crowds gathered to see it. It was moored at Sion Vista, and during the unusually high tide of January 10, landed on the Thames tow-path by the Clerk of the Woods of Kew and his staff, and safely erected during the year. It was the greatest flagstaff the world has ever seen made from one piece of timber, and probably the greatest the world ever will see.

The gentlemen of the timber trade of Vancouver had worthily carried on the tradition set by Captain Stamp, even as they had that of Jerry Rogers, for when the great staff first flaunted the flag of Empire in the Empire's capital, there were already incorporated in the Imperial Palace at Peking a set of dimension timbers from Vancouver such as even Jerry never shipped—Douglas fir 64 feet long and five feet square, of absolutely perfect quality. No other lumber port in the world could boast such triumphs as these.

In 1959, one hundred years after Edward Stamp's first gift to Kew Garden, the lumber industry and the government of B.C. shipped a second replacement timber to renew the giant flagpole at Kew. The tradition, maintained, spans Vancouver's whole life.

The city was noted for its lavish reception and enthusiastic acclaim of royalty and vice-regality, from the 21-shotgun salute that greeted Lord and Lady Dufferin in 1876, to the magnificent welcome of the Duke and Duchess of York (later King George V and Queen Mary) in 1901. There was, however, a more practical turn to its patriotism.

In 1893, Captain T. O. Townley, Vancouver lawyer and later mayor, was authorized to raise No. 5 Company of the British Columbia Brigade of Garrison Artillery in Vancouver; other units of the brigade were in Victoria and New Westminster. Townley had been promoted to major before uniforms and equipment arrived, and he attested 80 men January 16 and 17, 1894. The first parade was held January 18 in the Imperial Opera House on Pender Street. A creditable guard of honor was turned out for Lord Stanley, the governor-general, in November of that year. Recruiting was rapid and in 1896 No. 5 Company became the two-company 2nd Battalion, 5th Regiment, Canadian Artillery, reorganized as the 6th Battalion of Rifles in July, 1899.

Patriotic enthusiasm in B.C. was whipped to a fury as the Boer War opened, and it was a great disappointment when only 17 Vancouver men were selected for service with the Royal Canadian Regiment in South Africa. They left (with seven more from New Westminster) after a wild parade through town, in which a milk cart with a boar's head mounted on a pole appeared. Eight months after their departure, the Duke of Connaught became honorary colonel of the Vancouver unit, which assumed the title of 6th Rgt. Duke of Connaught's Own Rifles.

With the rest of B.C., Vancouver grew righteously indignant when the Province's offer to equip a battalion for the war on its own was rejected by the Laurier government, and when, on the last day of the century, December 31, 1900, seven of the detachment returned, they were greeted at the CPR station by one of the largest crowds in Vancouver's history. The Vancouver men had taken part in 37 battles and skirmishes and the capture of three defended cities. For them the Rifles were on parade, Colonel C. A. Worsnop and Mayor Garden made speeches and a procession accompanied them to the Royal Theatre, where they were welcomed home by Lieut.-Gov. T. R. McInnes. A further progress in the evening, under arches erected on Cordova Street and with searchlights playing from the top of the B.C. Electric Building, ended in the Opera House, where each veteran was presented with a gold watch and a new suit of clothes. Said the *News-Advertiser* next morning, "They were surrounded on the stage by the fair faces of the youth and beauty of the city, which set off to admiration the bronzed, bold and manly faces of the heroes who had suffered and conquered on the burning veldt for Queen, Home and Empire!"

After two cataclysmic world wars and in the shade of universal nuclear death, it all seems a bit tinselly and theatrical, but this was the biggest and best war the Empire had had since Waterloo. It was something else, too, but it cast no shadow over the wild rejoicing of the last night of the Ninteenth Century that 15 years later, men would know what the Boer War had been—a rehearsal for Armageddon.

The toll had been small; a captain and two privates dead, four privates invalided home. (Three more of the original 17 were to return later.)

The militia grew with the city during the 1900's. In 1909, Company 18 of the Army Medical Corps was embodied; in 1910, the 72nd Regiment, Seaforth Highlanders; in 1912, the 6th Field Company, Canadian Engineers, and Company 19, Canadian Army Service Corps; in 1913, the 11th Irish Fusiliers. A new drill hall had been built on Beatty Street; in 1904 Rifleman S. J. Perry had won the King's Prize at Bisley, and in 1913, Major W. Hart-McHarg of the Rifles won the title of World's Champion Marks-man at a meet in the United States and came home, ironically, with Kaiser Wilhelm's Palma Gold Trophy. When the boom reached its height in 1912, total authorized strength of Vancouver militia units was 1182; their actual strength about two-thirds that.

In the last days of 1912 the world was plunged into an economic depression, and the Vancouver boom came to what the president of the Board of Trade euphemistically called "a pause". It was more than that, it was a dead halt that lasted all through 1913 and 1914. Internationally, the depression was more serious than that of 1907, and bade fair to equal that of the 90's, but Vancouver was in better shape to meet it—the city now had meat on its bones. There was hunger, deprivation and suffering, and still no conception of welfare and unemployment relief on the modern scale, but a far larger proportion of the people remained self-sustaining and the city did feel an obligation to the unfortunate. That more were able to tide over the bad times was due chiefly to the fact that Vancouver had become simply too large to shut down. The same applied to its major industries; they could not shut down without collapsing altogether, and now they had the resources to enable them to keep alive.

In 1913, a photograph taken at Hastings and Granville streets, looking south on Granville, was scarcely distinguishable in its main features from one taken today; among the larger structures there was lacking only the Imperial Bank Building at Dunsmuir, and that was compensated for by the large and architecturally-distinguished "new" Hotel Vancouver at Georgia, which no longer exists.

A new CPR station—still in use—was being constructed; the CNR had $10 million to spend on terminal facilities, most of it in Vancouver; the PGE and Kettle Valley Railways were being built, with Vancouver as their major supply depot. The population, exclusive of Point Grey and South Vancouver, which were growing rapidly, was 134,000.

There were between 300 and 400 industrial plants, large and small. The B.C. Electric, having made the switch-over to hydro power in the 1903-05 period, was delivering 76,125 horsepower from its Buntzen No. 1 and No. 2 Plants on Indian Arm at 20,000 volts, drawing stored water from Coquitlam Lake; with substations in the West End and on Earls Road. The company's new head office and interurban depot was rising at Carrall and Hastings Streets. It had nearly 250 miles of street-car lines operating in the city and its suburbs, though a dispute with Point Grey Municipal Council had led to shutting down of service on the Sasamat line and on the Shaughnessy line south of 16th Avenue. Consumption of electricity in 1913 was over 213 million kilowatt hours.

The city had over 49 miles of paved streets and 153 miles of sewers. Most of it was served with domestic gas from 50 miles of mains. It had 16 main-office banks, with 47 branch offices. H. H. "Harry" Stevens, a former alderman, was a member of Parliament and secured for the port its first grain elevator, Dominion No. 1, of 1.3 million bushels capacity, costing $1,750,000, on which construction began in 1914; for years it was known as "Stevens' Folly", but history vindicated him. School enrollments were over 12,000, with 337 teachers. The Panama Canal was about to open.

The port's activities were immense. The CPR's new *Empresses of Asia* and *Russia*, largest liners the Pacific had ever seen, replaced two of the three old Empresses in 1913; the Canadian-Australasian Line was running a monthly passenger liner service and semi-monthly cargo service to Honolulu and the Antipodes; 14 ships were on the CP coastal runs, besides numerous tugs and barges; the Grand Trunk Pacific had five vessels in coastal service; Ocean Steamship Co., Mutual Steam Navigation Co. and Harrison Direct Line had 20 deep-sea vessels running to the U.K. and Continent

via the Orient and Suez on a regular schedule; Royal Mail Steam
Packet, seven; East Asiatic Line, six, on a bi-monthly service
via Cape Horn; Pacific Coast Steamship Co. had coastal liners
departing every five days for San Francisco and southern ports; Union
Steamship Co. had 10 passenger vessels in the coast service; five
deep-sea vessels serviced the northern halibut fleets, and Vancouver
was an important halibut-landing port. Grain exports (all sacked)
were 1,250,000 bushels in 1913 and this was just an experimental
opening of the trade.

On the outbreak of war in 1914, the Admiralty took over the
Canadian Pacific liners and in that year, for the first time in the
history of the city, the port business declined. Customs receipts
were down from $8.2 to $5.2 million; building permits from $10.4
to $4.4 million; bank clearings from $605 to $420 million. The
city now had reserves of strength it lacked in 1893, but it had to
call on them to the limit to make good its stand against what, at the
end of 1913, its business leaders called "the pause," declaring that
the banks "had put the brakes on" in order to keep the boom
from running away out of control. A year later, Jonathan Rogers,
President of the Vancouver Board of Trade, had changed the tune,
and in the meantime the Dominion Trust had failed and created a
major financial panic.

The City of Vancouver was spending $150,000 on unemploy-
ment relief during the winter, public works were cut down, and before
spring the provincial government had to come to the assistance of
the city in caring for the jobless. Rogers made the unconvincing
plea that the depression had "shaken down" the financial structure
and business was again on a sound basis, but from there went on to
admit that speculation was extinct, no capital and little credit available
for even the soundest business and that the board was pressing the
provincial government for that last relief for a business community
on the ropes—a moratorium on debts and taxes. The "pause" had
become a depression, and the depression perilously close to being a
calamity.

The one thing Vancouver had escaped was large-scale labor
trouble, but the shadow of it hung over the city. Mackenzie and

Mann, notoriously "friends" of the McBride government, had taken over the Dunsmuir mines at Nanaimo and Ladysmith, with their history of labor trouble. They were using Japanese and Chinese as strike-breakers in a major stoppage, backing them up with "special police." After wild rioting in Nanaimo, W. J. Bowser, the Vancouver lawyer who was acting premier, reverted to the old B.C. pattern and threw 1000 militiamen into the town to break the strike. Strictly limited Oriental immigration for six years had made Chinese and Japanese much less of a threat to Vancouver workers in hard times and the Dominion government now banned immigration in B.C., but the threat was to be suddenly and dramatically revived.

The ban on Chinese and Japanese immigration was within the powers of the government of Canada, but that imposed on East Indians by order-in-council in 1913 was found invalid by Chief Justice Gordon Hunter of the Supreme Court of B.C. The crucial point was that the East Indians were British subjects, which, as such, Canada could not exclude. Special new orders-in-council applied only to entry into British Columbia and were complicated by a requirement of "direct passage" from the land of the immigrant's nativity. The ban affronted the pride of the Indians, and a Sikh, Gurdit Singh, determined to test it. He was variously identified as a wealthy landowner, as a "Punjabi agitator" and as a secret agent of the Japanese government, which was also proud, and also affronted by Canadian immigration policies and resentful of the riots of 1907. Gurdit Singh recruited 375 Sikhs, partly farmers and partly time-expired veterans of the Indian Army. The East Indians chartered the Japanese steamship *Komogata Maru*, boarded her at Hong Kong, and arrived at William Head quarantine station May 23, 1914, after stopping at Yokohama en route. The ship was granted pratique and sent on to Vancouver, where she was anchored in the stream pending immigration examination.

May 26 and June 9, the examiners allowed a total of 34 "return men"—previous immigrants returning from visits home—to land. May 28, the Board of Trade asked assurance the remainder would be excluded, and the fact that the examiners took three days over the case of a single applicant indicated that the assurances Ottawa at once gave were to be relied upon. The examinations continued, all applicants were rejected, and June 1 the Sikhs of Vancouver had raised a fund of $70,000 to fight each case in the courts. The vessel and its passengers were held incommunicado; June 3 immigration officials were removed from the ship for their own protection and the same day Gurdit Singh refused to pay 8000 yen due the owners until he and his men were landed. The following day, the Sikhs appealed to King George V personally, refused to let Immigration Superintendent Malcolm J. Bird aboard, and the patrol launches arrested two Vancouver Japanese and two local Sikhs trying to board the *Komogata Maru*.

For three weeks the affair dragged on, amid rumours the immigrants were starving, but they refused to allow immigration patrol launches to put stores aboard. June 25, a test case was brought before Mr. Justice Murphy, who upheld the ban. The case was taken before the full Court of Appeal, and Murphy's decision upheld in a ruling delivered July 5. Upon this, the city's East Indians withdrew their support of the immigrants. The following day, an attempt was made by the immigrants to kidnap an immigration official, to hold him as hostage for supplies of food and water, but this failed. July 18, when the Japanese master and crew attempted to set sail, the Sikhs took over the ship, locking the master in his cabin and threatening to cut the throats of any stokers trying to get up steam. An attempt by the immigration authorities to board the ship was repelled.

Upon this, the police were called into the case and July 19, aboard the tug *Sea Lion*, 150 city police under Chief M. B. McLennan (shot and killed by a Negro drug addict in 1916) and 50 special police under Captain Warden, attempted to board the *Komogata Maru* and provision her for her homeward voyage. The *Sea Lion* got a grapnel aboard and police with a firehose prevented the Sikhs casting it loose, but on trying to board the police were met with a barrage of coal, bricks and old iron. Eleven policemen were seriously injured, but all, though armed, obeyed orders not to fire on the Sikhs. After this repulse, aid of the military authorities was requested.

It was provided immediately. In Victoria the dismantled cruiser *Rainbow* was immediately re-gunned and supplied with a crew of sailors and Garrison Artillery gunners; in Vancouver 100 men of the Irish Fusiliers and 40 each of the Rifles and the Seaforths were called out. With the troops on the wharf and the *Rainbow* beside her in the stream, on the morning of July 23, the *Komogata Maru* surrendered. All Vancouver, crowding the housetops and the beaches in anticipation of the inlet's first full-scale naval battle, watched her hoist anchor and peacefully sail away. Everybody heaved sighs of relief; the city was still ashamed of its excesses of 1907, nobody wanted a repetition, and both local Sikhs and whites had behaved with admirable restraint while sitting on the powder-barrel.

Eleven days later the *Komogata Maru* was forgotten. Canada was at war.

To a generation of citizens which remembers only the Second World War, the impact of the First World War is difficult to convey. There had been no conflict of such magnitude and menace for a century, since the wars of Napoleon; even the American Civil War, bitter and destructive as it was, could not be compared with it. To Britons, war had become a gallant, gay and only occasionally fatal game, directed by professionals in an atmosphere of pageantry and hero-worship. To no man alive had its threat ever been any more than the possible collapse of a single nation; certainly to none had it meant the likely end of an entire civilization and of his own way of life. During the next five years, that threat was to come closely home to every citizen of the Western World, and Vancouver did not escape it.

Much more than the Second World War, it was an intensely personal conflict to the people of Vancouver. Canada's casualties in 1914-18 were greater than those of the entire United States forces. There were streets in Vancouver where every house had a man overseas, and in which every block mourned its two or three dead before the Armistice came. For sheer grinding, continuous, merciless slaughter, the Hitler war never approached it. Death or disablement were not matters of "if," but of "when," battalions consisted of approximately 1,100 officers and men and could be "used up" in two battles. In three years at the front, the 7th Battalion passed 9000 human beings through its ranks—1400 killed, 7000 wounded. The last original officer of the 16th Battalion was killed two years after it arrived in France. In two years, the 47th Battalion lost 22 officers and 639 men killed, 2000 wounded. Unlike the Second World War, these were local units, recruited locally, and largely composed of local men; when a battalion was thrown into an immense set-piece First World War battle and consumed, the dreadful casualty lists filled long columns in the papers day after day; practically every name brought mourning or anxiety to a city home, and regret to scores of citizens for a man known personally to them. It was a war that struck home and struck hard. The Second World War was a war of anxiety and frustration; the First World War a war of sorrow and hatred. The Second had been anticipated and was never quite as bad as expected; the First—its reality, at least—an unparalleled nightmare, and its every new terror a stroke at unprepared hearts and minds.

On the declaration of war, Vancouver shared with the rest of the province alarm over the known presence of the German cruisers *Leipzig* and *Nuremberg* off the coast. Bank gold reserves were sent to Seattle and to Winnipeg, and arrangements made to burn all stocks of currency in case of a raid on the city. Armed protection was demanded for the harbor; eventually it was made a closed port, and small coast defence guns were mounted on concrete emplacements at Siwash Rock in Stanley Park.

The B.C. militia was placed on active service August 8, two days after the remainder of Canada, and Vancouver's first contribution to the war effort was a detachment of 350 sent to guard the port of Prince Rupert. Local units were held under arms until September 12, when British naval forces arrived in the North Pacific and the emergency was over. In the meantime, recruiting was pressed for the 1st Contingent, Canadian Expeditionary Force. In 10 days, with Vancouver contributing its full share, British Columbia had on the rolls more officers than any other province, and more men than any other military districts except the 2nd Divisional

Area (central Ontario) and MD No. 10 (Manitoba and Saskatch-
ewan combined). Throughout the war, B.C. contributed more
volunteers in proportion to its population than any other province.

On August 19, the first detachment, 75 British reservists, left
Vancouver for active service. Three days later two special
trains pulled out with 46 officers and 1022 men. These consisted
of 25 officers and 516 men from the Seaforths, 14 officers and
350 men from the Fusiliers, two officers and 50 men from the 18th
Field Ambulance, one officer and six men from the Corps of Guides.
They were followed August 26 by 20 officers and 350 men from
the 6th Regiment, DCOR, and a detachment of the 6th Field
Company of the Engineers, travelling with a large number of Victoria
volunteers.

These detachments included the bulk of the peacetime militiamen, and almost all the militia officers. What remained was merely
a recruiting cadre engaged in funnelling volunteers into the CEF,
where they were trained and assigned to battalions with little concern
for their place of origin. In the 1st Contingent, most of the
Vancouver men found themselves in either the 7th Battalion,
commanded by Lieutenant-Colonel Hart-McHarg with Major
Victor W. Odlum second-in-command, or the 16th Battalion,
commanded by Lieutenant-Colonel R. G. Edwards Leckie. Other
battalions recruited later in the war and containing substantial numbers
of Vancouver men were, with dates authorized and commanding
officer in brackets: 29th Bn. (November, 1914—Lieutenant-Colonel
H. S. Tobin) 47th Bn. (March, 1915—Lieutenant-Colonel
W. N. Winsby) 62nd Bn. (July, 1915—Lieutenant-Colonel H.
B. Hulme) and 72nd Bn. (September, 1915—Lieutenant-Colonel
J. A. Clark). After the war, when the militia was reconstituted,
its regiments were designated "continuing units" of certain of the
battalions and carried their battle honors; veteran officers and
men of the battalions concerned naturally gravitated to the appropriate
"continuing unit" if they joined the militia, but none of the
battalions were formed from or in any way represented militia
units during 1914-18; typical is the 7th Battalion, continued after
the war by the 1st British Columbia Regiment (DCOR), which

was formed in 1914 from 250 men of the 6th Regiment (DCOR), 250 from the 11th Irish Fusiliers, 250 from the 87th Fusiliers (Victoria), 150 of the 104th Westminster Fusiliers and 150 of the Rocky Mountain Rangers (Kamloops). Nevertheless, the 7th, 16th, 29th and 72nd Battalions Vancouver considered particularly its "own" throughout the war, and such exploits as those of the 72nd at the taking of Vimy Ridge were proudly marked up to the credit of Vancouver's "boys."

The progress of the war itself is beyond the scope of the city's story, but its continuing impact may be indicated by the baptism of fire at Second Ypres in which the 7th and 16th were blooded.

After an introductory tour of duty in a very quiet sector, the Canadians went into the line in the critical Ypres salient. Trenches were practically non-existent and the artillery was limited to three shells per day per gun; the infantry's Ross rifles were already proving difficult to manage with ammunition manufactured to the greater tolerances permitted by the British Lee-Enfields. At 5 p.m., April 22, 1915, the Germans launched the first gas attack in modern warfare, and the French on the left of the Canadians fled to the rear, leaving the untried "colonials" the only shield for 50,000 Imperial troops penned in the salient. Their only orders were, "You must hang on and take care of your own left."

In the face of furious German attacks, during the night of the 22nd the 16th took part in the famous counter-attack on Kitchener's Wood. When dawn came, five officers and 263 other ranks of the 1100-man battalion were all that were left, but they continued to hold.

The following day, the 7th, which had been in reserve, found itself holding the peak of the salient under heavy bombardment. Lieutenant-Colonel Hart-McHarg was killed that evening, and Major Odlum took command. In the morning of April 24, the German shelling rose to an unprecedented crescendo and a second gas attack was launched. Between 3:30 and 4:30 a.m., wave after wave of Germans were thrown back by rifle fire. The bombardment was resumed and, by 6 a.m., the 15th Battalion, on the 7th's left, was wiped out to the last man; the 7th was now holding the critical apex of the line. At 6:30 a.m. another attack was repulsed by the 7th, but the line was broken on the right flank; the battalion, with remnants of the 13th and 14th, was surrounded. At 9 a.m. the shelling was officially recorded as "tremendous." At 10 a.m. German field guns were brought up on the right to within 200 yards, and the two right platoons were wiped out. Lieutenant E. D. "Smoke" Bellew and Sergeant H. N. Peerless, alone, with the battalion's only two machine guns, held the flank. When Peerless was killed, Bellew dragged his body in front of his own gun for protection and continued to fire, beating back several attacks. When his ammunition was exhausted, he destroyed both guns, stood up, fired his last clips of ammunition from his rifle and charged the advancing Germans, killing three with the bayonet before he was shot down and taken prisoner. So the Vancouver battalion won its first Victoria Cross.

By 11 a.m., the battalion was able to make a fighting withdrawal of 300 yards, during which the two left platoons died to the last man. A second short withdrawal was made at 12:30 p.m., at which time six Canadian battalions had so shattered the attacking units that 20 German assault battalions and the 51st Reserve Division were withdrawn from the battle. At 1:40 p.m. 3rd Brigade troops nearby were withdrawn as a result of a garbled order, and the remnants of the 7th and 10th Battalions stood alone. General Currie, commanding the 2nd Brigade, ordered them to retire, but both officers and men refused, declaring they would die where they stood rather than give way any further. "Hang on, then, and—good luck," was Currie's reply.

Imperial commanders, refusing to believe the Canadians could still exist in the hell of shellfire, prepared a counter-attack and shelled the Canadians from the rear; some "lost" Imperial units were shepherded into the line, but withdrawn again at 7 p.m. The remnants of the 16th had been withdrawn from Kitchener's Wood, and a German attack from the wood broken up by rifle fire; later rifle fire forced the Germans out of the village of St. Julien. The night was passed in bringing up ammunition and repairing wire, the troops receiving no rest after 60 continuous hours of fighting.

The 150 remaining men of the 7th were taken out of the line, fed, shifted to Bombarded Cross Roads with the remnant of the 10th, Major Odlum in command. A German attack was thrown back at dawn, shelling was more intense than ever from 9 a.m. to noon, and two companies of the 8th Battalion were brought up to reinforce the 7th and 10th. Three more attacks were thrown back that afternoon. That night, Imperial troops managed to form a line to the rear, and the Canadians made a fighting withdrawal to it—those who were left of them.

They had held the line for over 70 hours, mostly without food, always short of ammunition, lost three men out of every five, survived two gas attacks without respirators or any other protection and broken five German divisions. Declared Sir John French's order of the day, "These splendid troops have averted a disaster. . . ."

Many and many a Vancouver home was in mourning after the Second Battle of Ypres, but there was not a Canadian who did not bear himself more proudly. The period of tutelage was over; Canadians were Canadians, and no longer "colonials." The Canadian forces had started the long climb up the road of savage and intelligent heroism that by 1918 made the CEF, with the Australians, the aristocrats of the European battlefields. It called for blood and it called for guts; Vancouver gave her share.

At home, the city rolled up its sleeves to back up its fighting men. The careless happiness of the boom days vanished; social life was non-existent except where it aided the war effort.

Red Cross work took up the time of housewives and society women alike. Debutantes stood on street corners tagging for prisoners of war, for soldiers' comforts, for the families of men overseas. Businessmen in the hundreds drilled in the Horse Show Building with the Home Guard. When Georgia Street Viaduct was opened July 1, 1915, it was one continuous carnival, end to end, organized by the United Commercial Travellers to aid war charities.

At first the strains of war intensified, rather than relieved, the depression. By April, 1915, the city considered itself "in a state of siege," with relief gangs working in the parks for $1 a day, paid in groceries, and relief funds almost exhausted, a condition which was temporarily relieved by a provincial grant. South Vancouver and West Vancouver were in financial difficulties; assessments in the former had dropped 20 per cent to $37 million in a single year; only wealthy Point Grey claimed to be in good shape, chiefly because there were fewer men on its relief rolls and the majority of its residents were people of some substance.

The population of Greater Vancouver that year showed its first decline in 22 years; it dropped 34,000, to an estimated 172,230. The opening of the Panama Canal, long looked forward to, did little to increase the port's shipping, due to the scarcity of vessels in the Pacific; the grain railway freight rate differential remained 20 per cent to 31 per cent above the rate on eastbound shipments from prairie points and largely cancelled out the one-third drop in ocean rates. Tax sales of forfeited land were general, with the municipalities, particularly South Vancouver, buying in the land rather than disposing of it on a real estate market that for all practical purposes no longer existed.

That winter the news was almost all bad, both from the war front and the economic front. In the city, R. H. Alexander and later in the year, H. B. Abbott died; on April 29 the Connaught (Cambie Street) Bridge was almost destroyed, and Granville Street Bridge lightly damaged, by simultaneous fires blamed on enemy sabotage. The Cambie Bridge went long unrepaired. It was not until mid-summer that people began to feel things were picking up.

In the fall, optimism was plainly visible. Under President F. F. Wesbrook, the long-awaited University of B.C. opened in shacks and tents on the General Hospital Grounds, pending post-war completion of its Point Grey buildings; the official student gowns were piped with khaki cord to mark its wartime birth, and no sooner had students begun to attend classes than they began to leave them to enlist in the Western Universities Battalion for overseas service. That same September, the city got its first major war contract, a $2 million order for shell casings, split between Wallace Shipyards and North Shore Iron Works. The old *Empress of Japan* was released by the Admiralty to take up its trans-Pacific service again, and in November, the first Canadian Northern (soon to be Canadian National) train left the city depot on Main Street. The Great Northern was building a depot, and CPR trains had been running to Penticton on the Kettle Valley line since June 1. At the year's end, the Board of Trade called for conservation of resources, an end to monopoly control in industry, but also reported that business was sound, construction dead, but trade picking up.

All through 1916 the upsurge continued, with the provincial government, under W. J. Bowser of Vancouver, providing laws and funds to aid shipbuilding, mining, farmers and seaport, all of which helped Vancouver. The city, however, was not properly grateful; when Tisdall joined the cabinet, it threw him out in the subsequent by-election, returning Liberal M. A. Macdonald, and a good deal of criticism was aroused over Bowser's confession that in the questionable ousting of the last Squamish from Kitsilano Indian Reserve, "I knew that . . . not only with Indians, but other people, a bit of greasing sometimes has to be done."

Prices were rising steadily, with little or no increase in wages, but nearly everybody was back at work. The fish pack was fair, the lumber mills working to capacity, not a miner was left on the skid road. City building was up to $2.4 million from $1.5 million in 1915, but it was almost entirely large industrial construction; permits for the year had dropped to 434, from 612. Bank clearings rose from $238 million to $321 million, and customs receipts to $6 million from $4.7 million. Shipping was picking up, with large consignments of munitions and other war material going to embattled Russia via Vladivostok; this trade vanished with the outbreak of the revolution in 1917 and for years immense dumps of machinery and steel sat rusting on the city's outskirts. H. H. Stevens secured the city its first shipbuilding contracts; J. Coughlan and Sons were to build six 8800-ton steel vessels on False Creek, and Wallace Ship-yards six wooden auxiliary schooners, several small steel vessels and an immense floating drydock in North Vancouver. The auxiliary schooners were a new departure in ship designing, abandoned in the post-war slump, but not before they had made a considerable repu-tation on the deep seas as economical, if temperamental, cargo carriers.

W. H. MALKIN
Mayor 1929-30

L. D. TAYLOR
Mayor for eight terms

SEN. G. G. McGEER, K.C.
Mayor 1935 - 36 and 1947

J. W. CORNETT
Mayor 1941-46

GEORGE C. MILLER
Mayor 1937-38

CHARLES JONES
Mayor 1948

CHARLES E. THOMPSON
Mayor 1949-50

F. J. HUME
Mayor 1951-58

CHARLES E. TISDALL
*At Stanley Park reception to
President Warren G. Harding
Mayor 1922-23*

DR. J. LYLE TELFORD, M.D., M.L.A.
*With HRH the Queen on May 29, 1939
Mayor 1939 - 40*

The first, the *Mabel Brown*, was launched January 20, 1917. The total of the first shipbuilding contracts exceeded $10 million.

For the rest, the year was marked chiefly by a vote in favor of prohibition December 20, the death of John Hendry, president of Hanbury Mills (which now owned, among other properties, Hastings Mill), and an election scandal. Macdonald, the first Liberal member from Vancouver in the new Brewster government, was accused of accepting $25,000 for his personal campaign from the Canadian Northern; he was dropped from the cabinet and J. W. deB. Farris took his place as attorney-general. Jitneys, too, had appeared during the year; they were chiefly Model T Fords which, crammed to the limit with passengers at five cents or ten cents a head, mounted colored signs corresponding to those of one or another street-car route and gave fast and furious competition to the B.C. Electric. Giving many persons their first experience of automobile riding, they proved popular with the citizens, but not with the transit company.

Concerned with the battles overseas, its war work at home, its patriotic appeals (the Red Cross had collected nearly $1 million in the city) and the growing manpower shortage, the city was scarcely aware of the change that had taken place since the happy, patriarchal days of the great pre-war boom. But the change was great, and it altered the fundamental character of the city. Vancouver was no longer a land-crazy circus, filled with beneficiaries and hangers-on of a boom in which everybody was going to get rich overnight. It had become an active industrial city and the bulk of its inhabitants a wage-earning proletariat. For most of its workers the weekly or monthly pay-cheque no longer represented part of a "stake" to be accumulated as rapidly as possible for an adventurous speculation, which would lead to independence. Now a job was a steady and perhaps life-long occupation, and the pay a closely-calculated and anticipated income.

The city had been remarkably free of labor trouble during its early years, but during the past decade it had absorbed a vast number of British and European immigrants highly conscious of economic theory and trade union practice. Wages were still largely at pre-war levels, the cost of living had shot up 50 percent, the work day, except for a favored few, remained at nine or ten hours. Job security was non-existent, and outside a Workmen's Compensation Act passed during the year and as yet untried, modern "benefits" were unknown. The city's rulers were blissfully sitting on a powder-keg, while contemplating the inevitable boom coming in 1917.

The boom arrived on schedule. New businesses opened. Board of Trade membership jumped 100 percent to 1000. Coughlans launched two steel ships and contracted for 14 more; Wallaces launched four schooners and contracted for 27 more wooden ships; the yards had 5250 men and women employed and a backlog of $31 million in orders. The prices of milk, bread and meat soared; meat was so scarce, "meatless days" were decreed in August. Women were working everywhere, even in the shell factories. The people of Vancouver bought $7,250,000 worth of Victory Loan bonds, and the Dominion was building a great military hospital in the Shaughnessy district. Mothers, church members and business-men hailed the economic and social benefits sure to arise from pro-hibition, when it came into effect October 1; amid all the excite-ment they scarcely noticed an unusual epidemic of infantile paralysis (polio) which sent nine children to hospital during August.

But the powder-keg surprised everybody by going "Boom!" too. In February, the boilermakers struck, and won a wage increase. In April, employees of the B.C. Sugar Refinery went out for 16 days. In May, employers growled when the city, already pioneering with the eight-hour day, increased civic wages. The same month, equal pay was won by police and firemen. In July, the fishing industry was paralyzed by a strike at Rivers Inlet; simultaneously a sea-men's strike shut down coastal shipping from June 27 to July 16. On July 7, an alarming work-stoppage of several hours was staged by city firemen. Apartment owners put up rents 20 percent July 31, giv-ing point to the wage demands of longshoremen, who walked out for a week, halting war shipments to Australia and Mesopotamia. The Coughlan shipyards were struck in October.

But what really turned the city upside-down was the B.C. Electric walkout June 13. The men had had no wage increase for two years. Trackmen were getting 29 cents an hour, and many of the employees less than $60 a month. The union demanded five cents an hour increase in the lower categories, and five percent in the higher, to bring top wages to $84 a month. The company declared jitney competition had hit it so hard it was losing money on the transit system and could afford no increases. The strike lasted eight days, and the people of Vancouver, whose sympathies were largely with the men, rode jitneys or walked while both sides remained adamant. The company finally gave in on the promise of the city to investigate the jitney situation.

The investigation was carried out by Dr. Adam Shortt, but the basic situation was unchanged and carried on the following year when the men again went out July 2. The union feeling was bitter. The company refused to budge, conciliation under Mr. Justice Macdonald failed, the men refused to accept an arbitration award in favor of the company and the provincial government brought pressure to bear, on the strength of the Shortt findings, against jitney competition. The strike was settled July 11, with the men receiving a pay increase, and the city granting a one-cent fare increase, at the same time abolishing jitney licences. The hostility between men and company was long-lasting and the repercussions of the two strikes were still visible as late as 1934, when Mayor Taylor, in his unprecedented eighth term of office, appealed to the company on behalf of the men and staved off a threatened wage cut by the counter-threat to again license jitneys on the city's streets.

The labor troubles of the war and post-war years culminated in a bitterly-fought longshoremen's strike in the winter of 1923-24, but Vancouver fortunately escaped the impact of any upheaval such as the Winnipeg general strike of 1919. Nor did the Canadian veterans, as in U.S., and apart from one raid on Labor Temple, turn on the unions as "betrayers of men at the front." Canada had been at war almost three years longer than the United States, and its fighting men had mostly been working men during some period of 1914-18, either before enlisting or after they returned wounded; a very large proportion of the union men were returned men by the war's end.

The last year of the war saw the trends of 1917, apart from

strikes, intensified. There was full employment, business was "the soundest in history," with bank clearings up to $545 million, prices went higher, stocks of goods were low, housing was scarce. The main war industry continued to be shipbuilding, with 39 vessels, large and small, completed, six still on the ways, and 33 wooden and 12 steel ships contracted for. There had been 39 tag days during the year, which had raised $105,000 for various charities; people were complaining about the frequent appeals.

News of the armistice arrived just after midnight, early in the morning of November 11. The town went wild; every light blazed, every whistle howled, elderly housewives danced in the streets, dignified businessmen yelled and shrieked and beat on tin cans. All day long the streets were filled with people; at noon traffic could not move at Hastings and Main. The step-seated, open B.C. Electric sight-seeing car, so long piloted by fast-talking, wise-cracking Teddy Lyons, careered all over town, a band jam-packed aboard, blaring out all the wartime songs. The civic parade that afternoon made its way through massed crowds of hoarse, happy, tired but still yelling and cheering men, women and children.

There were 100,000 people in town that afternoon, and the only ones not watching the parade were either marching in it or the motormen and conductors of the street cars which were stalled for three hours. One of the most prominent and notoriously tight-fisted financiers in the city stood on the curb in a fur-collared overcoat as the parade passed. One hand waved his bowler hat in the air; the other held a cheap tin horn, on which he was blowing lustily as he danced a little jig.

"Where'd you get the horn?" inquired a passing acquaintance.

"Last one in town," exulted the financier. "Had to pay a feller a dollar and a half for it." His face took on a puzzled expression, " . . . an' you know, it ain't worth two bits." Out in the roadway drums thundered and trumpets blared as another band went striding by; the tycoon responded with another yell and toot on the horn and shouted to his friend, " . . . but what's a dollar on a day like this?"

As the parade passed by and the crowd began to melt away, he wiped the moisture off the mouthpiece, carefully stowed the horn in an inside pocket and settled the bowler in place with a firm final tap on the crown, then solemnly addressed his acquaintance. "You know, George," he remarked, "it's the first time in my life I ever said anything like that."

That night the celebration had spent itself. On the waterfront, every flag was at half-mast as the *Princess Alice* glided slowly in to her berth at the CPR's Pier D.

At seven o'clock the next morning, quiet, shuffling bearers began to unload her ghastly cargo—157 roughly-shrouded bodies that were laid in long rows on trestles in the gloomy, cavernous wharf-shed. At 9 a.m., small groups of stern-faced men and weeping women filed through the improvised morgue to identify the first victims recovered from the wreck of the *Princess Sophia* in Lynn Canal, the worst marine disaster in the history of the Pacific Coast.

On the night of October 24 the *Sophia,* pride of the CPR coastal fleet, had driven on a reef in a blinding snowstorm. There she lay all the next day with numerous ships and fishing-boats in attendance, but she seemed reasonably safe and the weather was so bad that none of the passengers and crew were removed. That night the gale increased to tremendous force and the *Sophia* drove clear over the reef, going down like a stone with every soul on board. Three hundred and forty-three lives were lost. There were few Vancouver people aboard, most of the passengers were Yukon-ers and Alaskans "coming out for the winter," but the Vancouver of 1918 was pre-eminently a seaport, and the tragedy struck home very sharply to the city; the arrival of the *Alice* on the evening of a day of such unrestrained celebration caused an abrupt change of mood, and as the quiet, slow procession of still, dark, stiff bundles passed through the dock-shed, it brought memories of another cara-van of death, many thousands strong and four years in passing—blanket-shrouded, silent, ominous—the sons, fathers and husbands of this far city of the West, laid to rest in the graveyards of England, the mud of Flanders and the depths of the sea, or who had fallen, flaming, from the skies.

The years of blood were over, but "at the going down of the sun, and in the morning," the city remembered its dead.

13

The Dizzy Decade

THE GIRLS CUT off their hair, shortened their skirts and rolled down their stockings.

The boys wore turtle-neck sweaters with pants 22 inches around the cuffs, and grew sideburns. Grown-up veterans of five years of war went back to school.

Everybody read "The Sheik," danced the Charleston and drank bathtub gin.

The citizens of Vancouver subscribed $15 million to the final Victory Loan, prepared to "bring the boys home" from overseas, and wondered what the world was coming to.

What was coming to Vancouver was the dizziest ten years of its history.

First, the boys came home. The Dominion government and Premier John Oliver's provincial government had old-fashioned ideas, and were going to settle them all down on the farm—but the boys had seen Paree. Most of them agreed, however, to settle for Vancouver. With little help from the senior governments, the city had to cope with what became, even during the most frenzied of boom decades, a permanent sub-stratum of unemployed. Typical was the winter of 1925, with 1800 men on relief, getting a dole of 25 cents a day for meals and 25 cents for a bed. This was in the best of times; in 1920 there had been nearly 10,000 jobless, with 3500 more in the Chinese community alone; unprecedented bank clearings of $867 million were announced in a month when the unemployed were holding mass meetings, retail stores reported a "buying strike" and married civic employees were getting two days' work a week. It was the "starvation amid plenty" that U.S. President Roosevelt was to dramatize a decade later.

Through all the fabulous Twenties this illogical discrepancy between fantastic prosperity and never-quite-overcome destitution kept gnawing at the city's subconscious.

The prosperity, indeed, was fantastic. Like all the rest of the world, Vancouver shared in the Wall Street frenzy, and fortunes were made on the stock market. In addition, the Province's basic industries—mining, fishing, lumbering—were coining money hand over fist, and the city shared in this spate of wealth. Large financial interests and politicians worked hand in hand to create wealth, and if the wealth was unequally and sometimes illegitimately shared, almost everybody got some of it. Some part of the prosperity came to some citizens whose enterprise took the form of rum-running to the States via Ensenada, Mexico. In that coterie, business and crime were allied—and some Vancouverites in those days gained their wealth in league with smugglers.

As the war ended, Vancouver was viewing with some amusement a politico-financial comedy that created one of its larger business assets—Granville Island. This artificial and highly profitable mudbank in False Creek had first been proposed by Robert Kelly, city grocery wholesaler and Liberal boss of Vancouver in the pre-war days of the Laurier government. When the Conservative regime came into power the project was dropped, but with some assistance from H. H. Stevens, revived. Originally it had been a plan to dredge the creek and fill in the swamp at its head, east of Main Street. Sam McClay, chairman of the Harbor Board, became the leading promoter of the subsidiary fill at the south end of the Granville Street Bridge, and on his own initiative, borrowed $300,000 to build the necessary bulkheads. The dredging firm took two separate contracts—one, to dredge a channel in the creek 300 feet wide and 21 feet deep, and dispose of the spoil in deep water; and the other to fill in Granville Island. Combining the two, it made a very neat profit indeed by disposing of the spoil in the area it undertook to fill. When the smoke of political controversy cleared away, the firm had its profits, the city had 50 acres of new industrial sites, and the island an autonomous existence, paying city taxes only by consent, and making a profit of $35,000 a year in rents. There seemed to have been considerable hanky-panky about the business, but nobody was unfavorably publicized in the easy-going city and everybody was happy with the results.

Anyway, there were other things to worry about, such as the evolution of a new species of criminal—the automobile bandit. By January, 1919, gangs of youths in autos were roaming the streets at night, staging as many as five or six holdups per gang in one evening. Coincidentally, the theft of automobiles became common, and in 1920 was running up to 60 and 70 a month. Crime rose to a climax in 1922, during which bank holdups occurred, a police court clerk absconded with over $3000 and bandits in the middle of a September afternoon held up City Paymaster Schooly and Assistant Paymaster Armstrong on the steps of the City Hall, escaping with the $76,000 city payroll. Drug addiction flourished, and during October a constable and detective were shot down by a Negro in a drug squad raid. That winter, Chief Anderson put armed patrols on the main streets to curb the holdup men, but it was not until 1925 that an efficient prowl-car service was finally organized and the police were again on a reasonably even footing in their war with the auto bandits.

Prohibition posed some problems all of its own. By the end of 1918, an enquiry held in the city produced some remarkable evidence in spite of the tendency of witnesses to forget a great many important details, and the committal of the provincial liquor commissioner to Oakalla for refusing to answer any questions at all. One prominent Vancouver businessman involved blew out his brains with a shotgun in a New York hotel; draymen and teamsters testified to delivering cases of "canned goods" and barrels of "oil" from liquor warehouses to scores of citizens, both notorious and respectable; freight cars of legitimately imported liquor were mysteriously spotted on lonely sidings and arrived at their destination minus a half or two-thirds of their consignments. Particular interest was displayed in the delivery of 40 cases to a Shaughnessy address which was never exactly identified, and in the straight-faced declaration of the manager of the provincial "prescription store" that nobody, at any time, had ever suggested he sell a pint without a proper medical prescription.

The chief of police confessed that his force was unable to cope with the problem of enforcing prohibition. It was little wonder. In December, 1920, the dry squad raided 108 bootleggers and 18 disorderly houses and collected $9750 in liquor fines. The booze flowed free from Chinatown to the Fraser, and from West Point Grey to Boundary Road; even Sikhs with pint bottles wrapped in their voluminous turbans stood at the entrance to downtown alleyways, retailing questionable intoxicants by the drink. The inception of government sale of liquor, and of club licences and beer parlors in 1921, gave the harassed police some relief, but the bootlegger had become an established civic institution and remained so.

A related problem was caused, not by provincial, but by U.S. liquor laws, for Coal Harbor became the rendezvous of one of the finest assemblages of adventurers, pirates, skilled seamen, gangsters and downright murderers the eastern Pacific had seen since Woodes Rogers sacked Guayaquil and plucked the original Robinson Crusoe off Juan Fernandez Island. "Mother ships" and prohibition blockade runners from Vancouver operated from the Gulf Islands to San Diego while certain Vancouver liquor exporters, distillers and brewers made fortunes. Not all the exports went by sea, for the tide of illicit (in U.S., but not in B.C.) liquor lapped over the border from Blaine to Grand Forks by auto, pack-train and even mountain-scaling human packers. Romantic and exciting it was, a game rather than a crime, but the disregard for the law nurtured by the game culminated in one of the coast's most celebrated crimes in 1924 when the fishboat rum-runner *Beryl G.* was found adrift off the southern end of Vancouver Island. Captain W. J. Gillis and his son had both been murdered and the cargo hijacked. Mounted Police, Provincial Police and U.S. officials co-operated in a manhunt that eventually resulted in the hanging of the hijackers, Owen "Cannonball" Baker and Harry Sowash, January 14, 1926.

The early 20's were a time of violent and lawless change everywhere, but not all change in Vancouver carried the flavor of crime and irresponsibility. We noted in the winter of 1884-5, the arrival of Seraphim Fortes of Barbados, to be porter, handyman and second bartender of the Sunnyside Hotel. "Seraphim" was a bit too-ornate a handle for pioneer Vancouverites, so it was "Joe" Fortes who lived through the fire, saw the first train arrive, and graduated during the subsequent boom to a steady situation behind the bar of the Bodega Saloon where the Rainier Hotel now stands at Carrall and Cordova Streets. There the burly, chocolate-colored ex-seaman became a popular citizen, and known for his habit of discouraging excessive drinking. Sometime during the 90's, Joe discovered English Bay. Giving up his good job, he estab- lished himself in a squatter's shack on the shore side of Beach Avenue, a little to the east of the present Alexandra Park, that pleasant triangle fronting on the bay near the bathhouse. He supported himself by casual laboring jobs, but the work of his life became the bay and its beach.

Every morning, all year around, he swam in the bay and drank his "medicine"—a cup of salt water. All day, when not working as necessity demanded, he "managed" the beach. As the West End filled up, he became known to the elders as "English Bay Joe," to the children, simply as "Ol' Black Joe." And the children were his delight; scarcely a tyke who was raised in Vancouver in the 90's or 1900's but learned to swim with Joe's hamlike fist gripping the back of his or her cotton bathing suit and that deep, mellow voice ordering, "Kick yo' feet, chile—kick yo' feet." When the time came that the Park Board needed a lifeguard, there was no other possible candidate, and when Joe was not among the children, his little boat swung and danced from wave to wave amid the throngs in the water; how many lives he saved over the years will never be known, but he has been credited with over one hundred witnessed rescues, some of them in desperate circumstances. When —as was bound occasionally to happen—his utmost efforts failed, his grief was shattering to behold. Mothers confidently shooed their children away to the bay for the long summer days with the simple command, ". . . and don't go away from where Joe is."

Joe belonged to the beach—and the beach to Joe. From dawn to dark and long after dark, he was host to picnickers, chaperone to courting couples and a terror to the bum and the hoodlum. His cottage was spick and span within and without; the children visited him; for them he kept a tin full of all-day suckers; beside his bed there was his only book, Thomas a Kempis' "Imitation of Christ," and he left the bay only on Sunday morning to attend Mass, for he was a devout Catholic. The city gave him the authority of a special constable, and when the houses were cleared away from the shore where he lived, by popular demand Mayor Buscombe had the little cottage moved up beside the bandstand in the park, to stay there as long as Joe should live.

In January, 1922, Joe became ill. At mid-month he was carried to Vancouver General Hospital with a severe case of pneumonia, halting his stretcher on the way to give minute instructions to the constable on the beat for the care of "his" bay. To all the city, the news came as a shock, for he had become a permanent and indestructible institution. The hospital telephones rang constantly, and his room was knee-deep in flowers every day. February 4, Death came for Seraphim Fortes, far from the sunny isle where he was born.

They took him to the cathedral, where he had so long worshipped his good and kindly God. High and low, rich and poor, laborer and merchant prince, logger and miner, housewife and socialite, policeman and pickpocket, old, young and toddlers filled the grim impressive pile while the priests chanted requiem for "Our Joe." Many of the motley throng were ill at ease during the service which, to a large number, was unfamiliar and in strange surroundings. As the priests fell silent and the bearers lifted the coffin to begin the slow, quiet, inevitable procession to the doors, some Power or Principality must have inspired the mind of the organist — for undoubtedly the first, and surely the last time on so solemn an occasion in so sacred a place—the deep pipes rumbled into the fine, swinging, strains of "Old Black Joe."

Then the great assembly crowded to the aisle, women with handkerchiefs to their eyes, men with tears streaming down their faces, and all Vancouver followed Seraphim Fortes of Barbados to his last, long home while the organ called him, sobbing with the voice of angels.

In the quiet little park where he had lived and served so long, there is a simple granite monument—a drinking fountain, low enough for the smallest of the children that play nearby, and over it a modest bronze plaque with the head and shoulders of a cheerful, heavy-set brown man and three just such rowdy little youngsters, below, as Joe delighted in. On the granite is carved only:

"Little children loved him."

It was not only the children who loved Seraphim Fortes, for there spoke the heart of a Vancouver that lived and grew and toiled and built and loved and played quietly and decently and honestly amid all the frenetic excitement that superficially characterized the Roaring Twenties.

This was the Vancouver that was building row after row of small, undistinguished houses all through Fairview, Kitsilano, the East End and out into South Vancouver, on 33-foot and 50-foot lots. It was the Vancouver that was overflowing into North Vancouver and West Vancouver every morning and evening and crowding the ferries and the gasoline rail-cars that ran out toward Howe Sound on a detached fragment of the PGE Railway. The latter service was augmented by the West Vancouver ferries which ran from the dock at the foot of Columbia Street out through the Narrows to Ambleside, Hollyburn and Dundarave. This was the Vancouver of laboring men, artisans, clerks and small business owners, chiefly newcomers from Eastern Canada and the British Isles, who radically changed the character of the city as it expanded. Their sober and cautious industry submerged the reckless daring of the pre-war years; politically, they opposed to the factious "plunderbund" which had dominated provincial politics a Liberalism which contained the seeds of a welfare-state philosophy; economically, they resented and fought the concentration of power in the hands of a fortunate few.

In the cynical licentiousness which marked the early 20's throughout Canada and the United States, the battle lines were soon drawn and the fundamental issues overlaid with a moralistic fervor which often obscured them. In Vancouver, the moralist aspect predominated in the dramatic clash which took place in the latter half of 1924, for the Janet Smith case was in all its aspects so theatrical it might have been the script of a playwright dedicated to social reform. Janet, a Scottish immigrant girl of unblemished reputation, was employed as a maid in a Shaughnessy mansion by a young couple of considerable means who were closely related to influential "old families" in the city and were among the leaders of the wealthy and boisterous junior socialites of the "flapper era." The morning after a gay party in her employers' home, Janet was found dead at the bottom of the stairs to the basement where Wong Foon Sien, the Chinese cook, had a room. After a hasty inquest the following day, in which a verdict of accidental death was returned, she was buried.

Very shortly, rumors circulated through the city that there was more to the incident than had been allowed to appear at the inquest. Since the girl was without relatives or close friends in the city, her case was taken up by the Scottish societies, largely formed of the new class of immigrants. The protests and accusations grew so vociferous the case was taken out of the hands of the Point Grey municipal authorities by the attorney-general, and the Provincial Police placed in charge. The body was exhumed and a second inquest held, at which it was indisputably proved that death was due to a gunshot wound in the head, and a verdict of murder was returned.

The subsequent proceedings, when read in the cold perspective of 50 years' distance, are so redolent of buffoonery and cynical disregard of law they are almost unbelievable. They began with the blanket absolution of the municipal police and other authorities who were responsible for the original verdict of accidental death in the case of a woman shot through the head. Much, then, was made of the fact that she was found in the basement near the Chinese cook's room, and he was severely questioned despite the fact that the body showed unmistakeable evidence that, living or dead, she had been thrown down the stairs. As investigation proceeded, some of the guests at the party were found to be absent from the province on extended travels. Finally the cook disappeared. A hue and cry was raised and he was sought diligently by the authorities until one night he was unceremoniously and in a state of considerable disrepair, delivered at Provincial Police headquarters in Vancouver. A private detective subsequently confessed that he, two Chinese (one of them a court interpreter) and two city detectives, had kidnapped Wong and held him prisoner, convinced that "only third degree methods would serve to produce the truth from an Oriental." The three detectives were tried for kidnapping; the private detective was convicted, the other two acquitted.

Finally, Wong was brought to trial for murder, an alleged confession under duress—which he had repudiated as soon as he had been placed in lawful custody—was inadmissible, and the obvious verdict of "not guilty" was returned. The Scottish societies concurred in the verdict.

For years afterward attempts were made to reopen the case, but none succeeded. In refusing to do so, the authorities seem to have been justified, as no evidence was ever submitted to clear up the state of utter confusion into which the case had been allowed to fall. Janet Smith remained unavenged. Legally, at least.

However, the social and political repercussions of the affair were profound. The prestige of the police (never great in Vancouver) and the legal authorities, suffered badly. The influence of the "old families" in civic politics was reduced to a point where they never again could openly assert their sway; mayors like W. H. Malkin and Gerry McGeer were elected on their own merits, in spite of, rather than because of their connections. Politically, the city hardened into "east" and "west"; for years radical candidates carried the polls east of Ontario and Carrall Streets, while the more conservative and "respectable" office seekers could hope for success only if they carried large majorities in the western division— which did not always occur. Finally, the "high society" which had developed in the pre-war and post-war booms was shaken to its roots and lost the respect of the community, falling an easy victim to the onslaught of the depression in the 1930's, never to be revived in its old brilliant extravagance. Doubtless these changes would have taken place eventually more or less in the same form if Janet Smith had lived on, unregarded and unknown, to be a grandmother, but her murder provided a focal point upon which the forces at work coalesced and exploded into action.

Against the background of these eventful years, the city itself was building toward its modern form. Its objectives were increased commercial traffic, increased industrial activity, and eventual amalgamation with its dormitory suburbs, Point Grey and South Vancouver. While seeking these goals, it remained economically dependent on its basic primary industries, lumbering and fishing, and on shipping. Throughout the decade it shared in the increased immigration and commercial activity common to all Canada, and particularly British Columbia. Much of the city's progress was, therefore, the result of federal and provincial policies and politics, but on the local level a vigorous press and persistent civic administration played important parts.

The city's newspapers had a lively history, with many minor and often eccentric publications taking on a brief existence, but by 1925 the Fourth Estate had assumed essentially its modern form, with the *Sun* and the *Province* dominating their field. The *Province*, originally a Victoria weekly, began daily publication in Vancouver in 1898, under the management—later the ownership—of Walter Cameron Nichol, an enterprising editor noted for his readiness to invite libel suits at the drop of an adjective. Nevertheless, Nichol had a sound appreciation of news values and reader interests and, by valid newspaper policies, soon had Carter-Cotton's pioneer *News-Advertiser* in such distress it eventually gave up the ghost. The *Province's* main competition became Louis D. Taylor's *World*, which, when Taylor became absorbed in municipal politics, passed into the hands of John Nelson. Struggling to cope with inadequate financing, it endured until 1924. "Both are good papers," was the opinion of the neutral weekly, *Saturday Sunset*. This was in the years when Nichol had restrained his editorial ebullition and, with the assistance of F. J. Burd and Roy Brown, was producing a paper noted for its sound conservatism and comprehensive news coverage.

The *Sunset* itself, founded in 1907, fell upon evil days. It was taken over by a syndicate headed by F. C. Wade, a prominent Liberal, and on February 12, 1912, put out its first daily edition as the *Morning Sun*, under a charter which tied it hand and foot to the Liberal Party and the party's policies. It continued with scant success, its creditors foreclosed and it was snapped up by Colonel J. W. Stewart, then a railroad contractor much concerned with the construction of the PGE Railway, and by him conducted more as a political organ than a newspaper. By some freak of chance, however, Stewart selected an accountant whom he employed, Robert Cromie, to manage the paper and appear as its publisher; the contractor, all unknowingly, had been nursing a newspaper genius in his bookkeeping department.

When Stewart went overseas to become a general in 1917, in a series of moves that have been the basis of numerous legends but have never been publicly elucidated, Cromie emerged as owner of the paper and quickly began to make his mark on the city's history. Mistakes he made, but with his chief competitor the now ultra-conservative *Province*, what impressed so able a judge as D. A. McGregor, veteran *Province* editor, was that "he was never afraid to make mistakes." Within a few years, Cromie was to be saluted by Sidney Walker, the historian of North American newspapers, as "the last of the great individual publishers." Eccentric, bold, ruthless, resourceful, he determined to identify the *Sun* with Vancouver and Vancouver with the *Sun*. In this he had a great measure of success, particularly after Nichol disposed of the *Province* to the Southam newspaper chain in 1923, and the older paper was subject to the reproach of being "foreign" controlled. In 1924 the *Sun* absorbed the ailing *World* and issued morning and evening editions.

The evening edition was soon challenged by the *Evening Star*, a new paper taken over shortly after its birth by the Odlum family and managed by General Victor W. Odlum; in 1926 a deal was made whereby the *Star* shifted to morning publication and absorbed the *Morning Sun* circulation while the *Evening Sun* absorbed the *Evening Star's* circulation and became the *Sun*. The *Star* lingered on until, when it suspended publication, some of its staff replaced it with the *Herald*. In subsequent form of the *News-Herald* the struggling journal went out of existence as one of the few failures of the Roy Thompson chain; but except as a training ground for news-

Downtown Vancouver with False Creek in the foreground, Stanley Park, Burrard Inlet, North and West Vancouver and the North Shore mountains.

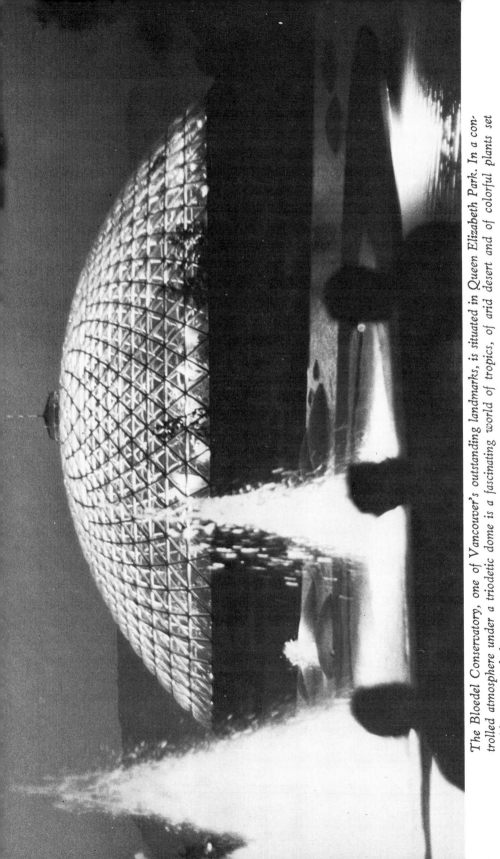

The Bloedel Conservatory, one of Vancouver's outstanding landmarks, is situated in Queen Elizabeth Park. In a controlled atmosphere under a triodetic dome is a fascinating world of tropics, of arid desert and of colorful plants set amidst a seasonal theme.

From English Bay looking north towards West Vancouver and the Upper Levels highway.

The prow of a once proud Empress boat, a familiar landmark on the sea-wall walk at Stanley Park.

A model of the Van Dusen Botanical Garden, a living museum demonstrating the rich diversity of form and function in the plant kingdom. The administration and education complex to the left will contain auditorium, classrooms, library, laboratory and staff offices. The building in the foreground will house the information and exhibition areas.

papermen, it was at most a negligible factor in the city's life. The *Sun* and the *Province* had become "the" papers—and waged incessant war.

The *Sun*, under family management after Cromie's death, maintained his policies in mellowed form and passed the *Province* in circulation during the disastrous strike of the International Typographical Union against the Southam chain in the late 40's. It maintained its ascendancy until 1957 when, simultaneously with the negotiated demise of the *News-Herald*, the two papers joined forces in the Pacific Press, the *Province* taking over the deserted morning field and the *Sun* continuing as the only evening paper.

During the 20's, however, these events were yet undreamed of, and Cromie was establishing his paper by continually hammering at provincial and federal governments to facilitate the grain trade of the port by cutting the mountain freight differential and improving port facilities, and to "open up" the Peace River Block by extending the PGE. Locally, he was always in support of large and even grandiose projects, insisting on the necessity of a bridge over First Narrows, a civic centre and auditorium, a civic airport and construction of the University of B.C. in Point Grey. The *Province* was consistently less vociferous than the *Sun*, but in reality, it was little less determined in seeking advantages for the city and it is probable that its measured deliberation of tone carried greater weight, both locally and abroad. In any case, during the period between the two World Wars, the city was ably served by a vigorous press. Such diverse editorial personalities as Jim Butterfield, Francis Bursill (Felix Penne), Bob Bouchette, Lukin Johnston and cartoonist J. B. Fitzmaurice enlivened the newspapers' pages.

More difficult to assess is the quality of the various civic administrations, particularly those headed by the dominating figure of the 1925-35 decade, Louis D. Taylor. In the first post-war years, from 1918 through 1921, R. H. "Harry" Gale, a railroad and real estate promoter and speculator, was mayor. He was a fast-talking, colorful and popular personage, but showed little capability of dealing with the pressing problems of the transition period after the war. In 1922 and '23, he was succeeded by Charles E. Tisdall, who improved the efficiency of the civic organization and maintained a sound, if conservative, financial position. W. R. Owen, in 1924, had an uneventful term. When Taylor took over in 1925 the great boom that was to continue until the end of 1929 was in full swing and many of the problems of finance which had faced his predecessors had solved themselves. Nevertheless, the city had need of the perennial optimist to set things in motion.

Already Taylor had made his mark. He had been mayor in the boom years of 1909 and 1910, again in 1915. His experience of civic office and of civic politics was large; it had begun with his election as licence commissioner in 1902 and his defeat for the same office in 1903; never an alderman, though he twice sought the post, he had five times unsuccessfully run for mayor, besides the three times he had won. His policies were liberal and progressive (without capital letters) and he favored and was favored by organized labor. Born in Ann Arbor, Michigan, he had arrived in Vancouver in 1896 and was now, at the end of 1924, 67 years old; he had a pleasing, rather gentle, personality and preferred to gain his ends by negotiation rather than open conflict. However, the vast knowledge of the city and its people which he had accumulated made available to him many sources of subterranean pressure which he was never reluctant to apply to gain his ends; as a consequence he had a reputation for deep and sometimes unscrupulous intrigue which more than once worked to his disadvantage when his enemies charged him with dishonesty. But in his declining, poverty-stricken years even his most determined foes acquitted him of profiting personally from his eleven years as chief magistrate of the city.

He had a puckish sense of humor, and a talent for creating legends about himself, such as the time in 1915 when he kidnapped ex-President "Teddy" Roosevelt and Mrs. Roosevelt, when they visited Vancouver, out from under the nose of a flabbergasted Board of Trade delegation. The board had decided to freeze out the mayor from the official reception of the distinguished couple in the CPR station. Taylor boarded the train at Heatley Avenue, took the Roosevelts under his wing and, when he ushered them off the train, condescendingly introduced a few board members to them before whisking them off in a borrowed limousine for a drive around Stanley Park. Again, there was the election of 1923, when he lost to Tisdall because of a sudden and complete power failure in the East End during the late afternoon. With the street cars immobilized, the workingmen who were the bulk of Taylor's support could not get home to cast their votes before the polls closed; the next day the B.C. Electric, whose officials had no particular love for "L. D.," produced an extremely dead woodpecker which, they claimed, had penetrated the internal workings of a transformer and paralyzed the power system. Taylor lost the "woodpecker election," but gained in the story a powerful political asset with which he made great play in future years.

Later in life (1928) he was struck on the head by an airplane propellor at the inauguration of B.C. Airways passenger services and after a long convalescence, dramatically presided over council meetings from a wheelchair while still partially paralyzed; a year later he narrowly escaped drowning on a five-week canoe trip north of Prince George—he was then 72—and while again mayor, in 1931 after attending the opening of Sea Island airport, contracted a lingering illness which brought him to the verge of death.

Taylor's connections with pioneer Vancouver went far back beyond his own arrival in 1896, for he married as his second wife Mrs. Alice Berry, the widow of the pioneer teamster, Harry Berry, who was one of the heroes of the Great Fire, and the daughter of Jonathan Miller. On all ordinary occasions he wore a bright red necktie, which became his personal trademark. A slight and quiet man with little timbre to his voice and no gift of oratory, it was a tribute to his dogged personality that he made so great an impression on the electors.

In the six years between the end of the war and Taylor's fourth term as mayor the city, of course, had not been standing still, and several notable events had occurred. In 1919 the provincial government had agreed to press construction of the University of B.C. on Point Grey; the university, still functioning in the General Hospital "shacks" under its new president, Leonard S. Klinck, had to mobilize its friends and exert much pressure before it finally moved to its permanent location late in 1925. Otherwise, in the cultural field, Vancouver lagged; the city's Symphony Orchestra was organized by Henry Green in 1919, but the years went by with the Public Library and the City Museum housed in wretched quarters, no art gallery, and no proper auditorium built. A vast new YMCA building on Georgia Street, construction of which had been halted by the war, stood as a steel skeleton until, in post-war years, it was sold and completed as the present Ritz Hotel. The "Y" remained housed in a rickety but memorable frame building at Dunsmuir and Cambie Streets where several generations of youth played, exercised and fraternized.

Industry had expanded. Shipbuilding dwindled away, with four vessels still under construction at the end of 1921, but by 1925 there were some 500 established industrial operations with 14,000 employees to take its place; these were mostly small plants, but in the total comprised an investment of $95 million, with an annual output of $85 million. Power was supplied by the B.C. Electric from its Buntzen plant, and by the Western Power Co. of Canada, Ltd., from three generating units at Stave Falls. The Western installation had been begun in 1912 and continued in competition with the B.C. Electric until 1920, but its distribution facilities were insufficient and the B.C. Electric shared water rights with Western on the Stave River, so it was a logical consolidation when the latter was sold to the BCE in 1920. The transit service continued to be plagued by labor troubles, and a strike was narrowly averted on the very day of the complicated changeover in the rule of the road on January 1, 1922, when all traffic began to keep to the right, instead of the left.

The 20's saw the power company playing a much larger part in the home life of Vancouver, for besides providing industrial power and public transit, the city was swinging over, first to gas and then to electricity, for cooking, and electric appliances were making great strides in domestic use. When a new franchise was negotiated in 1922, it provided for the innovation of motor bus service, and the pioneer buses were placed in operation on Grandview Highway in 1923. By 1925 the city was using 700 million cubic feet of gas a year and the old cluster-globe and arc lights on the streets were being replaced by the first of the modern 1,500 to 2,500 candle-power single lamps on ornamental standards. That year the B.C. Electric, through a subsidiary, was operating bus lines as far afield as Haney, Ioco, White Rock and Seattle.

Some scattered events in the passing years were worthy of note. During 1920, plans were made to erect the present Cenotaph on the old courthouse site at Cambie and Hastings, to be renamed Victory Square; Dave Black became the Pacific Northwest golf champion; a pioneer Dominion air mail flight successfully reached Minoru Park landing field and Major Clare McLaurin and Lieutenant Templeton made the first flight to Victoria (McLaurin and a companion were killed in an air crash in 1922 in English Bay). South Vancouver, its finances all awry, was languishing under a commission form of government. Daylight saving time for summer was endorsed by a public vote, and the B.C. Electric employees won the eight-hour day, which was becoming general, but would not be established in the mills for several years yet.

In 1921 the city made a brief excursion into proportional representation voting at the civic elections, but it was soon abandoned as too complicated; the Vancouver General Hospital treated 13,000 cases during the year, and its budget rose to $1 million; printers struck for and won the 44-hour week, first of Vancouver workmen to obtain it; the Peace Arch at Blaine, a project vigorously supported by Vancouver women's organizations, was completed and dedicated; Mrs. DeBeck, that energetic pioneer of Gastown, died in Marpole at the age of 107, and on the first of December, Vancouver was introduced to a unique B.C. custom—three Doukho-bors startled the city by disrobing in the CPR station.

In 1922, a camp for 3000 unemployed men was opened at Hastings Park in the exhibition buildings. In 1923, a second grain elevator was started in the harbor and westbound grain rates were cut 10 percent; Burrard Drydock was under construction. Grain shipments grew over the years, until in 1924 they reached 53 million bushels, a substantial backlog of port business. Much of the credit for this was given to a Vancouver lawyer, G. G. McGeer, K.C., who, as an MLA and special counsel for the Province, had been arguing furiously at various Dominion conferences and hearings since 1916 for adjustment of the freight rates, until he had made himself a considerable reputation as a fiery and persistent advocate.

When Taylor took over as mayor at the beginning of 1925, the population of the city proper had grown to 126,000, its property assessments were $211 million, Point Grey and South Vancouver each claimed between 25,000 and 30,000 residents, the city budget exceeded $4.8 million. Unemployed in the city had dwindled to a mere 1800 and the civic cash relief dole had been discontinued. The first Second Narrows Bridge was near completion, and West Vancouver had pushed a road as far west as Whytecliff.

Taylor was elected again for 1926—carrying in with him as alderman Angus McInnis, who was to become famous as a CCF stalwart—and for 1927-28, when a two-year term for mayor and aldermen was an innovation. His two previous terms had seen the general prosperity of the city continuing, the financial recovery of South Vancouver, the opening of the Second Narrows Bridge, and the start by North Vancouver of the Grouse Mountain Highway and Chalet, an enterprise later changed to private hands. Grain shipments had increased 50 percent, the tourist traffic scored its first million visitors in a single year, and the city boasted 50 miles of ornamental street lighting. But Taylor's main achievement was the passage of the amalgamation vote which provided for the union of Vancouver, South Vancouver and Point Grey on January 1, 1929. The citizens of all three areas decisively rejected a metropolitan-type "county council" and approved full amalgamation, for which preparations were made during the ensuing two years.

Already, instituted by Tisdall during his last term and carried out by Taylor during his first, one utility had been organized on a metropolitan basis—the Greater Vancouver Water Board came into operation in 1925, and with it, an amalgamated sewer system. Dr. E. A. Cleveland was placed in charge and began building up the vast watershed and distribution system which was to give

Vancouver one of the finest water supplies in the world and remains a monument to his name. One of his proudest boasts was, "No case of disease has ever been traced to this city's water supply." His method was complete isolation of the watershed, with meticulous exclusion of all possible human disease carriers; during the Second World War, at the insistence of the U.S. Navy in contracting for port facilities here, the city's water was first chlorinated and a wild public protest arose, many citizens travelling far afield to obtain their drinking water in jugs from untreated sources. Cleveland was heartbroken, seeing his life's work brought to naught. Certain public health officials declared the coliform bacteria count made chlorination mandatory; Cleveland retorted this only proved dangerous bacteria could live in the water, not that they did, and pointed to the perfect record of the system. Nevertheless, once the furor over the original chlorination died down and the war ended, the treatment was maintained, though on a much reduced scale, and is continued to this day.

One project Taylor took in hand was the hotel which the CNR was obliged to build in Vancouver under the terms of the agreement of 1912, which also included an obligation to build a $20 million tunnel approach underneath Grandview to the station on Main Street. The CNR was still using the Great Northern tracks to enter the city, and had begun neither the tunnel nor the hotel. Taylor compromised, and by yielding on the tunnel, persuaded Sir Henry Thornton to agree to a 600-room, rather than a 500-room, hotel. In December, 1928, work was begun on the present Hotel Vancouver at Georgia and Burrard Streets.

His four years in office also saw the old City Hall abandoned for a temporary location in the Holden Building, the institution of civic planning under the late Alexander Walker and the projection—never carried out—of a magnificent civic centre on the slope at the north end of Burrard Bridge, planning of the bridge itself, and the appearance of the city's first automatic traffic signals. The first signals were installed at Main and Hastings, the second at Robson and Granville; previously police had directed traffic at the busy corners, often equipped with portable "stop-go" signs which they operated by hand.

In 1927 and '28, the city's material progress took place amid an ostentatious prosperity such as the province had never experienced. Electric signs made the night garish; at the B.C. Electric station on Hastings a three-storey bottle forever poured golden beer into a two-storey glass that filled, foamed white, blinked out and began to fill again; on Granville, an immense, scintillating rooster marked the elegant Chanticleer Restaurant, where young social lights congregated for afternoon tea, or after the theatre. One New Year's Eve, 1000 merrymakers danced at the Hotel Vancouver, 400 at the Elysium Hotel; lavish parties were staged at the Terminal City Club, all the private golf clubs, at Harrison Hot Springs' new hotel, at Grouse Mountain Chalet, and the Rotary Club took over Stanley Park Pavilion. The parties were white-tie-and-tails affairs, though some of the younger generation were tending to become regrettably slack and show up in dinner jackets and black ties.

The event of the evening was, however, the magnificent fancy dress ball in Hycroft on the brow of the Shaughnessy hill, where General and Mrs. A. D. McRae annually entertained in baronial magnificence. Next day the McRae party became celebrated with two picture-filled pages of the social sections of the newspapers, and all the ladies who had not been there almost died of envy. They recovered, however, in time to gossip about it at the Wednesday tea-dance in the Spanish Grill, or over cocktails at the golf clubs.

In less exalted circles the occasion was also fittingly celebrated; 16 automobiles were stolen, 73 drunks arrested and the next morning 18 sturdy citizens were photographed half-submerged in English Bay, the chill waters of which one lady endured for 33 minutes, to set a record. A belated traveller noted that, as the New Year came in, the city's lights were visible, reflected against the overcast, as far east as Chilliwack.

So 1928 arrived and passed, and when October came, the first elections of the new Vancouver were held, in order to give the incoming council time to organize administration of the 11 wards which now stretched from the University Lands on Point Grey to Boundary Road, and from Burrard Inlet to the Fraser River. The city had grown from 9.35 square miles in 1886, to 44 square miles. Its population jumped "overnight" from 142,000 to 220,000. There were 75,075 voters listed, 15,000 of them in South Vancouver and 12,000 in Point Grey. Assessments of the combined areas totalled $314.5 million, building during 1928 had reached $23,750,000, bank clearings passed the $1 billion mark, a permanent airport had been established on Sea Island and grain shipments touched 80 million bushels.

W. H. Malkin campaigned vigorously for the mayoralty, denouncing an alleged "vicious professional vice-ring" and promising yet another searching investigation of the police force and its alleged participation in gambling and prostitution. He pledged construction of a new City Hall, of the Burrard Bridge, and elimination of the vexatious CPR level crossing at Carrall Street, which several times a day held up traffic on Hastings, Pender and Cordova as trains shunted backwards and forwards between the False Creek yards and the main line along the inlet. Taylor's ambition long had been to be the first mayor of the amalgamated city, and he was bitterly disappointed over Malkin's victory by a modest 2000 majority, but somewhat mollified by a public testimonial in the shape of a gift of $5000—even his political foes contributed—which he was urged to spend in a tour around the world. January 1, 1929, the veteran mayor gracefully handed the reins to his successor and departed on his travels, leaving the city and its problems to the new regime.

14

Rock Bottom

THE DEPRESSION couldn't have happened to a nicer mayor—that was the shame of it.

Mayor Malkin was universally respected. Having made his fortune in wholesale groceries, he undertook public office as a service to the city he loved. He was a sound businessman, had no axe to grind and had great plans for Vancouver. An intelligent and astute philanthropist with a strong moral code and sense of civic obligation was just the man to take over the helm at this juncture, for the city could stand some improving.

It had just finished 11 years of growth against the background of a fantastic world boom. During that time it had to repair the ravages of the war years. In addition, it was faced with all the problems of trying to shape the pre-war boom town into a rational, 20th Century industrial city; it was trying to do the work of decades in mere years. Moreover, it existed in a hostile setting; a very small city by world standards, it was an immense concentration of humanity by contrast to the remainder of the Province. It had to face political and economic jealousy. A very fair example of the picture seen by British Columbians on the outside looking in, is conveyed by the official Centennial historian, Miss Ormsby, in her account of the city as it was in 1929. Her graphic, but perhaps overly sombre description follows:

"In downtown Vancouver . . . the air was heavy with grime and soot as boats and trains, sawmills and flour-mills, breweries and food-processing plants, shoe factories and clothing factories belched clouds of heavy black smoke. Just how busy the sawmills, iron plants and machine factories in the False Creek district were, every roomer living in the now shabby and smoke-stained frame houses of the West End was only too conscious. Sometimes, by a shifting of the wind, the great activity at the Eburne and Marpole sawmills was also drawn to the attention of the wealthy residents living in timbered mansions near the old McCleery farmhouse on Marine Drive. Only the office-workers who nightly crossed Burrard Inlet by ferry to North Vancouver and West Vancouver really escaped the polluted evidence that the city was now held fast in the toils of industry—industry constantly expanding to satisfy the apparently insatiable demands of the export markets.

"During the first months of 1919, almost all the previous records for economic endeavor were broken: The employment index rose to 111.5; the value of manufactured, agricultural, fish and lumber products reached record heights; trading in oil and mining shares became frenzied; bank clearings in Vancouver approached the figure of $3 billion dollars, and the department stores not only permitted, but encouraged, the buying on credit of automobiles, radios and the new mechanical and electrical aids. It was the greatest boom Vancouver had yet known, and its magnitude was reflected in the spectacular development of new suburbs. Eastward, southward and westward the city was stretching out up Kingsway and on to Burnaby and New Westminster, it pushed its shops and working-class homes south along the interurban tracks to Kerrisdale and beyond it devoured the truck gardens once kept by Sikhs and Chinese . . . sacrificing grace and harmony for quick profits, the building contractors reaped fortunes. . . .

"The spirit of the city was still, as it had been at the beginning, predominantly materialistic. An eager, grasping, acquisitive community, it squandered its own resources of natural beauty, all the time extending its economic power until it held most of the province in fee.

"To its harbor, and away from Prince Rupert, it had drawn the freight cars filled with prairie wheat which spelled prosperity. Its stockyards set the price of beef for the Cariboo cattle industry, and its Water Street jobbers determined the price of apples for the Okanagan fruit industry. The city provided the processing plants for the dairy industry of the Lower Fraser Valley, and it supplied the head offices for the great fishing companies. It had the stock exchange and the head offices of the banks and insurance companies. Each year the lines of its commerce radiated further inland to reach the almost inexhaustible mining, forest and agricultural wealth of the province. And year after year the private fortunes of its leading citizens increased; by 1929 it had 83 millionaires, not a single one of whom, as Duff Pattullo remarked, had yet been known to make a gift to the university or sponsor a major civic enterprise.

"Not content with drawing the wealth of the province and even of the prairies, toward itself, Vancouver came close, through its press and radio, to imposing its political views on all of British Columbia. The Vancouver newspaper editors were powerful men; they could aid or almost smash a provincial political machine; and at the drop of a hat, they could stir up agitation for 'provincial rights'. But they could never completely dominate the thinking people of the province."

Miss Ormsby is sometimes a severe critic of Vancouver. The city had virtues which she could have mentioned, met challenges she left unmarked, and had justifications which she failed to examine, but her judgment of its state in 1929 reflects a fact of great importance in the Hungry Thirties: it is an accurate picture of the way the remainder of the province then and for some time later regarded Vancouver. The city's plight received little sympathy, and when it needed assistance, it got only what it could fight for, tooth and nail.

In 1929, for its size, the city was very much under-industrialized, a condition which continues at the present time. It depended— and still does—too much on constant population increase and a continuing influx of outside capital for its prosperity. Outside the "ash-belt" which surrounded False Creek and did not extend much into the West End, it exhibited few of the evidences of industrialization. A great deal of what industry there was had been electrified. The only real export manufacturing in the city was in the lumber mills on False Creek and the mill-owners were already beginning to shift operations out of the heart of the city. The concentration of commercial operations here was only natural. It was uneconomic to ship grain out of Prince Rupert because of the simple fact that the northern port had no inbound cargo trade and ships would have to proceed there in ballast. Commodity brokers could not very well operate any place else than in Vancouver; their business called for them to be at the major concentration of population in the area they served. The producers, as always, considered the middlemen their natural enemies, but the conditions which resulted in the forming of the great fruit and milk co-operatives during the decade after the First World War were the nation-wide conditions of the trade. While the Fraser Valley dairymen were naturally most concerned about the metropolitan distribution of fluid milk, the Okanagan horticulturists had little quarrel with the Vancouver distributors—their battle was with the organizations which controlled operations on the prairies and in Eastern Canada.

That the Vancouver newspaper editors really could make and unmake provincial governments is open to doubt. They could exert a powerful influence on public opinion in the city itself; not so outside it. While the *Province* enjoyed a fairly wide provincial circulation, that of the *Sun* was for practical purposes non-existent for years to come. In a close contest over important issues the papers might produce a majority one way or the other in the city, but only because they spoke the mind of Vancouver and pointed out where Vancouver's interests lay. For that very reason, they were open to suspicion from readers in other communities, who were unlikely to neglect their own interests at the call of a Vancouver newspaper editor. British Columbia voters have always had a highly-developed sense of self-protection.

Miss Ormsby's understandable regret at the destruction of natural beauty in the city's expansion is shared by all who love a natural, unspoiled bit of scenery. It can be pointed out, however, despite men's defacements many of the beauties remained and received assiduous care. Here we are up against the dilemma which faces any growing city. The beauty of the wilderness cannot be preserved in the heart of a metropolis; nor can the metropolis substitute an unbroken expanse of palaces and magnificent boulevards for the wilderness. Land use must be economical, as well as aesthetic; poor men must have homes, as well as rich. If the city did not achieve architectural grandeur, neither did it build tenements and slums. It became a city of middle-class homes of good quality for their time, and of streets adequate for the traffic which existed. Much was done to preserve the natural beauties of their setting, and if some areas decayed with time (50 years is about the average use-life of wooden buildings), Vancouver never has developed any conditions to equal the slum areas of such cities as Montreal and Toronto.

It is not an apology, but only justice, to point out that a rich city is not a city of rich men. Inevitably, the bulk of its residents are people of modest means. They must cut their coat according to the cloth; taxation must be held to a level that is endurable to the poor, rather than placed at a height that punishes the rich; particularly civic taxation which is forbidden to establish graduated levies. All in all, Vancouver has been conscious of and proud of its natural beauty and has preserved it well with the resources available.

Perhaps Pattullo's "83 millionaires" deserved his criticism, but even this is questionable. Most of the millions were the paper millions accumulated in the frenetic years of the great stock-market boom. The wealthy men of more solid riches were engaged in building their fortunes. They had not the consciousness of great wealth and its powers which existed in long-settled communities where major fortunes had become hereditary trusts. As we shall see, their attitude changed as time progressed and the first generation of rich men became solidly established and gradually retired from active participation in business.

This, then, was the community with which the new civic administration had to deal. The axe, of course, fell in October, 1929. The "Black Friday" of the stock markets was not at first recognized for what it was; by December all the economists and market forecasters were agreed the temporary setback was over, and the boom under way again. The voters of Vancouver, who had in May approved by-laws for raising of $5,850,000, sanctioned another $4,200,000 in December, including bonds for the construction of Burrard Bridge. Civic revenue for 1930 was estimated at $18,985,344, and the $25 million expenditure proposed for the year, Malkin observed with pride, equalled the provincial budget. Sewers, streets, waterworks, the airport, a new juvenile home, city morgue and fire-alarm headquarters, were to benefit. The mayor and the *Sun* declared that renewed and increased prosperity lay just around the corner of the New Year. Malkin predicted building would reach $50 million in the city during the coming 12 months, and announced plans to secure a fireboat for the harbor, abate the smoke nuisance and limit parking on the city streets.

Summing up the past year he drew attention to a $10 million grant from Ottawa for harbor improvement, construction of the $2 million English Bay interceptor sewer, start of construction on the Marine Building skyscraper at Hastings and Burrard Streets, plans of Dominion Bridge Co. to build a $1.5 million plant in Burnaby and of Boeing Aircraft Co. to open a plant at the city airport, start of construction on the CPR tunnel from Coal Harbor to the False Creek yards, which would eliminate the Carrall Street crossing, purchase of Little Mountain for a park, completion of the $1 million Midland Grain Elevator, start of construction on the $1.7 million Royal Bank Building at Hastings and Granville Streets, completion of the Hall Building, purchase by the S.S. Kresge merchandising chain of $1 million worth of retail store sites, grant of Spanish Banks foreshore to the city for park and beach development, launching by the CPR of the new *Empress of Japan*, the Pacific's largest ship, and purchase of the airport site on Sea Island. It was an impressive list of achievements for a single year.

What his New Year message did not mention was the tripling of the relief rolls, the unemployed raid on the relief office, the parades and arrests of the destitute on downtown streets. During January, the demonstrations and arrests were multiplied, the city relief officer was exposed as accepting a rake-off on meal tickets and the "Communist" red herring was worked overtime to account for the disorders. Victoria refused to assist the city with its relief problem and in spite of pressing on with all authorized public works, the decline of private industry placed more and more men on the relief rolls; by the year's end there were 7000 receiving assistance and hundreds more were riding the rods into town on every freight train. The city justly complained that all the rest of Canada was dumping its unemployed into Vancouver. "Jungles" grew up under Georgia Street Viaduct and on the False Creek flats east of Main Street; on one occasion, 1250 men were counted in the First United Church breadline. It was an impossible situation for any administration, but the blame rubbed off on the incumbents anyway, particularly as the mayor, in the public mind, represented the business community which had so obviously failed. When Taylor, refreshed and revitalized by his world tour, ran against Malkin for the 1931-32 term, he won by a handy 5000 votes.

Not that the workingman's friend had any solution for the depression, either. He stayed in office for four years, and only in the last was there a partial up-turn in the economy. At the beginning of 1931 there were, besides transients, 807 families and 640 single men on relief, all city residents; at the end, 2588 families, 175 single women and 4664 single men. The senior governments had removed all transients to work camps, which took a load off the city's shoulders in the autumn, but the relief bill for the year was $1,300,000.

By the end of 1932, the assessment rolls were dropping, taxes were remaining unpaid and Burnaby and North Vancouver District were under commission government; North Vancouver City had defaulted on its bonds, and the bondholders demanded a commissioner take over there, too. Vancouver was paying relief rent for families only on a "shelter basis"—none was paid until eviction was threatened, and then only enough to stave off eviction.

The winter of 1932-33 the city hit rock bottom. The Second Narrows Bridge, its centre span out of commission after being unseated by a ship in 1930, lay idle and rusting. The gaunt bulk of the big new Hotel Vancouver, on which work had been suspended, hung over the city's skyline like a cloud of gloom. Idle men stood around the street corners, beggars walked from door to

Two units of the Bentall Centre with the Marine Building in the background. The beauty of the Bentall Centre has contributed greatly to the miraculous change wrought to what was once a drab Pender Street of bygone years.

Efficient and beautiful, Vancouver's $32-million jet age air terminal was opened in October, 1968. Buttress at right is a cleverly disguised intake tower for building's air conditioning system.

Entrance to Royal Centre on Georgia Street. Below street level is a mall of interesting specialty shops.

The MacMillan Bloedel Building, headquarters of one of the world's largest forest products companies, designed by Arthur Erickson, renowned Canadian architect.

the
silversmith
shop

Gastown scene, a revival of the past century for the pleasure of today's shoppers.

door, streetwalkers were three or four to a block on the main streets in the evening and the breadlines shuffled interminably up to every soup-kitchen. Particularly noticeable to visitors from the interior and up the coast, was the absolute hopelessness and despair of the city unemployed—they had no notion of helping themselves; men and women shivered over empty stoves two or three blocks from beaches littered with driftwood, or if they had garden space, did not cultivate it. The pioneer spirit had been lost, the working people had become a city proletariat without enterprise or resource once the pay-cheques were no longer coming in regularly; efforts at co-operation or attempts to find new sources of income were the exception, rather than the rule.

Nor were the worried business leaders a whit better. The Board of Trade, the Retail Merchants Association and five Vancouver service clubs were represented in a delegation of business men which pressed on the Provincial Government the necessity of allowing the business community to advise emergency steps in this crisis. The result was the briefly famous Kidd Committee Report. If the people who had nothing were in despair, those who had everything could be judged to be in a panic. The report urged that the provincial budget be cut from $25 million to $6 million, that university funds be cut off completely, that free schooling be cut down, the PGE be abandoned, depression-born extraordinary relief be cut off and social services reduced. Fortunately, nobody in authority was foolish enough to attempt to carry out the recommendations. A year after their document had been "filed and forgotten" the business men who authored the report doubtless would have been willing to admit that it was extreme and impracticable. But the report was indicative of the sense of disaster that was abroad at the depth of the depression.

Some signs of revived business were seen the following year, after President Franklin Roosevelt took office in the United States, and a more hopeful frame of mind prevailed in spite of the fact that the actual impact of the depression was even more severe, with 34,000 persons on relief in the city. Tax collections had dropped to less than $10.5 million, from the $18 million of Malkin's first year of office, and the relief bill had risen to

$2,390,000. Property was worth nothing; in the East End, a lot assessed at $1500 would sell for $150; on Howe Street, an assessment of $30,000 indicated a sale price of $5000; premises on Granville that rented for $4800 in 1929 were let for $1800.

The best that the voters could think of was a change of management. Gerald Grattan McGeer, spellbinder, son of a pioneer, veteran of the freight rate fights, ousted L. D. Taylor from the mayorality by 34,521 votes to 8978. It was a sad departure for the old man, aged 77. He had been chief magistrate of Vancouver eight times, for a total of 11 years. Now, old, alone, a widower for the second time, he could not give up his dreams of civic glory and he continued to fight elections until 1938, when he was dismissed with a contemptuous 429 votes out of a total of over 42,000 divided among a five-man field. From then on he lived until 1946, barricaded in his flat in once-fashionable old Granville Mansions, at the corner of Granville and Robson, and opening only to a secret knock. He was penniless; a friend paid his rent until he died, and old political foes and friends clubbed together, each chipping in $5 a month, to support him. He died at the age of 88, convinced of the ingratitude of the city he had loved. But he had been its mayor more times, and for longer, than anyone else in its history.

If Taylor's role had often been enigmatic, McGeer's place in the city's history is also difficult to define. He was a man of ebullient enthusiasms and forceful personality, but little judgment. His platform during the mayoral election was sheer anarchy beside that of Taylor, the veteran leftist. It consisted of "investigation, shake-up and repudiation," aimed at the police force and the city's bondholders. He demanded that the Provincial Government authorize a 50 percent cut in the interest on all the city's debts. A revealing estimate was that of Lord Macmillan, the astute British advocate and investigator, who was in Vancouver in 1933 to conduct the Dominion Royal Commission on Banking and Currency; he wrote:

"We sat next at Vancouver, where we were enlivened, if not enlightened, by a local enthusiast, Mr. McGeer, whose views on monetary reform were expressed with no lack of vigor."

It was just that vigor that Vancouver needed at the time. There had been some slow and small progress during the previous year— the Second Narrows Bridge had reopened, the city was able to restore partially the pay cuts imposed previously on teachers, and civic finances had been stabilized at a point that permitted cancella- tion of tax sales in October. Payments into the sinking fund had been suspended, but in a period when other cities were defaulting on their debts, Vancouver met its obligations. Nevertheless, the atmosphere of despair and apathy continued.

McGeer came into office like a whirlwind, grabbed the city by the seat of its pants and collar and stood it on its feet. He began with yet another shakeup of the police force, in which two magistrates and the chief of police were dismissed, 17 officers suspended, pending an inquiry. The mayor made an excellent choice for the new chief—Colonel W. W. Foster. When it proved impossible to finance a new City Hall by orthodox methods, McGeer devised "baby bonds" and sold them locally. The handsome $2 million hall long dominated the south skyline of the city—the sight of it rising in the midst of the depression was a shot-in-the-arm for the citizens. Somebody was doing something at last; it didn't matter very much just what he was doing. McGeer was the man to fill the bill— he was always doing something.

All through 1934 a slow but steady improvement was visible in world conditions, which was reflected in the city. By the end of the year the mayor was whooping it up for Vancouver's Golden Jubilee and easily won a second term of office. The relief budget had dropped to $1,214,000, and he was promising to secure $12 million in construction projects for the city during the coming year, including a Post Office extension and a bridge over First Narrows. His promises were backed up by the fact that he had been elected to the House of Commons during the past year.

The Golden Jubilee celebrations were a marked success, "featuring" in almost Hollywood style the visit of Sir Percy Vincent, Lord Mayor of London. McGeer received Sir Percy dressed in robes, with tricorn hat and chain of office and accepted from him the gift of a most handsome city mace. There was an attractive

McGeer panache about the affair that added to the dignity of the City Council and gave the citizens as a whole a better conceit of themselves.

The mayor's most questionable actions were in connection with the relief problem, and occurred in April, 1935. The men in the relief camps, on 20 cents a day and board, had for a year and a half been dragging out lives of hopeless monotony. They struck for "work and wages," and about 2000 marched on Vancouver. In an organized demonstration, they marched to grocery warehouses and eventually the Hudson's Bay Co. department store, where they began to smash showcases and merchandise. Driven out by the police, they moved to Victory Square and sent a delegation to the City Hall, but McGeer refused to see them and ordered their arrest. He described the occurrence as "organized revolution," proceeded to Victory Square and read the Riot Act, after which mounted city police spurred down Hastings Street, clubbing and dispersing the men. It is still debated whether or not the mayor meant to authorize the police and, if necessary, the armed forces to fire on the demonstrators, but such is the purpose of reading the Riot Act. It would appear to have been a case either of unjustifiable panic or unsuccessful bluff, for in the subsequent hurly-burly along Hastings Street hardly anybody concerned was aware of what the mayor had done. The demonstrations soon petered out, though many of the men remained around the city "tin-canning" on the streets for contributions.

This, however, was only a preliminary to the occupation of the Post Office and Vancouver Art Gallery in 1938 by about 1600 men under the leadership of Steve Brodie. They had been cut off relief during the spring and "tin-canned" in the city for a month before George C. Miller, then mayor, banned collecting on the streets; 108 of them were arrested and sent to Oakalla. May 11, the men moved into the gallery and Post Office and also the Georgia Hotel. When the city promised them $500 in relief, the group in the hotel left May 21. The others sat tight until June 20, "waiting for money from Ottawa."

At 5 a.m. that Sunday morning, the Royal Canadian Mounted

Police moved in, using tear gas. City MLA Harold Winch persuaded the men in the Art Gallery to leave without doing any
damage, but with the militant young Brodie at their head, those in
the Post office started to riot. Swinging clubs, the Mounties cleared
the building, but the men spread through the streets, smashing
store windows. They were not dispersed until $30,000 worth of
damage had been done. Apart from its dealing with the men in the
Georgia Hotel, the city played little part in these events; the police
action at the Post Office was ordered from Ottawa and carried out
entirely by the Royal Canadian Mounted Police, with the city
police kept in the background. The city reacted violently; many
had been apprehensive of disorders when the men first staged their
"sit in," but the police action caused a revulsion in their favor.
A great protest meeting was held at Powell Street Grounds during
the afternoon, release of those arrested was demanded, and windows
were broken in the police station. Appeals to Victoria and Ottawa
gained nothing for the men.

This was the last surge of the depression; by 1937 its worst
effects were over. It had made a remarkable change in the city's
outlook on life; all classes shared in what was almost a moral
revolution. The New Deal philosophy of Roosevelt had taken deep
root in Canada, and nowhere more than in Vancouver; in addition,
the action of wealthy Americans who bought property in B.C. to
retire to when "comes the revolution" which they seriously expected
in the United States, gave the fearful confidence in the stability
of Canada and the despairing a measure of consolation.

In all the tribulation there had grown an active social conscience
and a conviction that the distress of one individual was a matter
of concern for all. Even to the most conservative and reactionary,
the Kidd Report of 1932 would have been unthinkable in 1937.

Not all was sweetness and light, of course, but associations
devoted to civic reform and social betterment multipled and
carried much weight; service clubs were less business associations,
re-discovering the wider meaning and obligations of "service"; the
83 "millionaires" (many of them the paper variety) whom Pattullo
had scourged in 1929, were sadly reduced in number, but Malkin

Bowl in Stanley Park, the new Vancouver Art Gallery, bequests of scholarships to the university and of park land to the city, testified that the premier's criticism was no longer valid. Women's associations assisted students in the arts and in music, and private benefactors shouldered the main burden of maintaining and improving the Vancouver Symphony Orchestra.

Among the mass of the people, community associations were formed to organize recreation, to co-operate in assisting the less fortunate and to take part in cultural and educational movements, such as the adult education programs instituted by the university. As access to the North Shore mountains and the outer beaches became easier, outdoor sports grew in popularity; ski villages rose on Hollyburn Ridge and Grouse Mountain and summer cottages filled the shores from Pender Harbor to Boundary Bay, until the Union Steamships' "daddyboats", carrying husbands away from the city to spend the weekends with their vacationing families, became a famous local institution.

The rise of the CCF was a part of this general movement which was reflected in civic politics. "Labor" representation on the city council had been sporadic and local, but the advent of such aldermen as Alfred Hurry and Helena Gutteridge, openly representing a national political party, broke with a tradition that, in form at least, had been observed throughout the city's history. In 1937 the Non-Partisan Association was formed "to keep politics out of the city hall." It has been so successful in its results that inevitably it has been accused of being a political party in itself. But party politics, as such, has been left to the senior areas of government.

Mrs. Gutteridge's election was a new breakthrough for women in Vancouver. Previous to Mrs. P. McNaughton's triumph in 1912, when she led the polls in the School Board election, the city's women had been active in the traditional fields of "women's work", ever since Susan Patterson was the neighborly nurse of Gastown. Mrs. R. H. Alexander led the first, informal hospital auxiliary in 1886. Mrs. C. M. Beecher and Mrs. James Macaulay were thanked by Lady Aberdeen for their work in establishing the Local Council of Women

in the early '90's, and notable in its long history of achievement was
the resolution of the Vancouver Council of Women in 1896, which
led to the founding of the Victorian Order of Nurses in 1898 as
Canada's Memorial of Queen Victoria's Diamond Jubilee. Women
such as Mrs. J. Z. Hall, Mrs. B. T. Rogers (in music) and Mrs.
Jonathan Rogers (in art) played prominent parts in welfare and artistic
movements and led groups of associates in gifts of time and money.

After 1912, women regarded the School and Park boards as
legitimate fields of community service, and were not reluctant to seek
office, but the City Council remained a male preserve. This despite
the fact that Mrs. Helen Gregory MacGill became a judge of the
Juvenile Court in 1919, and Mary Ellen (Mrs. Ralph) Smith had
been elected to the Provincial Legislature a year earlier. Mrs. Smith
pioneered in her field indeed, for in 1921 she became minister without portfolio in the Liberal government—the first woman member of
a legislative cabinet in the British Empire. Mrs. Dorothy Steeves of
the CCF and Mrs. Paul Smith, a former president of the University
Women's Club and of the National Council of Women, also served
in the Legislature before a woman had even become an alderman of
Vancouver. Mrs. Laura Jamieson, who, like Mrs. MacGill, had
been a Juvenile Court judge, and Grace (Mrs. Angus) MacInnis,
daughter of J. S. Woodsworth, founder of the CCF, also became
MLAs. Mrs. Buda Brown, a former Conservative converted to Social
Credit, became B.C.'s second woman cabinet minister. For the
Conservatives, the late Mrs. Tilly Rolston was an able debater in the
Legislature and effectually voiced the woman's viewpoint.

After Mrs. Gutteridge, however, not an election passed without one
or more women seeking a seat on the City Council. Mrs. Jamieson
became an alderman in 1947; Mrs. Anna Sprott served long, Miss
Evelyn Caldwell, a newspaper columnist, held office for one term,
and Mrs. R. M. E. Linnell and Mrs. D. Marzari hold seats in 1974.

Women in the public life of Vancouver have been strong advo-
cates of social reform—Judge MacGill set a notable precedent here—
and in politics have usually been somewhat left of centre, but they
have rarely been the "anti-" this or that type characteristic of reform
groups in the United States. Typically, they have taken to politics as

the logical method of achieving constructive reforms. They have fought the tooth-and-nail battles of the hustings on equal terms with male politicians, and as competent politicians themselves. As a result in part, at least, of this professional approach, the reforms they have achieved have usually been embodied in sound and lasting legislation.

As the CCF strove to penetrate the City Hall, Dr. Lyle Telford turned his attention to civic politics. The doctor had a devoted personal following in the East End, where his jovial and kindly personality had won many hearts, but as a CCF member of the Legislature, he had proved a maverick and somewhat of an embarassment to his party.

During 1936, serious irregularities had been found in the Pacific National Exhibition finances and Mayor McGeer had been challenged in City Council itself with condoning and even attempting to conceal them. Telford, in company with Wilfred Tucker, an accountant who had brought the mishandling of funds to light, began a crusade during which both appeared at numerous public meetings. Telford in the role of an avenging public-spirited angel, determined to purge civic politics of evil, and Tucker, a rather mousey individual, was hauled on midway through the oratorical fireworks to stammer out his quota of facts and figures.

The doctor thoroughly enjoyed the performances; he was a silver-tongued spellbinder rather in the style of a junior William Jennings Bryan, and besides, the crusade gave people an opportunity to forget the doctor's unfortunate connection with the co-operative "Plenty for All" grocery project which had collapsed after mixing sodium fluoride in its baking-powder, with fatal results. For some reason Telford was convinced Chief of Police Foster had profited illegally from his engineering firm's connection with the construction of Bessborough Armouries and the crusade took on an anti-Foster complexion. The doctor provided the oratory, but a clerk, G. W. Gilbanks, provided the alleged facts. Foster retaliated by laying a charge of defamatory libel and established his rectitude to the satisfaction of the court and the public at large. Gilbanks went to jail for six months.

Mayor Miller's term in 1937-38 was relatively uneventful, marked chiefly by the general upturn in the economy and the resumption of work on the CNR hotel as a joint CNR-CPR project, the construction of the First Avenue Viaduct at the east end of False Creek Flats, and the beginning of construction of the Lions Gate Bridge over First Narrows. This handsome suspension span had been first projected in 1932 by the British financial interests which erected the Marine Building and went on to develop the British Properties luxury suburb in West Vancouver— it was an integral part of the development. However, it met with determined opposition from shipping interests and the Conservative government in Ottawa resolutely refused to permit its construction. The city and the newspapers of Vancouver exerted all possible pressure, until the span was authorized in 1937, with work starting March 31. The bridge and roadway through Stanley Park were opened to traffic in November, 1938.

Telford's opportunity came as Miller's term drew to a close. He campaigned vigorously, capitalizing on the unemployed disorders, reviving charges of civic corruption, and defeated Miller for the 1938-39 term by some 2000 votes, while Colonel Nelson Spencer cut heavily into Miller's support. The NPA candidates carried almost all other civic offices. As soon as he was firmly in the saddle, Telford revived his attacks on Foster, charging him with neglect of his duties as chief of police and with incompetence, but an extended inquiry completely discredited the charges and redounded to Foster's credit. The council, over Telford's objections, paid the chief's legal expenses as a gesture of its confidence in him, and there is little doubt that during his term of command, terminated by his return to military duties during the war, the harassed force had perhaps the best leadership of any time in the city's history.

Telford's last year in office saw the visit of King George VI and Queen Elizabeth, and the outbreak of war with Germany. The royal visit coincided with the opening of the new Hotel Vancouver, but was otherwise remarkable chiefly for a 50-mile automobile tour which sadly taxed the strength of the King, who was suffering from food poisoning. Inept arrangements spread out the crowds until the welcome Their Majesties received was thin and tepid compared to previous occasions of a similar nature.

Telford finished his term during the "phoney war" period of disillusionment. There were still 9972 persons in the city on relief, which during 1939 cost $1,546,352, of which the city's share was $747,897. This remained a heavy drain on Vancouver's finances; the sinking fund was $14.5 million in arrears, and there had been no levy for it since 1935. However, the depression was past, and Vancouver had weathered it. It was now "a shabby and battered city, more scarred by the depression than any other in Canada." But it had paid its way, fought its battles, held up its end, and if it had had the hardest fight, it had the most right to be proud. The city had changed profoundly, but it still had its courage and its strength.

15

The Metropolis

So, THROUGH tribulation, Van-
couver reached the period of its flowering into a metropolis. Of this
phase, the story cannot yet be told with the dry judgment of history.
Those aspects of civic life which, previous to the outbreak of the
Second World War, can be treated as more or less admittedly historical, from 1940 onward are still much involved in current political
controversy. More, the forces and processes at work even yet have
not fully completed their courses, nor is their impact completely
understood. As we have seen in the period from 1914 on, more and
more of the city's history becomes inextricably mingled with the
history of the Province and of the nation, both of which are beyond
the scope of a purely civic study. It is necessary, therefore, to speak
in very general terms and deal only briefly with affairs of magnitude.

The Second World War revived in some particulars the civic
problems of the first, but in the main its effect on the city and its
people was much less direct and personal. Very little of the military
organization was on the local level; for much of the war, the Canadians overseas were not in combat, and after the invasion of Sicily, no
matter how heavy on the battlefield, losses did not assume the same
proportion to the city's population as they had in the previous
struggle. The citizens again threw their support to charities and
war loans, but even in these fields individual efforts played a smaller part; the work that had been done by volunteers on a local
level in 1914-18 was to a great extent taken over by the national
government on a national basis. It was in the economic and industrial
field Vancouver was to play its part.

Before Pearl Harbor, the war scarcely intruded upon the city. It shared in the growing economic activity of the country, and during 1940 a small boom developed, with building rising from $6,253,000 in 1939, to $8,043,000, and continuing in 1941 to establish a record for the city, with $9,206,270 worth of construction, including 2125 new homes. This was almost peace-time life, and there was no urgency in war production. The civic administration of the period 1940-46 was under Mayor J. W. Cornett, a veteran alderman and previous reeve of South Vancouver, whose financial policies were conservative and directed toward erasing the ravages of the depression period. In this he succeeded; during 1941 there were still over 5000 persons on relief, with a total cost of $1,228,616, but the tax levy was kept down to 50 mills and an operating surplus of $1,135,000 was used to start restoration of the sinking fund.

Nevertheless, as the flames of war blew up in Europe after the "phoney war" period, war industry began to grow in Vancouver. It was sufficient in 1941 to bring a noticeable increase in population as men and women from the prairies and the interior of B.C. moved into the city. In subsequent years as Canada struggled to remedy the "too little and too late" policies of 1939 and 1940, the tide of migration became a torrent. The industrial achievements of Vancouver were remarkable. It was not just that 20,000 men and women were working in the shipyards in the place of the 5000 of the First World War, or other thousands in the Boeing Aircraft plant on Sea Island, or that the port was daily setting records for shipping metals, timber and foodstuffs from the busy piers; there was a change in quality, as well as an increase in quantity.

New techniques revolutionized old industries, and new industries grew up overnight. Iron foundries undertook and completed huge ship-member castings of a size and complexity they had never before attempted; boilers, winches, condensers and engines, previously imported, were made locally. Aluminum and other metals were worked, and new plywood techniques evolved for airplane parts. Entirely new electrical and electronic processes were devised and utilized. Refugees with superior technical skills, who had been grudgingly admitted to Canada and relegated to farm or domestic work, became worth their weight in gold, and flocked to the city. Capital for new plants and for entirely new industries, unobtainable during the depression, was made available as a matter of course by both private sources and the national government.

The war really began for Vancouver, however, on December 7, 1941. The galvanic reaction of the United States to the disaster of Pearl Harbor was reflected in the city with almost the full force felt to the south. Vancouver was no longer the lone metropolitan outpost on the distant Pacific of a Europe at war; one could no longer slip across the border in an hour into a land at peace, with "business as usual". The immediate effect was an excitement—almost a panic —with the city blacked-out, night shifts in the war plants cancelled, guards on bridges and railways doubled, the Japanese fishing fleet immobilized and 10,000 volunteers swamping the previously-anaemic Air Raid Protection organization.

This phase soon passed, and December 11 the city resumed normal life under a "brownout", but with road traffic still running with shielded headlamps under a 15 m.p.h. maximum speed.

There had not been the same rapid exodus of troops as at the beginning of the previous war; complete military formations—with headquarters in the old Hotel Vancouver at Georgia and Granville— remained, and expansion of the Royal Canadian Air Force establishments at Jericho Beach and in Kitsilano and Sea Island, and of naval installations in the harbor and on Deadman's Island, were rapid. American army offices were established in the city and the U.S. navy promptly completed an agreement for use of the harbor as an outlying base. With the allied unification of procurement services, the city's war industry was co-ordinated with that of the entire Pacific coast of Canada and the United States.

Immediately Japan came into the war, Vancouver's Japanese colony of 30,000 persons became an object of doubt and suspicion, inspiring fears that amounted to hysteria. There was some reason for this. "Little Tokyo" was a tight, clannish community, well disciplined and energetic in maintaining its Japanese schools and traditions. Its inhabitants mingled very little with the white population and made little secret of the resentment they felt at the discrimination which confined them to inferior occupations, to wage rates and status below those of white men doing equivalent work. Japanese dominated the fishing fleets, monopolized much of the "corner store" trade and had never sought nor encouraged the half-contemptuous affection with which the Chinese were regarded.

Shocked by the Pearl Harbor raid and fearing attack, the city, joined by Lower Fraser Valley communities, at once pressed for and obtained the removal of all Japanese, both alien and Canadian-born, to relocation centres or other Canadian cities and towns east of the Cascade Range of Mountains. There were no proved cases of treachery or subversion; the action was entirely preventive and, though injustice was involved, it was probably the wisest course possible under wartime precautions. What was discreditable to Canada in the aftermath was the virtual looting of the property and lands of the Japanese in the process of removal under government order and trusteeship; the owners were lucky to realize 10 percent of the value of what they were forced to leave behind. They accepted the situation as a backlash of war and philosophically made the best of their new surroundings, where most of them remained.

In itself, the proceeding was unjust, ungenerous and in some particulars indecent, but its ultimate results were beneficial, for it proved to be the last of the series of anti-Oriental incidents which had plagued the city from its beginnings. The much larger Chinese community, reckoned at 50,000, was ripe for better absorption into the life of the city. In the role of wartime allies, the Chinese found this process speeded and facilitated. Almost at once, with the hard-core of Japanese consolidation eliminated, Chinatown ceased to be a ghetto; its inhabitants spread out, found general social and economic acceptance and Chinatown today is little more than a tourist attraction, in the main kept alive by the Chinese themselves for commercial purposes as the "old Chinese" generation dies out.

Racial discrimination, to all intents and purposes, is a thing of the past in Vancouver. Occasional incidents, chiefly in connection with housing accommodation, give rise to sporadic outbursts of protest, but they are isolated and rare. There are no longer two wage

scales, for white and non-white; few unions (and those U.S.-domi-
nated) draw a color-line; there are no restricted occupations; schools
are integrated, not in name only, but in fact and deed; the city has
adopted and enforces a comprehensive anti-discrimination by-law. The
non-white is free to occupy the social, professional and economic
station he has the talent and energy to achieve. There do remain
"communities" of Sikhs, Chinese and returned Japanese, but
these are maintained by internal cohesion, not by external pressure.

As the war progressed, the natural strains developed, with an
acute housing shortage the major difficulty. The city's finances were
restored to a sound basis, but shortages of material and labor made
it impossible to keep the public services up to standard. Sewers,
streets, water mains, parks and utilities all suffered. Wage freezes
and price controls eliminated much of the labor trouble of the First
World War, but there was a good deal of unrest, culminating in the
B.C. Electric transit strike of early 1944, which set the town on
foot from January 9 to 26. In this case, the men's dispute was
with the National War Labor Board, rather than the company,
and the board was forced reluctantly to review its previous unfavorable decision. During the strike even the schools were closed for
a time, as the rationing authorities would not release extra gasoline
for teachers; however, the great increase in automobile ownership and
the speedy formation of "pools" proved surprisingly effective in
transporting workers to their jobs. This success also demonstrated for
the first time a fact that has since plagued the transit system—the
fact that Vancouver had become even then a city capable of transporting itself on its individually-owned wheels.

Not all the refugees whom the war brought to the city
were in distressed circumstances; a number of them had substantial
resources and a thorough knowledge of international business affairs
which they immediately put to use. When their enterprises were
successful, they added a new social and cultural depth to the business
community, for they had the European sense of the responsibilities
of great wealth. The philanthropies of the Koerner brothers, Leon
and Walter, are perhaps the outstanding example of this development, and the example they set is of even more value than the large

gifts they have made; in the post-war years, some of the possessors of great fortunes made in the hurly-burly of the Twenties and the stress of the years of conflict showed that they recognized a debt to the community which had made them rich.

With the end of the war years, there began the great explosion of population which again was to alter the fundamental character of the city, bring to it new power, new problems and new opportunities. Soldiers and airmen who had served on the west coast returned, bring-ing their families. The city and the province drew more than their share of the swelling tide of immigration from war-racked Europe. The city that in 1941 had 275,000 inhabitants, by 1951 had 345,000; by 1956, 398,000. The metropolitan area had grown from 377,000 in 1941 to 646,000 in 15 years, and to an esti-mated 820,000 in 1960. There was a new depth as well as greater number in the city's population: artists, writers, actors, fine architects, skilled artisans and, with the mushroom growth of the university, educators, students and professional men were attracted to the com-munity in substantial numbers.

The amalgamation of 1929 had been a natural development, Point Grey and South Vancouver, even before the union, had been integral parts of the city; utilities and public services did not halt at municipal boundaries, and until the area was unified under a single municipal administration, the tax structure was chaotic, industrial development hampered and intelligent planning impossible. Now a similar situation, but with a difference, was arising on a greater scale. What had been outlying suburbs were again becoming the city's dormitories. By 1956, there were 45,000 people in North Van-couver, 18,000 in West Vancouver, 78,000 in Burnaby and 33,000 in New Westminster; Richmond on Sea and Lulu Islands was filling up, so were Delta and Surrey Municipalities south of the Fraser, and Coquitlam and Port Moody to the east. Of these, only New Westminster and that portion of Surrey tributary to it could legitimately consider itself a unified and self-sustaining community; in the rest, the vast majority of the people worked in and drew their living from the industries and businesses of Vancouver.

There were stresses and strains during the period of growth. When

Totem Pole Park at the University of British Columbia includes some striking examples of carvings by Haida and Kwakiutl artists. The Park also contains a collection of plants and shrubs used by West Coast Indians for ceremonial and everyday occasions.

The drive through Stanley Park then over the Lions Gate bridge is a pleasant one for commuters and tourists — except in rush hours.

BELOW THE SNOWFIELDS — *Mile-high above Vancouver, reached by comfortable gondola cars of the Grouse Mountain Sky Ride, are snowfields where skiing begins in late fall and continues into spring — literally "only a few minutes" from the heart of the city.*

A TOUCH OF THE ORIENT—*Vancouver's Chinatown is second only to that of San Francisco in North America. A distinctive retention of quiet Oriental living patterns blends with the life of a thoroughly modern city.*

STANLEY PARK, A LOVELY HERITAGE—*Hard by the busy streets of Vancouver, like a Bois de Boulogne in Paris or a Central Park in New York, is the Admiralty reserve that became the world-famous Stanley Park. A thousand-acre wooded peninsula at the entrance to Vancouver Harbor was named a park in the first agendum of business of the first Council of the City of Vancouver. Today the park is one of the city's most valued treasures, a place of wooded quiet, sandy beaches, pleasant meadows, interesting aquarium and zoo collections and playing fields.*

servicemen first began returning from overseas or Eastern Canada, housing was in such limited supply they "sat down" in the old Hotel Vancouver and refused to budge until provision was made for them. The building boom that followed the war radically altered parts of the city; the old mansions of the West End were torn down and replaced by modern apartment houses; West Vancouver became the home of the wealthier class and proved to be the opportunity of gifted young architects whose handsome and harmonious designs for homes became famous throughout the continent; Burnaby and North Vancouver encouraged industries to locate within their borders in an effort to attain balanced development; Richmond attracted middle-class and working-class homes, and with the opening of the Oak Street Bridge across the Fraser's North Arm in 1957, its rural stretches of delta land urbanized rapidly. Surrey and Delta indulged in an orgy of subdividing to provide homes for people who wanted to "get out of the city"—but soon found the city was catching up with them in their rural retreats.

Later the opening of George Massey Tunnel (first called Deas Island Tunnel) under the Fraser River in 1959, though primarily designed to serve the new Vancouver Island ferry terminus at Tsawwassen, contributed to this growth. In the 1966 census, the population of Surrey was set at 81,826, and of Delta at 20,644. These figures were soon outdated, and the Delta-Surrey suburbs are among the fastest growing in the metropolitan area. This growth is almost entirely post-Second World War. It has given rise to a severe housing shortage despite the fact that from 1950 onward 5000 to 7000 homes were built annually in the city itself, and in Greater Vancouver in a typical year, 1967, construction of 13,897 private residences was begun.

As the surburban areas filled up, large shopping centres in the modern pattern were established and caused a marked decrease in retail business in the city's "downtown" area. Sewers and water services in many districts proved inadequate to serve the increased population, and a dozen communities pouring untreated sewage into Burrard Inlet and the Fraser River so polluted the waters that for a time the city's beaches had to be closed while construction proceeded on a costly diversion tunnel under Point Grey and Kerrisdale to link up with a sewage treatment project on Iona Island at the mouth of the Fraser. The public transit service, despite the switchover to trackless trolleys in the period 1948-55, was unable to cope with the demands of the sprawling metropolis; nearly everybody owned an automobile; by 1959 there were 179,000 registered in Vancouver itself, and 271,000 in Greater Vancouver; bridges and roads were inadequate and the city centre parking problem a severe headache. In addition, the sheer volume of private vehicle and trucking traffic impeded the already-inadequate public transit system.

In the following decade traffic congestion grew worse instead of declining. In the city 230,000 private automobiles, 32,000 commercial vehicles and 650 public transit motor and trolley buses competed for space on a road system that had been little expanded or improved. Georgia Viaduct reached the end of its useful life and complicated the planning of freeways, some projects for which called for an expenditure of $500 million. Opposition to the details of freeway schemes grew loud and vocal and demands for a rapid transit alternative increased. So bad did traffic congestion become that in 1968 a private company revived trans-inlet ferry service, for passengers only, which North Vancouver had abandoned as a public utility in 1958, and West Vancouver nearly two decades before that. Ironically, West Vancouver's veteran *MV Hollyburn* became the mainstay of the short-lived private service.

Another problem that arose was bitterly assailed by residents as "smog" but was chiefly fly-ash and industrial smoke and smell; the city's location, open to the winds off Georgia Strait, prevented the prolonged "temperature inversions" that at times seriously distress Los Angeles. With all the new construction, the city also had to cope with the decay of its inner residential areas built up in the boom of the pre-First World War days; in the West End and the city centre, apartments and business blocks replaced much of the obsolescent housing, but grim slum conditions developed in the area east of downtown Main Street, in Fairview north of Broadway, and in the eastern part of Kitsilano.

Slum clearance and renovation of blighted areas was slow to

develop, but the city expropriated and consolidated land east of Main Street for the erection of a major low rental housing project which rehabilitated much of the slum area on the eastern border of Chinatown, though many of the older Chinese generation protested bitterly at the loss of their long-time homes. As the 1960s progressed, private enterprise made a startling change in the West End. Multi-million-dollar office buildings proliferated west of Burrard Street, along Georgia, Pender and Hastings Streets, establishing a fine new commercial district, but leaving the city core along Granville and Hastings Streets shabby and run down. Long and frustrating negotiations took place and were even carried to court before the Blocks 42-52 project for a massive rebuilding of the two blocks west of Granville between Robson and Dunsmuir Streets was completed. This called for a vast complex of individual stores, hotels, office buildings and parking accommodation to be grouped around a new Eatons of Canada department store. First fruits of the optimism aroused by the project was a cleanup and refurbishing of Granville Street's "theatre row" in the two blocks south of Robson, with colored sidewalks, ornamental lighting and street plantings installed in 1968.

Coincidental with this commercial district development was the rapid construction of high-rise apartment housing in the remainder of the West End. These tall and often graceful buildings have altered the entire skyline of the city in less than a decade, and the Marine Building, Hotel Vancouver and B.C. Hydro Building which once dominated it are now almost lost in the forest of white towers which stretch from Stanley Park nearly to Granville Street.

A less serious problem, but still a major change in the city's habits, was created by the altered post-war pattern of transportation. Rising costs of operation and relatively cheap air travel almost wiped out the coastal shipping fleets. The Union Steamship Co. gave up the ghost entirely; the CPR fleet declined to a mere ferry service to Vancouver Island, finally retiring from even the Victoria run and confining itself to the Nanaimo shuttle service; the company did not resume its trans-Pacific *Empress* service after the Second World War, and old Pier D at the foot of Granville Street, burned down in a notable conflagration in 1938, has never been replaced. The Black Ball line and the Provincial Government compete in the Vancouver Island ferry trade, but aside from a pitiful remnant, the great coastal shipping fleets of the first half-century of the city's history have vanished. The port's business, however, remains immense. P & O liners provide oceanic passenger service, but with the national decline of Canadian deep-sea shipping, no vessels of consequence call Vancouver their home port. It is ironic that the young seamen of one of the world's greatest ports can go to sea in a tugboat, a fishboat or a ferryboat, but not otherwise except under foreign flags.

The expanding network of fine highways in the Province and the competition of air travel have cut into Vancouver's railway services. Freight shipments are well maintained, but the once frequent daily passenger runs have been cut to a melancholy minimum of arrivals daily. The opening of the PGE line to Squamish, tying the city into the line running to the Peace River district, has made little difference in this regard; that passenger service, inaugurated in 1957, has been cut to an irreducible point. On both water and land, however, airplanes, trucks and buses have substituted for lost sea and rail transport, and the change has not seriously affected the bulk of the city's business and industry; as wholesale supply centres, cities like Nanaimo, Kamloops and Prince George compete in a business of which Vancouver used to have a monopoly, but this has been a natural development of the growth of the Province; Vancouver has had ample compensation through increased trade for any loss it has suffered.

If the city's problems multiplied during this period of explosive growth, extraordinary efforts were made to meet them. Mayor Cornett, after six years in office, left the chief magistrate's chair with the civic finances largely restored from their depression state. His final year, 1946, was enlivened by the celebration of the city's Diamond Jubilee. If the Golden Jubilee in 1936 had marked the first signs of revival from the years of panic, the Diamond Jubilee was the guarantee of a full recovery. Optimism and confidence had returned in full measure and everybody felt the boom was coming, though few had any real notion of how great it would be.

Cornett was succeeded by G. G. McGeer, then a senator, who fought his campaign for another term of office from a hospital bed, to which he was confined by an emergency operation. It was, for the exuberant warrior, an unfortunate return to office. His election was marked by a bitter dispute with the *Sun*, his former supporter, over allegedly unfair tactics in the election. His only action of note was the appointment of a chief of police who later fled the country rather than face an inquiry into his ties with organized vice. The mayor died in his sleep at the age of 59 before the year was out.

McGeer's actions were never less than controversial, some of them have been proved unwise, but no one who felt the power of his personality and knew the city in its years of despair in the 1930's but must remember him as a dynamic force and the stimulant and tonic the city needed in its darkest days. When his friends and his enemies and his fellow-citizens turned out in thousands to bury Gerald Grattan McGeer, they remembered only that of him. He was succeeded in office by Charles Jones, an experienced former civic official, who finished the term; thereafter for two years by Charles E. Thompson, an active businessman; and then for eight years by Fred J. Hume, a former mayor of New Westminster. When Hume retired in 1958, his place was taken by A. T. Alsbury, a school principal long active in labor and civic affairs.

Alsbury was succeeded by W. G. Rathie, who served for two terms but was narrowly edged out in the civic elections of 1966 by T. J. Campbell, who took office at the beginning of 1967. Rathie, often frustrated by a factious council, did much solid work which was more appreciated after he left office than while he occupied the mayor's chair. Tom Campbell, younger and more theatrical, broke the Non-Partisan Association's hold on this high civic office, but his term of 1967-68 was marked by altercations in Council when his policies came under attack of aldermen as unpredictable. He was originally in opposition to the amalgamation of Burnaby and Vancouver, a project embraced by Mayor Emmott of Burnaby who resigned to contest the mayoralty of Vancouver in the 1968 election, with amalgamation as his major objective. Campbell changed his stand and proposed amalgamation be voted on in a plebiscite taken at the time of the civic election, and confessed he lacked information sufficient to make up his mind on the subject. Emmott opposed the plebiscite on the ground that more careful examination of the terms of any union was required before public opinion could be usefully tested. With the advent of the Regional Development Board for Greater Vancouver, the Vancouver-Burnaby merger proposal became, at least for the time being, a dead issue.

That Campbell, credited with getting action on the Museum and Planetarium complex and with facilitating final moves to bring about the spectacular Blocks 42 and 52 development, had improved his image of early impetuosity was indicated, perhaps, by the fact that the NPA conservatively-minded in its selections, was not unfavorable to his re-election in 1968.

When the Campbell mayoral era came to a close the Non-Partisan Association was in a slump and a rival group of mixed origin candidates under TEAM banners (The Electors' Action Movement) was swept into office, headed by financial consultant Art Phillips. Conversion of Granville Street to Granville Mall may be his most conspicuous influence on the face of Vancouver.

The post-war years were marked by the constant struggle of the council to meet the changing pattern of civic life and to maintain the city's financial integrity. A new charter was obtained from the Provincial Legislature in 1953, largely the work of Corporation Counsel D. E. McTaggart. It consisted of 600 clauses, consolidating some 50 acts and amendments concerning the city. Its main provisions broadened the electorate, increased the number of aldermen from eight to ten, provided for the adoption and financing of long-term projects and for closed-shop agreements with labor unions. The civic ballot was extended to tenant and resident classes, increasing the electorate from 172,000 to 212,000, or practically the entire resident adult population. In 1958, a civic board of administration, consisting of the mayor, an alderman and the two senior civic officials, was created by charter amendment; otherwise the 1953 charter remains the basis of civic government today.

One later amendment, designed to remove the police force from the sphere of civic politics, placed in charge of the force a commission consisting of the mayor and three commissioners appointed by the Provincial Government. This was in line with the general provisions of the charter, which favored the development of independent and semi-independent commissions, upon which the council is represented, to carry on much civic business. These took many and varied forms, such as the elected Park Board and School Board, the self-perpetuating directorate of Pacific National Exhibition, the Queen Elizabeth Theatre Commission, the Downtown Parking Corporation, which strives to cope with the traffic problem in the central business district, and the Greater Vancouver Water Board and Metropolitan Health Committee, which deal with essentially metropolitan problems and services.

Hardly was the Socialist Barrett government in power before it ran afoul of the PNE board of directors over race track policy, demanding that a contract with the long-established Jockey Club be abrogated and rewritten. The board resigned en masse and turned its mandate back to the City of Vancouver. A new and much less business-oriented board was appointed to carry on, comfortable in its task with the hefty revenues built up from one of the most extensive community facilities of its kind in North America. It was only the beginning, for Victoria became interventionist in municipal affairs, using available legislation to exert its dominance in final decisions over civic planning and city council decisions on use of lands always previously considered to be an inviolable municipal prerogative. Vancouver and Provincial Planning would not necessarily stay in line. A proud city watched the change with incredulity.

The system is criticized as cumbersome and inadequately co-ordinated and has given rise to a number of internecine feuds from time to time, but so far has functioned without more serious failures than arise from human frailties. Much volunteer help has been put at the disposal of the city by this means. Whether it is adequate for future needs, however, is doubtful. Like much else in the history of Vancouver's turbulent and Gargantuan growth, it was the best that could be devised at the time to meet the pressing problems of the time.

16

The Commercial Framework

THOUGH CITIES are made by men, the manner and the time of their making will always depend on geography, resources, industry and commerce.

Vancouver inevitably would have been a major seaport city. This was dictated not merely by her sheltered harbor near the mouth of a natural transport route afforded by the Fraser through the mountainous hinterland, but also by the location of an International Boundary Line, and the circumstance of no similarly suitable site existing anywhere else on the Pacific Coast in British territory.

When the Americans made good their claim to the Oregon country and took over old Fort Vancouver on the Columbia River, the Hudson's Bay Company had already prepared Fort Victoria on Vancouver Island and Fort Langley on the Fraser to replace the trading and transport centre farther south. The 49th Parallel became the boundary line and the new transport route from the interior debouched with Fraser's river on a wedge-like delta region that widened from the canyon to the sea. In this hundred miles or so were rich farming land and room for a great city to grow. Northward there lay no similar coastal site for settlement, the opportunities at the mouth of the Skeena River and at the Kitamaat River, much later developed, being slight by comparison. Thus, north of San Francisco Bay and Puget's Sound, this was the one logical mainland site where men could bring their enterprise to play aided, not handicapped, by natural circumstances.

The boundary was an added limiting factor concentrating commercial activity on this region.

At first the commodity of commerce was furs. The early forts, shrewdly located, were adequate for that trade and made no use of the harbor of Vancouver. Fort Victoria became the bustling commercial centre of the colony until the miners came in 1856.

Not until gold was found in the Interior, and on the bars of the river east of navigation at Hope and Yale, did Victoria begin to yield its position. It was an epic goldrush. San Francisco was in a frenzy of excitement. The gold fever struck indiscriminately and a motley throng of argonauts crammed northbound ships to Victoria.

The pioneers of pick and pan poured across the Gulf of Georgia in an invasion fleet of varied craft, many perishing as flimsy boats swamped or broke up in the choppy seas. Their supply base became the Royal Engineers' Queensborough, later to be named New Westminster. The fur era was ended and mining began.

As with all gold rushes, transport became the determinant of economic success or failure. The Engineers' road, precariously clinging to rocky cliffs, penetrated the Fraser Canyon, was pushed on to the new goldfields in the Lillooet and Cariboo countries.

No one then foresaw the mainland settlement at the mouth of the Fraser being centred elsewhere than on the shore of the tidal estuarial basin of the Lower Fraser. The men who were to make Vancouver were then children or very young adults, unaware of the challenge that would come to them.

When the logger's axe took its place with the miner's pick, Vancouver became inevitable. Perhaps nowhere in the world was there a finer site for giant softwood trees to grow than on the peninsula of land tonguing out into the sea between the muddy Fraser and the green waters of Burrard Inlet. Many great trees were by-passed at first, being too large for the sawmills to handle. This great "back bay" to New Westminster was wondrous logging country.

But before many were to gain a livelihood from lumber, another industry fed wealth into the young community. In countless numbers, hordes of spawning salmon homed on the Fraser River, milling about for a time in the waters of Puget Sound and Georgia Strait, then moving into the turbid Fraser. The best of the fish were strengthened to struggle hundreds of miles up the river to their destinations, firmly fleshed, wonderfully muscled to swim and leap against the rapids and cataracts to the self-same gravel beds from which they had originally come. Fishermen setting gillnets from manoeuvrable cat-rigged sailing craft worked this new and self-replenishing treasure trove.

Canneries at Steveston and Ladner and up the Coast employed Indians, Chinese and whites in a commercialized operation that greatly magnified the annual fishing and spearing parties of uncounted genera-tions of Salish and Kwakiutl Indians.

So it was that amongst the pioneers of commerce in Vancouver were cannery operators who welcomed the coming of the railway and shipped their products then by rail, as well as water, to distant markets. They were, with the pioneer mill operators, the new city's first foreign traders.

Fishing industry names like Bell-Irving, Ewen, Winch, Buttimer, Wallace, Gosse and MacMillan were in the business news and often appeared in the social columns of the papers when society lived in the West End. Later came Al Hager of Canadian Fishing, John Buchanan of B.C. Packers, Ritchie Nelson and others.

While the Panama Canal was building, Vancouver speculated on its coming new link with the old trade routes of the Atlantic. Lumber-men, canners and fish packers, shipping brokers and import-export agents all speculated on the seaport's growth once the sea route to Europe was greatly shortened and the Atlantic Coast of the United States and Canada came within easier trading reach.

In the pre-war years of Vancouver's greatest growth, the city thrived mainly on expectation of its coming commercial support. Its population swelled on sheer prospect and real estate values inflated in an unreasoning frenzy of anticipation. The Vancouver Stock Ex-change, opening its doors in 1907, was to achieve the proud boast that through subsequent conditions of all kinds, it never failed to do business.

The Balkan War and depression beginning in late 1912 left a be-wildered population trying to distinguish true from false in values and finding precious little to support it. But the real estate era had produced its men of substance and of bold imagination and speculation. Hundreds of citizens had no occupation other than buying or selling property for their own account. Their means of support was loosely described as being "in real estate" and this was accepted as adequate, understandable and respectable. The suicide bullet that killed personable promoter Arnold of the bankrupt Dominion Trust truly shattered the flimsy structure of the 1908-12 real estate boom in Vancouver. Leaders and followers alike were victims of their assumption that speculative demand for real estate gave it some basic value over and above commercial usefulness of the property. Prices plummeted. But in the annals of real estate in Vancouver, such names as J. W. Horne, J. Z. Hall, R. V. Winch, A. E. Austin, Waghorn, Gwynn & Co., C. D. Rand and Fowler, Count Alvo von Alvensleben, Williams and Murdoff, H. A. Roberts, W. H. Gallagher, Gillespie, Hart & Tod, Macaulay & Nicolls, and A. J. T. Taylor will long be remembered. Not all were "caught out" for there were conservatives amongst them who had kept some saving sense of proportion and continued in business long after the boom had exploded around them. There have been major increases in real estate values in the city since then, but for Vancouver that was the boom to end all real estate booms and never since has the business been so infected with ebullient optimism. Today's realtor little resembles the free-wheeling men of the big boom, of whom the Pierrot troupe at English Bay sang: "Freddie has lots and lots of lots!"

No industry has contributed more to Vancouver than forestry. But it was slow to make its truly important contribution. Until about 1920 it was chiefly supported by local sales, by cutting shingles for rail export to the Prairies and the United States and exporting some lumber overseas. The waterborne exports were, to a very considerable extent, handled by timber brokers in San Francisco, who at that time were doing business all over the world. B.C. mills occasionally would get windfalls in orders from that source, but for the most part, the real volume logically went to United States coast mills.

In the midst of the First World War, the still youthful chief forester of British Columbia, H. R. MacMillan, broke protocol and wrote to Sir George Foster, minister of trade and commerce at Ottawa, urging action on finding wider sale for B.C. softwoods. Foster arranged with the government of the Province to release MacMillan and sent him on an around-the-world trip of enquiry. He was instructed to find out why so little B.C. lumber was being sold and what was needed to sell more. His report: "It can be sold if we make the effort."

After a stint of work under Austin C. Taylor, director in B.C. of the Imperial Munitions Board charged with getting out airplane spruce, MacMillan, reluctant to go back into government service, was attracted to a London timber broker's suggestion that he set himself up in business to export the product of B.C. mills. Here was a chance to test the truth of his pigeonholed report. With able associates, he built his H. R. MacMillan Export Co. Ltd. from an idea in 1919 to a powerful force in the softwood lumber trade of the world in a space of less than 15 years. His theory had been sound.

Inevitably, the mills so represented decided that the selling job was one they could as well do for themselves. When Messrs. MacMillan, VanDusen, Scott and associates declined to become their employees instead of their brokers, the operators formed their own export organization and set up sales machinery. With orders for many millions of feet of lumber to be filled for Britain, MacMillan's export company found itself suddenly without suppliers. Then began a strenuous battle amongst the "majors" of B.C.'s lumber industry, which was to continue unabated for more than 20 years, widening B.C. lumber exports competitively in the process far more than if no such struggle had been joined. The MacMillan organization scrounged timber everywhere, produced some on its own account and filled its orders—then waded deeper and deeper into standing forests and manufacturing. In a dozen world markets the Seaboard-versus-MacMillan contest for sales raged vigorously, broken for a period in the Second World War when all timber came under control —and MacMillan was "immobilized" in Ottawa, setting up wartime timber control and rationing.

It is possible that in all the annals of B.C. industry and commerce no more free-swinging, globe-girdling battle of the giants will occur than this struggle for export markets. Vigorous men like Henry

Mackin, J. H. McDonald, Jim Robson, Prentice Bloedel, Bruce Farris, Leon and Walter Koerner, John Prentice, 'Poldie' Bentley and others supplied Seaboard with lumber and with initiative to sell it. They vied with MacMillan's for the output of large and small mills, especially when demand grew—and the demand did grow, partly because so much drive and energy went into the competitive effort.

In False Creek, along the Fraser River, in harbors of Vancouver Island and up the mainland coast, scows and ships loaded lumber for export. In Vancouver harbor grain ships "finished" with deckloads of lumber and, hard down to their marks, sailed out of the First Narrows, carrying timber that had made work and wages in the first-ranking industry of the province.

In a more sophisticated way, that battle still is fought. The Mac-Millan organization first merged with Bloedel, Stewart & Welch, then with the giant paper producer, the Powell River Company. The MacMillan Company, known today as MacMillan Bloedel Limited, still vies with Seaboard Lumber Sales for orders but the contest turns on competitive ability to load, carry and unload forest products destined for overseas markets under cost-cutting methods and in ships designed for the traffic. The Council of the Forest Industries of British Columbia has its headquarters in Vancouver as does the International Wood-workers of America B.C. Regional Council combining various locals. Vancouver, for all its growing-up in the decade of the sixties, was still a lumber town living chiefly on the ever more efficient converting of raw timber to finished forms of structural materials, pulps and paper.

Thus have the moderns built on the works of such pioneers as 'Sew' Moody, Edward Stamp, R. H. Alexander, John Hendry, John Hanbury, Eric Hamber, Chris McRae and the Hacketts.

After the Cariboo gold rush there was a long period when mining stagnated, then came the Kootenay and Boundary Country excite-ment. Camp McKinney, Rossland, Phoenix, Hedley, Greenwood, Salmo, New Denver and the Slocan were all producing their wealth of minerals. Spokane in Washington, being nearer, enjoyed more actual benefit from this mining activity than did Vancouver. Every Saturday a full passenger trainload left the Slocan to take miners and merchants on a grand and glorious excursion to Spokane and its fleshpots, bars and gaming tables. Later, however, the hard-rock miners trained in the Slocan formed the corps of skilled crew men, foremen, shift bosses and superintendents who spread over the Province and made possible the mining operations of the recent past and present. They were a durable, hard-working, hard-playing lot with "a stake" their goal and a "bender" all too often their downfall.

Vancouver newspapers recounted the comings and goings of colorful prospector Fred Wells, of A. B. Trites, "Roly" Wood, R. K. Neill and Dale L. Pitt of the fabulously rich Premier Gold Mine, of Dr. W. B. Burnett who mixed medicine and mining, of David Sloan and Austin C. Taylor, who made their millions in Bridge River Gold Mines, of popular "Blay" Blaylock—more properly described as Dr. Selwyn G. Blaylock — who changed prospector Paddy Sullivan's complex lead-zinc ore deposit into a great producer supporting the smelter city of Trail, and Gomer P. Jones, stocky, Welshborn manager of the Nickel Plate Mine at Hedley.

The British Columbia Chamber of Mines, for many years directed by its manager, Frank Woodside, a pioneer of the city, and latterly by Thomas Elliott, taught thousands how to prospect for ore. Some graduates of the winter evening classes made major strikes. In modern terms, the mining industry of British Columbia is describable as great and progressive and Vancouver remains its capital. Base metals, asbestos and coal mines are feeding the seemingly insatiable industrial machine in Japan on a scale unimagined as recently as the 1950's while continuing to expand sales to more traditional markets.

In the Port of Vancouver, a transport fraternity grew up, centred on the Vancouver Merchants Exchange. They bought and sold ship cargo space and the cargoes to fill them. Their members included some of the men who kept the fight alive for "equalized grain rates" and for removal of the so-called "mountain differential" in freight rates between British Columbia and points east of the Rockies.

They drew the Vancouver Board of Trade into their struggle and the Board of Trade brought in the redoubtable Gerry McGeer. Behind them all, with a prod, was R. J. Cromie, unpredictable crusading publisher of the *Vancouver Sun*. Let the struggle on freight rates or for grain elevators or for a railway to the Peace River sub-side for a quiet month or two and "Bob" Cromie front-paged a blistering editorial against the "do-nothings" who indulged in idleness while great opportunities languished. Cromie lived to see the grain elevators built, grain and other freight rates equalized and port traffic vastly enlarged. He died long before the PGE was completed to the Peace, but his economic crusades all had their eventual triumphs. Dry-witted wholesaler R. P. McLennan twitted *Sun* reporters: "Well, what are your instructions for saving the world today?"

Down through the years, the Vancouver Board of Trade, staunch-ly resisting the tendency to accept the newer, fancier name, Chamber of Commerce, has spearheaded most of Vancouver's campaigns for economic recognition and growth. Its leaders and supporters have been legion. To name any for achievement without naming all would be difficult, if not unfair, just as it would be impossible to name a few of the many community organizations of men and women that have been vitally part of the city's progress. Spanning a large segment of the Vancouver Board of Trade's career was the service of a man of vigorous, buoyant personality, W. E. "Bill" Payne, secretary to a long succession of presidents until his death in 1946. He began as office boy and served the business community there for some 37 years. Reg. T. Rose succeeded him as manager, followed by G. M. (Gerry) Morris.

The Rose regime as general manager of the Board ended as the organization moved into the towering Board of Trade Building on the Vancouver waterfront scarcely a stone's throw from where the John Morton cabin stood overlooking the harbor.

Only twice in its career has Vancouver lost ground through eco-nomic reverses. Once was before the turn of the century. The second time was after the bursting of the real estate boom and in the early part of the First World War. So many men enlisted and so many families moved away when there was no industry to support them, that the population dropped. But throughout the great depression and in the Second World War, the city's population grew every year.

Today in the City of Vancouver, there are few vacant lots. To build, something old must first be torn down.

The city has been disappointed in its ambitions to build ships, but so, too, have been all the other wartime shipyard centres on the Pacific Coast of North America and many on the Atlantic. Andy Wallace's little shipyard for scows and fishboats on False Creek grew into two great wartime shipyards on Burrard Inlet in the Second World War, managed at that time by his son Clary (Hon. C. W. Wallace) and more recently by his grandson; but modern costs are prohibitive for new ship construction on the West Coast except for specialized local purposes and the great facilities in North Vancouver are scantily but usefully employed, mainly in overhauls and repairs.

Wartime engineering created a great many metal working jobs in Vancouver. Most of these withered with the end of war contracts, but some engineering plants serve the forest and mining industries as, respectively, they have greatly increased their stature in production.

Along Burrard Inlet now, near the point where Captain Vancouver's longboat crew camped for the night, the Trans Mountain Oil Pipeline feeds a growing colony of oil refineries. These illumine the sky at night with their flares and blazing incandescents and emit their pungent petroleum odor, lending to that region the atmosphere of an Alberta or Peace River oil field. They are believed to be the forerunners of petro-chemical industries of the future, using the products of oil and gas fields of the city's farther hinterlands.

We have seen that the city's electric power, transit and gas systems began more or less simultaneously in 1887, in the year that followed its incorporation. British capital in the B.C. Electric Company, responding to R. Horne-Payne's guidance, developed the system in full pace with the community. One of the boasts of management under such men as George S. Kidd, W. G. Murrin, Dr. A. E. (Dal) Grauer, Dr. Tom Ingledow, W. C. Mainwaring and Dr. Harry Purdy was that the city never had a "brown-out" or turned away an industry for lack of hydro-electric energy to serve it. In many ways the B.C. Electric, when bought out by the Montreal-based Power Corporation of Canada and operated under the B.C. Power Corporation, was at the peak of its performance just before it came to an end as a private entity. It had surveyed and researched

*The penguin habitat at Stanley Park, a favorite of visitors from all over
the world.*

No university in the world has a more beautiful setting than the University of British Columbia — surrounded by the waters of the Strait of Georgia and English Bay and dominated by the Coast range to the north.

Contemporary architecture is exemplified in this Instructional Resources Centre at the University of British Columbia. Here students from a variety of disciplines are taught together, the aim of the program being to develop a team approach to the delivery of health services.

The Music Building is part of a three-building complex at the University of British Columbia making up the Norman MacKenzie Centre for Fine Arts. The sculpture in front of the building suggests a tuning fork.

the great Peace River Power Project, demonstrating feasibility, was planning to follow that, if permitted, with a series of dams on the Columbia and had started thermal power development at Ioco on Burrard Inlet. In Vancouver it had moved from its site close to the spot where the pioneers sat under the Big Maple Tree and had built a boldly conceived tower which at night was a shaft of light on Burrard and Hornby Street at Nelson.

Even before the great lake envisioned in engineering surveys launched by Grauer—the largest lake in British Columbia—had fully risen, Peace Power began flowing in September, 1968. The dam was officially named W. A. C. Bennett Dam and the B.C. Electric build-ing in Vancouver now is the B.C. Hydro Building for the initiators, unknowingly at the time, were building public power projects. A take-over by the Provincial government came swiftly in 1961 when the Bennett government contemplated with dissatisfaction two facts: One was that the Federal Government's tax levies against the B.C. Electric's profits were believed to be a burden on the power rate structure of the province; the other was that "Dal" Grauer and his board adamantly opposed a demand by Premier Bennett that the company agree to formulate and announce a plan to proceed with the development of the Columbia River for water storage and for power at the same time as it went ahead with harnessing Peace Power. The company management and directors strongly opposed doing more than one major project at a time. The "dynamic" Vic-toria policy was enforced with a take-over approved by a special session of the legislature. Dramatically, the change came on the very day A. E. Grauer's funeral was being solemnized in old Christ Church Cathedral. Under hard-driving Dr. Gordon S. Shrum, for-merly dean of science at the University of British Columbia, the government service elaborated on the private enterprise company's first plans and the city continues to have abundant energy. This new power is minus an income tax content in the tax rate, but it is also minus the participation in the city's affairs of men of the kind who headed the B.C. Electric and who were leaders of cultural, social and business life in the community. In Vancouver the event caused a stir but the tendency was to shrug off the happening as an inevitability in a province having a clearly established tendency to favor the principle of public power. What is perhaps most significant is that only a fraction of the hydro-electric energy potentially available at moderate cost to Vancouver has been developed. Few other industrial regions anywhere can say as much.

No other city in the world has available to it such a wealth of never-failing, self-replenishing hydro energy, still waiting to be harnessed. Who will develop the power is less important in the long run for Vancouver than the comfortable fact that, once the cost has been amortized with the passing of years, this will be truly low-cost power in great abundance. As yet, British Columbia has developed only a small part of its river power. Modern high voltage transmission can bring this energy within reach of the grid that serves the southwestern portion of the Province, within which is Greater Vancouver, and to other markets.

But it is not through hydro-electric heritage alone that Vancouver enjoys its position as the economic capital of the most richly endowed energy region of North America. It is linked by Westcoast Transmission and Trans Mountain pipelines with the huge natural gas fields of northern British Columbia and the oil fields of west central Alberta. Unused but in reserve is the Hat Creek coal field, a great lignite deposit which would produce relatively low cost thermal power for the southern British Columbia power grid whenever it was needed as an additional source. Falling water, natural gas, petroleum and coal —the raw stuff of power for progress—Vancouver and its neighboring cities of the Province possess for future needs to an extent that, in an era of worldwide energy shortage, spells growth.

When the pioneer city fathers chose for Vancouver's official emblem the motto: "By Sea and Land We Prosper" the sea to them meant the Pacific Ocean and the great opportunity for prosperity lay in trade with the Orient and Australasia.

With the coming of the CPR, the city's foreign commerce began promisingly to realize the first ambitions. It was to be onward and upward all the way in this trade with the myriad millions on those far Pacific shores. But the story of the years has been of hope often deferred and of a real growth in waterborne traffic coming first with access to the trade routes of the Atlantic through the opening of the Panama Canal.

Japan's conquest of the mainland of China turned that country's purchases away from North America and locked China behind as formidable a closed door as ever the first white traders found when they invaded China seas.

Vancouver became Canada's greatest all-year seaport virtually without dependence on Far East commerce. The communization of China has continued to make normal trade almost impossibly difficult, but Japan's defeat and withdrawal to her island empire gave Vancouver fortuitously another mouth-watering taste of the exotic fruit of Oriental buying power. As the 1960's opened, Japan, cut off from Manchuria, was selling Canada everything from Japanese oranges to giant generators, and in return was concentrating in the natural resource industries of British Columbia a volume of buying that made real at last the pioneers' hopes of their port one day handling a truly great volume of traffic to and from the Far East.

Meanwhile, the port's traffic has grown with traditional markets to the point where, in 1973, 29 million tons of dry cargo and 1 million tons of petroleum products were shipped, a figure nearly double that of 1960. But increasingly the expectation is that the Burrard Inlet harbor will be second to the Roberts Bank kind of deep-sea port.

First by a long series of politically-appointed harbor administration boards, reflecting the spoils system of politics, then, as from 1936, through the administration of the National Harbours Board, Vancouver has worked to keep its port facilities up-to-date. It forever has been critical of the results. But the dissatisfaction with physical plant and equipment, with inadequate planning for the future, and resentment against diversion of revenues from local application are criticisms that arise partly from impatience and ambition and bespeak the characteristic growing pains of a port always becoming too big for its previous provisions.

Still expanding its bulk cargo loading facilities, Vancouver harbor saw the advent of the "outer harbor" developing at Roberts Bank under the joint aegis of the National Harbours Board and the Provincial Government, to handle coal and bulk freight.

Pioneers of the modern towing and shipping industry out of Vancouver were the Mackenzies—captains Simon Fraser, Duncan and William, sons of a ship owner on Loch Ness in Scotland. They came to Vancouver in 1890 and built the tug Clyde, laid the keel for a sealing schooner, freighted between Vancouver Harbor, Steveston and Ladner. The firm of Mackenzie Bros. gave Andrew Wallace some of his first orders. Out of the little False Creek yard below old Granville Bridge grew Wallace Shipyards, of the First World War, then the great Second World War steel shipbuilding industry of Burrard Drydock Ltd. Andy's sons, Clarence and Hubert Wallace, and later the third generation of Wallaces have built ships for many purposes. Burrard Drydock, now a subsidiary operation of Cornat Industries, survives strongly.

The rise of Prince Rupert created the first real boom in coastal shipping and the Mackenzie fleet of tugs, coasters and barges pioneered vigorously. In 1910 Mackenzie Bros. sold out to the Grand Trunk Railway Company (forerunner of Canadian National Steamships Limited), and the Mackenzies piloted and skippered such famous craft as SS *Prince Rupert*, *Prince George* and *Prince John* in difficult coastal navigation.

Whatever else Greater Vancouver may be, it is not agriculturally minded. Without compunction it spreads out over the rich, black delta soil to build houses and factories, using up the all-too-scarce supply of land suitable for farming. Increasingly, it brings its food from the mechanized farms of the United States.

Planners foresee the day when the city will stretch from Hollyburn Ridge, Grouse and Seymour Mountains and the seashore to the United States border and up the Fraser Valley to Chilliwack and Hope. Unless land use, according to the character of the soil and the sites, is rigidly controlled, the megalopolis of the future would then have covered in urban development virtually all of today's dairy and mixed farming land and be wholly dependent on imported food products. The Barrett Government's controversial land act of 1973 froze agricultural land from subdivision. An immediate side effect was a rapid rise in cost of building lots.

A city, as it grows, draws nourishment from itself to sustain further growth. Visitors to Vancouver constantly ask: "But where are your industries?" and the Vancouver host is hard put to explain a city of its size so little industrialized. Its industries are many miles away. An unseen strength of Vancouver is in the constant intake of people from elsewhere in Canada who have made their competence in less favored regions and who arrange to live in Vancouver because it is physically pleasant to enjoy the relative mildness of a climate that seldom sees the thermometer above 80 degrees in summer or more than five or ten degrees below freezing in winter.

Thus, a great many people in Vancouver are in the service industries, attending to the needs of those who work in scattered primary industries or who merely live in Vancouver.

Some of these industries are of considerable magnitude and of first importance to the commercial and industrial life of the city. Typical is the B.C. Telephone Co.

We have seen the first phones installed in infant Vancouver by the New Westminster and Port Moody Telephone Co. The service was started by Charles Foster, an American real estate dealer, one of the Port Moody land speculators, but on collapse of the boom there it was taken over by J. C. Armstrong of the Royal City and extended to Granville. Dr. J. M. Lefevre, the CPR physician, became a shareholder, and by 1890 the firm had 500 subscribers, with switchboard in a bookstore at Hastings and Seymour Streets.

The same day the city was incorporated, it had become the New Westminster and Burrard Inlet Telephone Co. Service was extended to Hastings, Moodyville, Eburne, Steveston, South Westminster and Ladner in the years after the fire, and in 1893 the first cable was laid under the Fraser River, with links to Tacoma and Seattle completed the following year.

William Farrell, an English immigrant, took a large interest in the firm in 1895. Four years later, the Victoria and Esquimalt Telephone Co. was acquired. In 1904, the B.C. Telephone Co., Ltd., was formed and the Nanaimo, Kamloops, Vernon and Nelson systems incorporated with the coast group. From this time on, the company dominated the B.C. telephone communications field, and in 1919 acquired a Dominion charter, dropping the "Limited" from its name.

By 1924 it had installed 43,000 phones in Vancouver, with 52,000 in Greater Vancouver. William Farrell's son, Gordon, became president in 1928, and the company grew with the progress of the Province, having half a million telephones and an extensive radio-telephone network in service by the time he retired and was succeeded by Cyrus H. McLean in 1958. The latter, retiring, moving to chairmanship of the company, was succeeded as chairman and president by J. Ernest Richardson who, in 1963 had become president. With the advent of the Barrett New Democratic Party government to office, espousing socialist principles, hints were given of eventual take-over but Ottawa might or might not co-operate. Meanwhile the government's pension funds were buying B.C. Tel shares on the open market while the company went ahead with its business ignoring the threat that undoubtedly shadowed its position and especially its fund-raising responsibilities to keep pace with a fast growing province.

The coming of the air age confirmed Vancouver's key position already established in surface transportation. William Stark took newspaperman Jim Hewitt on a flight at Minoru Park on April 24, 1912—the first passenger flown in B.C.; but earlier William Templeton, later airport manager, built a plane by hand and flew it at Minoru on April 28, 1911. Planes, pilots and passengers willing to risk their necks were oddities at that time. It was when the fliers came back from World War I that commercial aviation got its start, and the bush pilots began their careers.

Out of this "bush league" of fliers came such great Western personalities and pioneers as wartime aces Don MacLaren and "Wop" May, "Punch" Dickens, Lee Brintnell, "Ginger" Coote, Russ Baker, Roy Brown and his brother "Bus", Milt Ashtown and others; with MacLaren leading a group into Western Canadian Airways, later to be a nucleus of Trans-Canada Air Lines and the late Grant McConachie of Yukon Southern Air Transport forming another segment into what has become Canadian Pacific Air Lines. Appropriately the Canadian Pacific Railway, which gave Vancouver its position in transport, has headquartered its world-girdling air service at Vancouver International Airport.

Out of a series of bush route companies has grown, too, Pacific Western Airlines, likewise with its headquarters in Vancouver and growing rapidly as the third ranking airline company of Canada.

Year by year the face of the Brickmakers' Claim changes as it fills in still more solidly with apartment buildings. Skyscrapers march westward to Stanley Park and as they rise, the ground about them is cleared of old wooden houses, many of them gracious mansions of the well-to-do pioneer families — and asphalt spreads in wide black aprons to accommodate the cars of office workers. But somehow the distinctive charm of the old West End transfers to the new. There is an atmosphere individual to Vancouver, perhaps because Stanley Park, Coal Harbor and English Bay are still there.

The city suffers from clogged arteries of traffic and, pondering the adequacy of its provision for parks, wonders whence will come the money for more elaborate provisions needed in serving its trading area population, so soon to be a million persons. In Stanley Park it has a thousand-acre playground and forested retreat almost within sound of the city's busy traffic. In all, parkland totals almost 3,000 acres and more must be acquired if the city is to have the ideal ratio of 10 acres per thousand of population.

Late in the decade of the 1960's and in a program to continue in some specific parts into the 1980's, Vancouver's downtown core area began an era of major construction unprecedented in its scope and effect on the visual character of the city. This would see whole areas of the work of building in the city's first two decades razed to make way for spectacular towers, plazas and shopping malls. Project 200 would sweep along the waterfront from the foot of Cambie Street to somewhat west of Granville Street and up from the water to Hastings Street. Thus it would begin quite close to the site of Gassy Jack Deighton's Hotel and end only a short distance from where John Morton had built his shack on the Brickmakers' claim.

Excitingly, Vancouver was destroying without a qualm the things of its childhood, the better to be prepared for full stature in a fast-changing world. For the first time the suggestions of becoming a great and beautiful city implicit in some scattered office buildings and the complex of modern tall apartment building in the West End would begin to be reality. Cohesion, integration, planning for a total harmonious effect would come to areas of the city's core large enough to give the whole a new dignity and beauty.

And that is precisely the way it has been happening — with almost dismaying speed. To make way for the Bentall Centre at Burrard, Pender and Eveleigh Streets the clearing disposed of a brick building where once the young business and professional men, in their bachelor days, boarded swankily. It had declined into the unglamorous role of sheltering masseuses, rooming house tenants and a Chinese vegetable store. At Eveleigh and Burrard was the office above Home Oil Distributors where millionaire Austin C. Taylor directed the affairs of his rich Bralorne gold mine and where he coordinated the wartime shipbuilding program of the Canadian government under his friend and temporary boss, H. R. MacMillan. The trio of tall office buildings and the plaza with its fountain, pool and flower beds are an impressive example of how, when the old order changes, it becomes a magnificent improvement.

So, too, with the two blocks where Pacific Centre has taken over. Down came the memory-rich old Opera House, and the remains of the old Hotel Vancouver were excavated to create Eaton's store (which long before had swallowed David Spencer's store on Hastings Street) and the Toronto-Dominion Bank Tower. The city cavilled at the darkness of the exterior finish of the tower, which took its style from the head office building of the bank in Toronto, but it was reckoned by the more philosophical that when, across the street, a new and greater and light colored Birks Building would stand on the historic Birks Corner — with the old Birks clock intact on its sidewalk green pillar — there would be character in contrast. Here, too, the city began to go underground with its first shopping mall below street level, a development to be repeated on a still larger scale at the corner of Georgia and Burrard, facing Christ Church, and where once stood the ivy-covered old Glencoe Lodge. There close by the lofty and shadow-boxed windows of the massive Mac-Millan Bloedel Building has risen the still higher Royal Bank tower and the Hyatt Regency Hotel. Under the bank and hotel are two complete floor levels of shopping malls.

Out of all this building Vancouver is to have the gift of convention-attracting capacity on a scale far beyond that of the 1960's. Hotel space and convention halls big enough to accommodate international meetings, hitherto beyond Vancouver's ability to cope with, have given the city a new dimension in that phase of its changing character.

In the plan there began to develop first stirrings of a concern that this emulation of Manhattan should avoid the mistakes of impossibly crowded New York in its skyscraper areas. There was talk of rapid transit versus a freeway system, a waterfront arterial traffic road, which would expose the blocked-off waterfront to view from the landward side, even of an eventual subway and especially of bridge connections across to the North Shore with both ends of the bridge— or tunnel—occupying ground that had been the habitation of Indians when Vancouver harbor was first settled. B.C. Hydro began speculating on using the old B.C Electric Interurban 'Marpole line' right-of-way for a rapid transit rail route to the Sea Island airport and to fast growing Richmond on Lulu Island.

If with all this metropolitanization the city were falling heir to the almost psychotic fear of the streets at night that exists in some major American cities, due to criminal atacks on peaceful citizens, appreciation of the spectacular change of the downtown scene would be marred. It would seem that the price of change was far too high. But except in a very few areas the streets are safe, the record of attacks on pedestrians being such as to compare with any well-ordered city anywhere. This, obviously, could change if people and their mores change or if the city falls victim to a slack immigration service or to a decline in police efficiency. But that time, happily, is not upon us yet.

Two things the visitor comments on after he has become used to the startlingly near and spectacular presence of the North Shore mountains and the salt air atmosphere. One is the cleanliness of the streets. The other is the courtesy of those who serve in our stores. These are carried on as "no big production" in Vancouver for heaven knows we should be clean and we should be courteous. But it is a comment one must hope will not be changed through any failure to be worthy of it. They are good distinctions to enjoy.

Nothing here should be taken to suggest that Vancouver loses its old landmarks without due hue and cry — even at times deep emotion and rancor. Christ Church itself is the subject of a suspended plan to erect a combined chapel and office building, linking God and Mammon, and only a plan to build a great apartment house complex on Georgia at the very entrance to Stanley Park exceeded this proposal in public protest. It is a mark of Vancouver's relatively few years that almost any building erected before World War I can qualify in agitations for preservation as "historic".

From its loftier elevation up on the Fairview slope close to where a deep gully once ran to False Creek, the City Hall looks down Cambie Street at the new spires of the central city and tries to think through the problem of disagreement about what to do about public transit made urgent by such density of office populations, about a subway some day and how it would tie in with a distributor street plan and a third crossing of Burrard Inlet.

In its wisdom city council gave up a city square idea west of Robson Street to make way for an Arthur Erickson designed provincial government building in terraced garden concept extending far west of the existing Court House. (Where the law is now talked and justice dispensed the Vancouver Art Gallery plans to live in its far more commodious quarters of the future.)

On the face of it there is not much room for the main city area to grow in if really massive projects are to continue gobbling space. Project 200 on the waterfront will absorb more buildings and even Gastown one day may give way to what now it thumbs its nose at.

But mainly the thrust of growth in Vancouver has been to the west and soon, it would seem, the office buildings must start rising across False Creek where Burrard and Granville bridges take the traffic south and west — south toward Richmond and Delta and west to Kitsilano and Point Grey. It is then, no doubt, that the agitation will begin in earnest for a subway and surface system similar to those of Toronto and Montreal. But engineers doubt it will happen in the next decade and Broadway between Main and Yew Streets is attracting more and more medium height office buildings and stores. It could, with Burrard and Granville Street help, see a satellite city centre arise on the south side of False Creek.

Vancouver continues to debate with its satellite municipalities of Burnaby, New Westminster, North and West Vancouver, Richmond, Surrey, Delta, Coquitlam and Port Moody what will be the manner of its growth, what forms of government it should have for a truly great metropolitan area. Proud New Westminster, which can't quite forget that Vancouver was an upstart when the Royal City was prosperously mature, bridles at the idea of metropolitan government. Progress in this direction may be slow for all its inevitability.

But even before metropolitanization, Vancouver is bigger than its boundaries. All the citizens who live in its defined area or in the municipalities that lie below the snow-capped mountains with ski-fields and hiking trails, consider they are first of all citizens of Canada's third city and only incidentally citizens of a suburban municipality.

17

The Realm of Sport

CONFORMING to the Anglo-Saxon behavior pattern in most things, Vancouver has always been sports conscious to a degree—and this has been so ever since the exuberant days when, playing against the Westminster Salmonbellies a remarkably vigorous variety of lacrosse, Vancouver defended its upstart precocity at old Recreation Park in many a contest that ended in grimly happy blood-lettings, with spectators mixing in the melee. There was little importation of strangers in early times sport and if a home-town boy was slashed with a stick, the gorge of the whole local populace rose loyally—and the visiting team did well to get off the field unmobbed.

Cricket at Brockton Point, English Rugby there and on the high school playing fields, sculling on Coal Harbor and the annual Caledonion Games tested sinews and stamina of Vancouver's youth before the First World War. And the Vancouver Amateur Swimming Club, later to be made famous by maker-of-champions, Percy Norman, sent its summer-bronzed youths into the waters of English Bay, swimming first the sedate breast stroke, later the Australian crawl and still later the speedy trudgeon-stroke. Wars interfered but it was in the zestful period of reaction after the First World War that the Patrick family's venture in the old Arena at Denman Street brought inter-city ice hockey to a clamorous pitch. The days of Cyclone Taylor, Mickey Mackay, Bobby Rowe, "Moose" Johnson, and many another well-loved skating and stick-handling hero saw perhaps the most genuinely patriotic upwelling of local loyalty in a mass fervor of completely dedicated enjoyment that Vancouver will ever know. True, it was commercialized sport but who thought of that when the face-off whistle sounded? And who thinks of it now?

When the arena, "home of hockey", was destroyed by fire, Lester Patrick took the game to New York, sparked life into a hockey league that featured major eastern cities, American and Canadian, and so the national sport of Canada became international. But a long time passed before events came full cycle and Vancouver Canucks became part of the National Hockey League.

On the basis that if one team is good in an international hockey league two would be twice as good, Vancouver today has its Canucks and its World Hockey League Blazers, both playing to ardently loyal crowds of hockey fans in the Coliseum at the P.N.E. grounds which once was old Hastings Park. Those stirring games are only a few hundred yards away from Empire Stadium where the never-to-be-forgotten first Empire Games in Vancouver were held while the sports world watched with astonishment as former records fell and the Landy and Bannister epics were written into the sports annals. Here the British Columbia Lions play to some of the largest crowds seen in Canadian football.

The Lions, Canucks and Blazers make the topics of talk everywhere in Vancouver after the games, at coffee breaks, in lunch hours and, to tell the truth, while work scheduled to be done has to wait a bit!

For Vancouver a brilliant meteor to light up the pre-depression era skies was a rather pale, not-very-competitive youngster who was handily winning high school sports events — Percy Williams. Enough enthusiasm and money were raised to get him to the Olympics of 1928 at Amsterdam and even in the boom times, that was not too easily done. At the outset in Amsterdam Williams was foremost only in the hearts of his quite localized countrymen, but incredibly he won his heats and a place in the finals. Those Vancouverites who were there and saw Percy Williams become a perfect running machine, with elbows tucked in and flashing legs in rhythmic beat eating up the metres, slipped their senses temporarily as suddenly the slight stripling pulled away from the world's best and flung himself into the finishing tape, a champion of champions. Then, to prove it no accident, he doubled by winning a second world's sprinting championship the same spectacular way, almost as inevitably as though he were in the inter-high schools sports meet at Brockton Point. He returned to a glorious home-town welcome that lionized him as a hero and profoundly embarrassed his rather retiring soul. But the Percy Williams episode belongs—with pictures—in Vancouver's book of memories.

In 1954 Vancouver hosted Empire Games in the new Empire stadium at Exhibition Park and in the fine new swimming pool at UBC. Television had arrived and the whole world stopped to watch as Australia's Landy and England's Bannister ran their record-shattering mile. That memorable day, too, the watchers suffered tortures along with the huge crowd at the stadium when wiry British marathoner Jim Peters came wavering into the home stretch at the park, fatigued and heat struck, wabbled, fell, rose, tottered, fell and painfully rose again to stagger toward the finishing line—yet never quite to make it before collapsing. That was a display of heart and spirit surviving when the body had failed—and it was an emotional tensity of hope and despair that all Vancouver shared with the world. The Jim Peters Fund was an almost automatic reaction of "doing something about it." A splendid Bannister and Landy bronze statuary stands at the entrance to Empire Stadium, immortalizing that great sports contest.

Empire Stadium made possible "big league" professional Canadian Football for Vancouver in a Western Cities circuit and the city broadmindedly (and with an eye to the box office) yielded up the name Vancouver to call its team the British Columbia Lions. Something of the old hockey fan loyalty was pentup awaiting wild expression at such time as the Lions could win a western championship and arrive at a Grey Cup final. It happened in 1964 when the Lions won the Cup. Football interest remains high but ice hockey in league series is under revival, backed by some of the original enthusiasts who brought professional football into popularity in Vancouver. It has not happened since . . . but Vancouver fans remain loyal to their team and the Coliseum rocks with their cheers and groans.

274

It is noteworthy that Empire Stadium and a splendid hockey rink in the new Coliseum are close to the site of the old Brighton House Hotel and New Brighton Beach where New Westminster folk came to holiday when there were only Indian settlements on Burrard Inlet.

As this is written, a professional football team, the Vancouver Whitecaps, is entered in the North American Soccer League, with summer of 1974 its opening season. This fills in any spectator sport gap that might exist in the summer season and will cater to the British and European soccer devotees as the core of a potential patronage.

In the existence of the Swangard Stadium, built by widespread public subscription to accommodate junior outdoor field sports, there is assurance of playing talent and team quality to come.

A new swimming pool under the Vancouver Parks Board at the entrance to False Creek, facing public cultural buildings at Vanier Park across the narrow waterway, will replace old Crystal Pool whence came the first parade of amateur swimming talent fostered by Percy Norman. The spendid new facility, with Olympic size pool, diving pool and spectator space, will further stimulate the remark-able flow of world contest swimmers out of Vancouver capable of finishing in top or medal-winning place.

But in golfing, swimming, figure skating, skiing, tennis, curling, bowling, badminton and every other recreational contest — not the least yacht racing — Vancouver plays so earnestly and vigorously that its reputation as a sports city is world-wide. Stars like skier Nancy Greene and skater Karen Magnusson in recent Olympics are worthy successors to Percy Williams, the runner. For any of many possible reasons, Vancouver is a city that takes its sports fun seriously!

This, perhaps, is why a Vancouverite, summoned to services of higher remuneration and greater scope in Eastern Canada, may be-come balky and refuse to go or, if he departs, does so with much inward doubting as to the price he and his family will pay in lost amenities of West Coast living.

18

Here Stands the City

THE TRAVELLER from the East has
motored through the aromatic leagues of sagebrush land in the
Thompson Valley, with its blue-green river and rounded hills, and
descended the swooping curves of the highway that threads its
way between the morose and menacing crags of the Fraser Canyon
and the grey-brown, boiling torrent below. At Hope, he emerges
upon the upper reaches of an extensive valley, where pleasant, green
farms alternate with shaggy, rugged hills—hills only in comparison
with the vast and snow-crowned peaks that tower behind them.
Thirty miles farther on, he passes through the busy town of Chilliwack, where the valley widens and levels out. One can drive straight
west to the seaport by freeway or follow the older road which runs
between flat prairies, dotted with comfortable farmhouses, immense
barns and grazing cattle; only here and there does a tree-clad wave of
rising land remind him of the forests and mountains he has left behind.

Now the villages and towns spring up and flow behind him at
closer intervals, until the roadway is lined with small homes, garden
patches, scattered stores and service stations, with the farms pushed into the background. He glides down a long hill amid thickening traffic
to a turn where the unmistakable salt marshes and familiar tang of the
tidal flat assure him the sea is near; then up one more long rise and
from the top he sees again the Fraser River, the turbulent course of
which he has followed for so long. But here it is a broad, calm,
placid estuary, spanned by the silver arches of the mile-long Port Mann
and Pattullo Bridges. The river is lined with docks and factories, mills

and warehouses; it is not until he sees the coiling bow-waves cease-lessly heaving up before and flowing away from the upstream side of the bridge piers that he knows the thundering rage of the mountain-pent Fraser still sullenly gnaws and tugs and worries its way to the sea below that quiet surface.

On the northern bank of the river, from its fringe of industry and above the penitentiary on the site of the old Royal Engineers' encamp-ment, tier on tier rise the streets and homes of New Westminster, mid-Victorian mansions, smothered in gingerbread-work, mixed with clapboard cottages and angular, glassy modern business blocks and apartment houses in a curiously appealing hodge-podge of ill-assorted architecture. One more abrupt and taxing climb, with the Fraser gliding away to the Strait of Georgia among a maze of delta channels to his left, or an even faster dash on the slow-curves of the 401 Free-way, and the City of Vancouver lies before him, Burrard Inlet in the distance and the great barrier mountains of the North Shore loom-ing across it, peaked, riven, blue with forest and starkly outlined against the sky. From the rising of the sun he has come to the great city of the West; here he completes the Great Circle of the world, the other half of which Captain Vancouver and his two small ships traced eastward through the oceans so many years ago. Here is the city that men, in a scant century, have built on the desolate shores of Sir Harry Burrard's Channel.

What have they made of it, as a century of settlement and 88 years of civil life are counted in the past?

The very statistics, dry, cold and mechanical, have an excitement of their own. The city — the living organism of some 14 municipal governments known as Greater Vancouver — as of 1969 was estimated to have 1,114,000 inhabitants. They transact their business in more than 6,000 retail stores, great and small, and over 60,000 of them earn their livings in more than 2000 industrial plants; three times as many are employed in all the other multifarious occupations of a great city — transportation, offices, banks, shops, services, arts and sciences. In one year they bury 9000 of their dead and give birth to 16,500 children. They worship in more than 300 churches and care for their sick in 12 public hospitals, one of them among the largest and best on the continent. Of the two universities in Greater Vancouver, University of B.C. accommodates 20,000 students and Burnaby's Simon Fraser University 6000.

Half of these people, some 440,000, live in the 44-square-mile core of the metropolis which is the city proper. They inhabit 86,000 family dwellings, 3465 apartment houses and 2729 hotels and lodging houses. On the voter's lists are 121,504 property owners and 131,000 tenants, the tenants now outnumbering the owners. They travel on 306 miles of permanently paved streets and are served by 847 miles of watermains and 901 miles of sewers. Their children are taught in 89 elementary schools and 17 secondary schools with an enrollment of 74,000 pupils and 3000 teachers. Night classes are attended by 43,000 adults. They play in 132 parks totalling 4154 acres, swim on eight public beaches, golf on nine courses and listen to 10 radio stations and two TV stations.

More important, how do they do these things? The visitor from Eastern Canada is probably first impressed with a breezy informality which he often fears—sometimes justly—is likely to develop into brash familiarity; the glittering masses of high-piled offices in the city's core push at the westward edges into a undergrowth of ramshackle rooming houses; he hears responsible businessmen soberly talking what in Toronto would sound like wild-eyed radicalism. The American tourist, on the other hand, is struck by the politeness of the citizens, the rugged individualism of a city where the unimaginative repetitious housing tracts are rare and where fences and walls divide gardens and homes of startling and sometimes almost comic contrast; much of the city and many of its people he finds quaint, friendly and old-fashioned.

Which, of course, is only to say that Vancouver is a city with a difference, the product of its history, its people and its surroundings. Its very magnitude is a constant surprise to its own people. They ripped the forests off the mountains of the North Shore and flung their homes up the sides of cliffs and hills, rank on rank of beautiful houses and gardens set among slopes denuded of forests which spawn occasional angry local floods, and served by bridges and roads which often are hard pressed to accommodate the daily flood of traffic into and out of the city.

They swarmed out into the farmlands of Richmond and Surrey, only to find they lacked sewers and water and had taken for unproductive residences the rich agricultural tilth upon which the prosperity of these once placid rural municipalities was based. Here, too, roads and bridges proved inadequate to the demands made upon them.

The result, indeed, does sometimes look like a slapdash recklessness, and is often the theme of professional planners' complaints. With all the certitude of hindsight the planners show how this and that mistake could easily have been avoided, how the one and the other amenity might have been provided. But it is not as easy as that. The city's growth was subject neither to control nor to anticipation. Even if it had been predictable, it could not have been provided for. The pattern has been consistent, a period of depression, a time of war and social upheaval, a boom and a great influx of population. The depression of the 1890's was catastrophic, the city's resources were exhausted; the Klondyke gold rush, the Boer War and the transition from the Victorian to the Edwardian age altered completely the patterns of life as the city knew them; the wild land boom of 1900-1912 was unpredictable and uncontrollable with the political and economic means then at hand. The depression of 1913-15 was severe; the First World War was a social and economic, as well as military, upheaval; the mining and oil-share boom of the 1920's was unparalleled in kind, as well as magnitude. The depression of the 1930's was a world-wide disaster; the Second World War altered the city beyond recognition; the following boom was of a type and extent previously unknown.

As a result of each depression, the city entered upon the succeeding period with its financial resources strained to the limit; before it could hope to provide for the future it had to repair the wounds of the past. Each time, while trying to do so, it found itself in an emergency to which it had to devote all its resources to duties above and beyond the needs of the city itself. As each boom developed, civic government was prepared in the light of experience to avoid the

Granville Square Office Tower at the foot of Granville Street, the first unit completed of Project 200 which will transform the appearance of the waterfront, once completely utilitarian and lacking in aesthetic appeal.

An artist's conception of the completed Pacific Centre. Beyond the complex can be seen the Birks Building and Hudson's Bay Company building.

excesses of the past, only to find the problems arising were new and unprecedented. In these three recurring cycles during 82 years, the population of the city grew from the 400 or 500 of Gastown's later years to the 960,000 of the metropolitan area today.

The sheer speed of this growth, coupled with the prevailing system of municipal government under which the city had to conduct its business, put planning—if planning for the unforeseen had been possible—out of court, for the simple reason it was impossible for the city to accumulate a financial reserve to implement an organized plan. Vancouver as a city may be rich, but it is comprised of a multitude of citizens, very few of whom are rich, and in whose lives civic amenities, outside the essential services, must take second place to their own homes, families and personal needs. This is a fact of civic financial life the social theorist is prone to overlook. The city is made for man, not man for the city.

The net result is that the city has to meet its problems as they arise, and usually not before they become acute. This is not necessarily improvident, since the terms of the problem are not always evident at an early stage; if the city had carried out some of the more ambitious plans made for it, such as the civic centre at the north end of Burrard Bridge planned in the Twenties, the results would have looked pretty silly in the Forties and Fifties. The most elaborate plan ever carried to completion, the "luxury suburb" of First Shaughnessy, is now neither luxurious nor a suburb, but a district of white elephant mansions, many of them degenerating into lodging houses against the grim but futile resistance of those who believed the plan was incorruptible.

The major problem which confronts the city now is metropolitan organization. There appears no doubt that some form of co-ordination is essential, but what services it will include, under what form of control, are yet a matter of speculation. The most probable appear to be police, parks, health, sewerage, water, land-use and roads. The regional district concept progresses slowly, with some opposition from favored areas which fear they will be called on to sacrifice advantages for the common good. This attitude is not completely unjustified, for some of these advantages have been gained by thrifty administration and the foregoing of luxuries at times when other municipalities were less cautious, but it appears that the only alternative to some measure of metropolitanization is increasing chaos. This, in a constricted area containing half the population of the Province, is a matter of more than municipal concern. The Provincial Government itself could not permit it, and there are signs the organization may be imposed from above if it cannot be achieved locally.

Certainly the problems of sewage treatment, air pollution and, above all, road traffic, cannot be solved under present conditions. The City of Vancouver, for instance, is faced with construction of a system of rapid transit, if its traffic is not to be stalled by complete congestion. The newest proposal of the Provincial Government is a return to street cars. Since the traffic complex includes the entire metropolitan area and congestion at the heart affects the outermost fringes, for the city to create and pay for such a system out of its own revenues is outside the realm of practical politics. Politics also dictates that the Provincial Government cannot give continual aid to the metropolian municipalities as a special case, unless they recognize they are a special case and take steps accordingly to help themselves.

The city's life has other aspects besides the purely material. In the last decade, education has moved largely under control of the Provincial Government and a system of school districts, rather than of the municipalities; nevertheless the sound early development of the school system has been maintained. In the suburbs, school construction has not always kept pace with the increase in population, but the city itself has largely avoided double-shifting and similar expedients.

The University of British Columbia, from its inception in 1915, has made large contributions to the city's intellectual life, not the least of these being its summer schools and adult education program. The latter endeavors have been shared by Vancouver School Board, which offers an immense variety of evening courses, from camp cooking to music appreciation, in classes which currently enroll 39,000 persons each winter. It is characteristic of the city that while some of these courses are strictly practical, the majority are devoted to opening new fields of interest and intellectual activity for leisure time. They have enriched the lives of many—an important achievement in a city where high proportion of elderly and retired persons. The public schools enroll some 69,000 in elementary and secondary schools and Vancouver City College about 12,000.

Newcomers from older and larger cities have often reproached Vancouver for a lack of cultural and artistic resources, but it is a reproach that was not merited. One of the first large public buildings in Vancouver was its Opera House, and in the rough pioneer settlement some of the shining names of the theatre and the music world appeared before appreciative audiences. Sarah Bernhardt, Pavlova, Paderewski, besides scores of lesser lights, saw the city when the forest was still standing on the skyline south of False Creek. No literary stars of the first magnitude have shone here. (Where have they, in Canada?) But in the early years of the century it was here that Indian poetess Pauline Johnson chose to live out her life, it was of Vancouver she sang, it was here she died and her ashes rest. One of the city's most appealing monuments is her modest memorial at Ferguson Point in Stanley Park, often overlooked by citizens and visitors alike. She has been followed by an appreciable number of capable writers, of which the city has never lacked its reasonable share.

Drama and the ballet have always had a strong attraction for the people of Vancouver. The city has contributed a Joan Miller to the English stage, and a Lynn Seymour to the ranks of the world's ballerinas, some notables to the world of motion picture, television and radio entertainment, but, as in painting, the lively arts for the most part have been a recreation rather than a profession. From the earliest days of the Little Theatre and the University of B.C. Players Club, the amateurs of the stage have been many and have maintained a high standard of accomplishment. Those of the brush are so numerous and their standards so high that the Vancouver Art Gallery is given much verve and color by their work. Music is on a more professional level. A competent and enthusiastic symphony orchestra is well established; the noted Theatre Under the Stars built up a fine summer light-opera and musical-play troupe which performed with much success over the years in the perfect setting of the Malkin Bowl in Stanley Park, but eventually it ran into financial difficulties and was liquidated in 1963.

The Queen Elizabeth Theatre and Vancouver Playhouse theatre, located almost on the spot where the Great Fire of 1886 began, have fostered legitimate stage efforts, good, bad and indifferent elsewhere in the city. Beached high and dry but not dead, as a suddenly aground rare whale might spread concern for rescue action, the large, ornate Orpheum Theatre becomes the subject of a plan for civic acquisition with senior governments making sizable contributions to assist in the achievement of the project.

A studio centre on the slope of West Vancouver was projected a few years ago to make films for the British and Canadian moving picture and TV quota requirements. It did not develop beyond preliminary stages.

Young Western architects, many from the School of Architecture at the University of BC., and all standing a little taller due to the brilliance of Vancouver's internationally famous designer, Arthur Erickson, are shaping now a city that could be magnificent.

Remarkably reminiscent in layout of Manhattan in New York and with a chance to benefit from monumental achievements and mistakes there, Vancouver's downtown peninsula is extraordinarily well bounded by waterfrontages. These can lend height, dignity and reflection to the structures man conceives and erects.

The towering apartment spires of the city's old West End as seen from the west across English Bay fairly burn with the flashing golden fires of sunset reflected in their plate glass view windows. The sight is often spectacular. Yet the street parking problems and the unplanned sociological consequences of a sudden and unexpected extreme density of population argue for a better rationale to go with the undoubtedly exhilarating picture.

The West End is almost entirely converted to apartment houses; some of these are mere chromium-plated rabbit-hutches, others are of impressive size in the clean, almost antiseptic modern glass-walled architecture, spectacular in the mass rather than in the individual building. West Vancouver has an extremely high standard of suitability and grace in its luxurious homes, but it is somewhat startling when a Greek temple in perfect miniature is glimpsed amidst the arbutus and pines crowning a rugged crag. For mile after mile of the city's streets, though, it is heart-warming to see still modest homes without architectural pretensions, set amid hedges, trees, flowers and well-kept lawns. Grandeur is imparted to them by the vast backdrop of seascape and mountains; no part of Vancouver but shares in the massive beauty of its setting, and to all of its people, this is an essential part of their lives.

Vancouver lives much out-of-doors. Often during the year it is but half-an-hour from skiing on the mountaintops to swimming in the sparkling bay. Boats swarm on the Inlet, on Howe Sound, on the Strait of Georgia, in the Gulf Islands. Hunters leave home and are shooting ducks and geese on the delta marshes before breakfast. Rugby, soccer and Canadian football are all-year-round games. Fishing in the streams and the sea (except for a fresh-water closed season) goes on every month in the twelve. Hikers, climbers and campers swarm in the Fraser Valley, in the mountains, up the Squamish Valley canyons.

The automobile and the outboard engine have opened up vast stretches of virgin country and in the mild climate, the eastern "summer cottage" often becomes an all-year-round weekend residence. The young push for the opening of the snowfields of Garibaldi Park and, with good reason, say it could become a world famous playground for winter sports and summer recreation.

Any city worthy of respect is conscious of its past and pays some debt of recognition to its pioneers.

This is happening in Vancouver, inspired to some extent by the words and pictures of the two earlier editions of this book. The men who were "first on the claim" that is downtown and west end Vancouver, Morton, Brighouse and Hailstone, will be immortalized as the Three Greenhorns. A posh restaurant borrowed this sobriquet for its own name. Its menu relates the story of the three. Many another restaurant, trying for a coloration legitimately Vancouver, has adorned its walls with large blow-ups of early photographs of Vancouver. This renaissance of the scenes that surrounded the townspeople of 80 or 90 years ago gives today's generation some degree of awareness of those who felled the great trees and burned out the stubborn stumps on the site of this modern city.

There is a pattern of life evolving here which has not yet become mature, a lively imagination can picture a possible future city which has become merely a machine-for-working, with its population's homes scattered far and wide over the south-western quarter of the Province. It is a development no more impossible than the city of today would have appeared to a citizen of 1886.

19

Tomorrow's Metropolis

As RECENTLY as in the past five years since the second edition of this book appeared, the basic quality, rather than the size, of the city altered beyond recognition. The city as an entity of itself has lost significance. Its individual history has come to an end. It can be considered now only as a part — still a major part, but only a part — of Greater Vancouver or, indeed, the entire Lower Mainland. In this it shares the future with Burnaby, Richmond, Delta, Surrey, the University Endowment Lands — where a new 1000-acre park is conceived as being another Stanley Park — and with farther away marginal municipalities invading the Fraser Valley farmlands.

The alteration of the city's character, economically and socially, may well have begun with the first "high-rise" construction; as this is written at the end of 1973, the changes have culminated in the civic and provincial elections of 1972. The long reign of Social Credit in B.C. politics was brought to an end by the New Democratic Party under David Barrett who occupied the portfolios long served by Premier W. A. C. Bennett. The dominance of the Non-Partisan Association in Vancouver's city hall lapsed more or less by default.

Provincial politics are beyond the scope of our study except as they directly affect the city. There has not yet been time to assess the effect of so-called "democratic socialism", so far as Vancouver is concerned, but certainly major changes in education, industry, commerce and social life are occurring and more lie just ahead.

Civic politics has entered a regressive period. Tom Campbell, in his final two years as mayor, became criticized for his many absences from, rather than his presence in, the city. The city, which did not appear to be suffering from this globe-trotting, found in him a person who frankly revelled in his job. In 1972 The Electors' Action Movement took over the majority of council seats with investment counsellor Arthur Phillips as mayor. The council's complexion changed from commercial to academic and professional. TEAM's objectives, chiefly concerned with social change and "citizen participation", were laudable but, during its first year in office, became honored in the breach rather than the observance. This gave rise to charges of apathy, timidity and incompetence. It might be more charitable to ascribe it to the growing complexity of the metropolis and the passing of effective power into the hands of regional and provincial authorities. The city retains the legal husks of local power but in more and more fields of government is obliged to follow decisions and developments in the larger community. The Greater Vancouver Regional Development Board, on which sit aldermen from various councils, is a major new force.

The rising population density in downtown Vancouver intensifies the city's traffic problems. Long cherished freeway schemes are likely to be abandoned, though the new Georgia Street viaduct was originally planned as a freeway link. The emphasis is now on plans for rail and bus rapid transit, with an underground railway talked of for the fairly distant future. An experimental pedestrian shopping mall on Granville from Nelson to Hastings Street will divert more traffic onto Howe and Seymour Streets. The mall is depicted in aesthetic terms but its real purpose is to try to arrest the rapid decline of upper Granville between Robson and False Creek. This area of a vital and respectable main thoroughfare had suddenly become an "instant slum", the habitat of prostitutes, dope pushers, knife-armed vagrants and 'porno' film theatres.

Some of this unwelcome change was due to the refurbishing of the old skid road on Cordova and Water Streets to produce so-called "Gastown". The location is right but re-created Gastown bears little resemblance to the original settlement of that famous name. Whereas

Gastown was hastily built of wood, this is a flourishing commercial complex with some 1890's decor and a good many arty-crafty shops, interspersed with restaurants and "niteries". Except that it is well patronized by Vancouverites it might be called, not inaccurately, an old brick tourist trap created from ancient stores and warehouses. The city once would have worried about the skid road association. But other cities have done conversions and Vancouver was ripe for it. This synthetic Gastown is in tune with the recent times. A project that 10 years ago would have been considered too large to under-take is now unremarkable.

The city today accepts in its stride the fulfillment of old visions. Typical are the Bloedel Conservatory in Queen Elizabeth Park, the H. R. MacMillan Planetarium on the south side of the entrance to False Creek, cheek by jowl with the new city archives building, and the new city museum.

Major gifts to the city, such as those of lumbermen Prentice Bloedel and H. R. MacMillan and W. J. Van Dusen and Leon Koerner are unostentatiously given and calmly accepted. There may not be money of that kind for civic munificances in the future for these were owner industrialists of an era that has passed.

Vancouver at this time may justly be compared to a man who, after years of sprouting adolescence, has come to maturity and is transforming his long-cherished daydreams into realities. At the same time he is incorporating himself into a larger world.

One example of this is the city's hospital system. Long inadequate to meet the demands on it, but consistently, from its early days, of high quality, it is being stimulated by greater support from the social service conscious government in Victoria. Control has passed from the hands of city council to the regional hospital district, in which a number of hospitals, such as Lions Gate General in North Vancouver, provide adequate general health care at a high level of competence to the people of their areas. In this, they at least equal the services previ-ously provided chiefly by Vancouver General and St. Paul's Hospital in the city, which accommodated many patients from the metropol-itan area.

Now, with Shaughnessy Hospital, no longer required exclusively for care of war veterans, added to the public hospitals, and with the rapid development of the University of B.C. medical faculty hospital, Vancouver General is becoming the major centre for both teaching and the concentration of equipment and eminent doctors for highly skilled specialist services. This specialization will be intensified by the separation of ancillary services such as the Children's Hospital, which is planned for the near future. Vancouver General is near the limit of effective physical expansion and can progress only by intensive improvement of special services. Thus in the medical field as in others Vancouver is becoming aware of and making use of its large reservoir of talent which no other part of the province can duplicate. It is a process evident in all aspects of the city's life, from the arts to commerce and industrial organization.

This is a natural heritage and as the core of a great metropolis, the role of Vancouver as a city has come to full flower. From the tiny seed of old Gastown the city has germinated, grown, blossomed and reseeded itself until it is no longer a solitary tree, but has become the patriarch of a forest. The city of Vancouver, from its humble beginnings as a milltown, has become a metropolis.

Epilogue

SUCH IS THE city that lies today where, 182 years ago, Captain George Vancouver saw "the low but fertile," forest-covered southern shore of Burrard Inlet, and "the sublime though gloomy spectacle" of the mountains to the north. The city is seen at its best and most impressive from the chalet on the brow of Grouse Mountain, as the evening shadows draw in. A mile below, the Inlet changes from a sparkling blue to a steely grey, and then to ink-black as the sun declines. Long, low and secret, the dark barrier of Stanley Park lies athwart the harbor entrance, even as it did when Peter the Whaler sought his monstrous prey in the waters it guards. But all else has changed.

The lights begin to twinkle on the lower slopes of the mountain, so near that even the window-squares can be seen. Farther down, they march away along the squares and curves of the streets, thicken at the water's edge until they reach the shining threads of brilliance where the bridges span the Inlet. Splashes and bursts of neon flare in the city's heart, the blossoms of an unearthly garden in the bosom of the dark.

And then, mile upon mile upon mile, the lights spring up in ranks and rows, ever thinner, ever fainter, until to the east and south they seem to vanish over the curve of the earth. To the west they dip abruptly into the luminous grey of the larger waters which lead the eye away to the stupendous barrier of the Vancouver Island ranges ranked against the faint and smokey orange of the dying day. Here are the jewels of the gods, spread on the velvet bed of Night. It is a beauty that tightens the breast and grips the throat.

There is movement, there, too; minute and winking lights crawling and forever crawling along all the threads of this Gargantuan cobweb of brilliance—unceasing, restless, irresistible. From this high distance, it is the city itself that is alive, nervous, quivering, tense with life in a dimension above and beyond its human corpuscles.

The massive mountain range stands as it has stood for uncounted thousands of years; the inland sea grumbles as it has grumbled forever around its points, dashes over its reefs, rolls through its narrows. But here, on the breast of the mountains and on the forehead of the sea, lies the jewelled city that men have built, all, amazingly, in the span of a single human lifetime — Vancouver.

Index